General Aviation Security

Aircraft, Hangars, Fixed-Base Operations, Flight Schools, and Airports

General Aviation Security

Aircraft, Hangars, Fixed-Base Operations, Flight Schools, and Airports

Daniel J. Benny, Ph.D.

CRC Press
Taylor & Francis Group
Boca Raton   London   New York

CRC Press is an imprint of the
Taylor & Francis Group, an **informa** business

CRC Press
Taylor & Francis Group
6000 Broken Sound Parkway NW, Suite 300
Boca Raton, FL 33487-2742

© 2013 by Taylor & Francis Group, LLC
CRC Press is an imprint of Taylor & Francis Group, an Informa business

No claim to original U.S. Government works

Printed in the United States of America on acid-free paper
Version Date: 20120518

International Standard Book Number: 978-1-4665-1087-6 (Hardback)

Library of Congress Cataloging-in-Publication Data

Benny, Daniel J.
    General aviation security : aircraft, hangars, fixed-base operations, flight schools, and airports / Daniel J. Benny.
       p. cm.
    Summary: "This book has been designed and written for the primary purpose of providing a single comprehensive source of information in order to provide for the protection of general aviation aircraft, hangars, fixed base operations, flight schools, and airports. Addressing all aspects of general aviation security, it supplies guidance to organizations such corporate flight departments, general aviation aircraft owners, pilots, flight school and airports"-- Provided by publisher.
    Includes bibliographical references and index.
    ISBN 978-1-4665-1087-6 (hardback)
    1. Airports--Security measures--United States. 2. Aeronautics--Security measures--United States. 3. Private flying--Security measures--United States. 4. Fixed base operators industry--Security measures--United States. I. Title.

TL725.3.S44B46 2012
363.28'760973--dc23
                                                                                              2012007592

Visit the Taylor & Francis Web site at
http://www.taylorandfrancis.com

and the CRC Press Web site at
http://www.crcpress.com

1997–2012

This book is dedicated to the memory of my beloved dog Magnum, who was by my side each day during the writing of this book.

CONTENTS

CONTENTS

FOREWORD

The ability to travel unhindered is one of the greatest freedoms Americans enjoy. Perhaps the apex of that freedom is achieved in general aviation. How extraordinary and wonderful it is to be able to pilot yourself to the destination of your choosing on a schedule set by you. Whether flying in furtherance of business, as part of a charitable endeavor, or simply for personal reasons, general aviation pilots and their passengers are exceptionally fortunate to be able to travel quickly and efficiently when and where they please.

But, with freedom comes responsibility—a notion the general aviation community has always taken seriously. Pilots must train continuously, learning new skills and honing old ones. Pilots understand that their lives and the lives of passengers and people on the ground depend on their willingness to accept responsibility for their own proficiency.

This same sense of responsibility serves the general aviation community, and the public at large, well when it comes to maintaining security. Pilots are, by nature and training, alert to their environment and what is happening around them. In fact, "situational awareness" is among the core skills pilots must learn and maintain.

At the same time, the general aviation community is both small and close-knit, with pilots typically knowing one another as well as what constitutes routine activity at their home airport. As a rule, general aviation pilots also know their passengers personally. The people who ride in general aviation aircraft are not strangers but friends, family members, and colleagues.

Taken together, these factors make the general aviation community exceptionally well placed to monitor activity at its airports, identify and report anything suspicious, and generally act to ensure the safety of airports, aircraft, and the people who use them.

In these security-conscious times, we must all be vigilant and alert to threats, from whatever quarter they may arise. But, we must also ensure that security solutions are appropriate, reasonable, and effective. Only by achieving this balance can we retain those freedoms we hold dear—including the freedom to fly.

Craig Spence
Vice President, Operations and International Affairs
Aircraft Owners and Pilots Association

ACKNOWLEDGMENTS

The following individuals and organizations have supported my effort in the writing of this book:

Patricia A. Benny, Harrisburg Area Community College, Harrisburg, Pennsylvania

Professor Elmer Criswell, Harrisburg Area Community College, Harrisburg, Pennsylvania

CXY Aviation, New Cumberland, Pennsylvania

Embry-Riddle Aeronautical University Worldwide, Daytona Beach, Florida

Kathleen R. Martian, Federal Aviation Administration FSDO, New Cumberland, Pennsylvania

Penn State Hershey Medical Center Life Lion, Hershey, Pennsylvania

Pennsylvania State Police Aviation Patrol Unit, Harrisburg, Pennsylvania

Andrew J. Portocarrero World Security Institute, Washington, District of Columbia

Reigle Aviation and Airport, Palmyra, Pennsylvania

Professor James Selgas, Harrisburg Area Community College, Harrisburg, Pennsylvania

Craig Spencer, Aircraft Owners and Pilots Association, Frederick, Maryland

ABOUT THE AUTHOR

Daniel J. Benny, PhD, CPP, PCI, CFE, CM, CCO, ACE, is the security discipline chair at Embry-Riddle Aeronautical University Worldwide and works from his home in Harrisburg, Pennsylvania. Dr. Benny holds a doctor of philosophy in criminal justice from Capella University, master of aeronautical science from Embry-Riddle Aeronautical University, master of arts in security administration from Vermont College of Norwich University, bachelor of arts in security administration from Alvernia College, associate in arts in both commercial security and police administration from Harrisburg Area Community College, and a diploma in naval command and staff from the U.S. Naval War College.

He is board certified in security management as a Certified Protection Professional (CPP), board certified Professional Certified Investigator (PCI), both by ASIS International; Certified Fraud Examiner (CFE) by the Association of Certified Fraud Examiners; Certified Confidentiality Officer (CCO) by the Business Espionage Controls and Countermeasures Association, and Certified Member (CM) Airport Certified Employee-Security (ACE) and Airport Security Coordinator by the American

Association of Airport Executives. He is also a licensed private investigator and security consultant.

He is the author of the forthcoming CRC books: *Cultural Property Security; Protecting Museums, Historic Sites, Archives, and Libraries; Industrial Espionage; Developing a Counterespionage Program;* and co-author with Dr. Paul Baker of *The Complete Guide to Physical Security.*

Dr. Benny has authored over 300 articles on security, aviation, and intelligence topics. He served as a U.S. Naval intelligence officer with duty at the Office of Naval Intelligence, Naval Criminal Investigative Service, Willow Grove Naval Air Station, Fleet Rapid Support Team, and Central Intelligence Agency.

He is a Federal Aviation Administration licensed private pilot and safety team representative. He is a Cessna C-172 aircraft owner and holds the rank of major with the U.S. Air Force Auxiliary Civil Air Patrol.

1

General Aviation

GENERAL AVIATION AIRCRAFT

General aviation aircraft are fixed-wing or rotary aircraft that are used for the private transport of individuals, company staff, or guests and cargo. These aircraft may be a general aviation aircraft such as a Cessna owned by an individual (Figure 1.1). They could also be general aviation aircraft rented as needed from a local general aviation airport for the pleasure of flying and to travel on weekends and holidays. General aviation aircraft also include aircraft utilized by corporations to transport staff, executives, and customers of the organization.

Aircraft are used by organizations such as power and water companies to conduct aviation security patrols. This allows the organization to cover large areas where power lines, pipelines, dams, and reservoirs are located. This allows for cost-effective security patrols of their property and facilities. Aircraft used in conjunction with this type of activity within the business or organization are also considered general aviation aircraft.

Local, state, and nonmilitary federal governmental agencies use general aviation aircraft for the transportation of staff and to carry out various missions of their respective organizations. These missions might include law enforcement and intelligence operations. They may comprise the use of aircraft for security or law enforcement patrols, aerial firefighting, emergency medical air ambulance service, and search-and-rescue operations. Governmental environmental agencies also use aircraft to monitor air quality and to conduct natural resource patrols to protect wildlife and the natural resources of the United States.

Figure 1.1 Author's Cessna C-172 at Reigle Airport, Palmyra, Pennsylvania. (Photo by Daniel J. Benny.)

Other uses of general aviation aircraft include private aircraft utilized for agricultural crop dusting. These aircraft provide a valuable service to ensure the quality of the nation's food supply by spraying the crops with pesticides. They may also be used for insect control along rivers, lakes, and other waterways near populated areas of the United States.

Aircraft used for flight instruction are also considered general aviation aircraft. This would include use at private flight schools operating out of general aviation airports in all fifty states. It also covers institutions of higher learning, such as colleges and universities that offer flight training and college degrees in aviation.

Universities such as Embry-Riddle Aeronautical University operate an extensive fleet of aircraft for flight instruction out of their Daytona Beach, Florida, and Prescott, Arizona, campuses (Figure 1.2).

There are nonmilitary corporate aircraft used by the Civil Air Patrol, U.S. Air Force Auxiliary, a nonmilitary congressional corporation. The Civil Air Patrol utilizes general aviation aircraft for one of their primary missions, national search and rescue for downed aircraft. Any aircraft

Figure 1.2 Embry-Riddle Aeronautical University Cessna C-172s at the Daytona Beach, Florida, campus. (Photo by Daniel J. Benny.)

that is reported missing or down is assigned to the Civil Air Patrol by the U.S. Air Force for the purpose of tracking, searching, and locating the missing aircraft. The Civil Air Patrol also operates a non-law enforcement counterdrug program. As part of its Homeland Security mission, the Civil Air Patrol provides the use of their corporate aircraft to local and federal law enforcement as surveillance and intelligence collection platforms to locate clandestine aircraft landing strips and drug-growing operations from the air. The aircraft take part in Homeland Security patrols as well as organ transport and the transportation of individuals during emergencies. The Civil Air Patrol aircraft are also used in its aerospace education mission. This includes orientation flights that originate from general aviation airports for Civil Air Patrol cadets (Figure 1.3).

There is another congressional, nonmilitary, corporate organization that uses general aviation aircraft. The U.S. Coast Guard Auxiliary is part of the Department of Homeland Security U.S. Coast Guard. The volunteer members of U.S. Coast Guard Auxiliary use their private general aviation aircraft to conduct search-and-rescue operations of navigable and costal waterways in the United States and on its coast. They also use their private aircraft to conduct Homeland Security patrols, support maritime

Figure 1.3 Civil Air Patrol Pennsylvania wing aircraft Capital City Airport, New Cumberland, Pennsylvania. (Photo by Daniel J. Benny.)

port security operations, and make environmental patrols along waterways throughout the United States. The Coast Guard Auxiliary transports individuals related to official U.S. Coast Guard business. Auxiliary members who are certified pilots use their own general aviation fixed-wing aircraft for the U.S. Coast Guard Auxiliary missions. These general aviation aircraft are based at general aviation airports.

GENERAL AVIATION AIRPORTS

General aviation airports are airports used exclusively by general aviation aircraft (Figure 1.4). These airports do not offer commercial air carrier service. The airports may be privately owned by an individual, family, or corporation. The general aviation airport may also be owned by a governmental agency or governmental airport authority.

While there are no commercial airline operations at a general aviation airport, there may be general aviation aircraft operations at commercial airports. This may include an area of a commercial airport set aside for general aviation ground operations and support. This support could

4

Figure 1.4 Reigle Airport (58 N), Palmyra, Pennsylvania. (Photo by Daniel J. Benny.)

include a general aviation fixed-base operator (FBO), a general aviation hangar, and flight schools. All general aviation aircraft, fixed-base operations, and flight schools will be subject to the Department of Homeland Security Transportation Security Administration (FAA) security requirement when operating out of a commercial airport. The most common security requirements include positive security identification badging and access control around the general aviation operations area of the commercial airport. This book addresses security issues for general aviation aircraft, hangars, fixed-base operations, and flight schools operating from general aviation airports with no commercial operations.

Fixed-Base Operator

A fixed-base operator is a term developed in the United States after the passage of the Air Commerce Act of 1926. The FAA defines a fixed-base operator as a commercial aviation business that provides aeronautical services. These services might include fueling, hangars, tie-down space, aircraft rental, aircraft maintenance, flight instruction, a pilot shop, and other aviation-related services at a public use general aviation or commercial airport.

Figure 1.5 Fixed-base operator CXY Aviation at Capital City Airport, New Cumberland, Pennsylvania. (Photo by Daniel J. Benny.)

A fixed-base operator is a primary provider of support services to general aviation at public use general aviation airports and at commercial airports. In some cases, the fixed-base operator owns the airport and flight school. The fixed-base operator might just be contracted by the airport owners to provide aviation-related service to the general aviation airport owner, pilots, and aircraft owners based at the general aviation airport (Figure 1.5).

Flight Schools

Flight schools provide the training required for an individual to obtain a private pilot's certificate. The pilot can then go on to obtain an instrument rating or more advanced aeronautical ratings. Flight schools are regulated by the FAA. A flight school can be a school certified by Federal Aviation Regulations (FARs) Part 61 or Part 141, which refer to the parts of the FARs under which they operate. The most common distinction between the two is the minimum flight time required for the private certificate, 40 hours under Part 61 and 35 hours under Part 141.

The most significant difference between the two is the structure and accountability. Part 141 schools are periodically audited by the FAA and must have a detailed FAA-approved course of study. This course of study must be in writing and must meet student performance rates. Part 61 schools do not have the same paperwork and accountability requirements. Many flight schools at general aviation airports are only Part 61 schools. The flight school can be both if it so chooses as long as it meets requirements for both Part 61 and Part 141.

The flight school can be owned and operated by the airport or fixed-base operation. The flight school may also be a stand-alone business operating the flight school at a general aviation airport under a lease agreement with the owner of the airport or the fixed-base operator.

IMPORTANCE OF GENERAL AVIATION

General aviation is critical to the security, infrastructure, and economic success of the United States. It supports many aspects of society. This would include public safety, business, agriculture, commercial airports, aeronautical education, and many aspects of the aviation profession. General aviation also serves as a valuable recreational activity to thousands of general aviation pilots and aircraft owners who utilize general aviation airports and fixed-base operation facilities across the United States.

Public Safety

General aviation plays a critical role in public safety. Fixed-wing aircraft and helicopters are used by federal, state, and local law enforcement agencies for a variety of missions (Figure 1.6). They are utilized for law enforcement patrols, Homeland Security operations, and traffic enforcement. General aviation aircraft and general aviation airports are used to support tactical and emergency law enforcement operations throughout the United States. General aviation aircraft are also used by law enforcement for search-and-rescue missions, counterdrug operations, and the transport of law enforcement officers and dignitaries in various situations and to counter or respond to terrorism.

Fire protection agencies utilize general aviation fixed-wing and rotary aircraft in firefighting. They are primarily used in rural areas to fight brush and forest fires where ground equipment cannot reach or when there is no access to water to extinguish the fire.

7

Figure 1.6 Pennsylvania State Police helicopter, Capital City Airport, New Cumberland, Pennsylvania. (Photo by Daniel J. Benny.)

They are also used to transport firefighters to rural areas to reach the fire line. Such aircraft can be utilized in urban areas in firefighting and for rescue from tall buildings. General aviation aircraft can also be used by the fire service to gather information on the fire operation and conduct damage assessment surveys.

Emergency medical services agencies and hospitals use helicopters for emergency medical evacuation operations. They are also used for critical transport for those already hospitalized but who need to be moved to another hospital for critical treatment in a timely manner.

General aviation aircraft are also used by the medical profession to transport donor organs that must reach the donor recipient in a judicious manner (Figure 1.7). General aviation can be used in areas where ground vehicles cannot reach the victim or when the victim must be transported to a specific hospital from the field based on the injury in an expedient manner.

Natural resources organizations tasked with the protection of the environment use both fixed-wing aircraft and helicopters. They are utilized for natural resource patrols to move personnel to remote areas

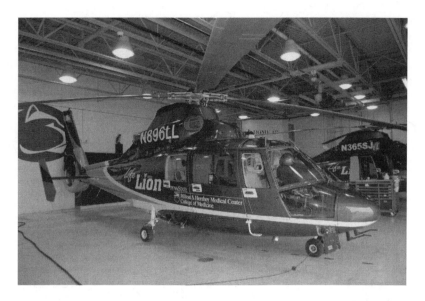

Figure 1.7 Penn State Hershey Medical Center Life Lion helicopter, Hershey, Pennsylvania. (Photo by Daniel J. Benny.)

during emergencies. Such aircraft are also used by these organizations for nonemergency situations to transport animals and for natural resource studies, tracking, and mapping.

Business

Organizations of all sizes use general aviation aircraft to operate and expand their business. Aircraft of all types, from a Cessna single-engine to a Citation jet aircraft, are used. Business enterprises also use helicopters in support of their commerce and for travel.

The aircraft may serve to carry executives and other company staff to attend meetings or trade shows or to travel to other company facilities. They are also used to transport possible customers to the corporate office or other meeting locations. The transport of company cargo and products is also a part of business aviation. Many businesses will locate their corporate office in an area that has a general aviation airport to facilitate corporate air travel needs.

9

Agriculture

The United States is the largest producer of safe food in the world. In part, this is due to the methods used to protect the agricultural products from pests. This is accomplished by general aviation in the form of agricultural spraying of the crops to ensure the proper growth and profit to the farmer. Because of the numerous acres of crops that need to be sprayed, it could only be accomplished in a cost-effective manner by general aviation aircraft for aerial spraying. These general aviation aircraft are based at general aviation airports around the United States to provide this service effectively to the farming community and the United States.

Economic Development

General aviation airports and aircraft contribute to the economic development of an area by attracting businesses that need the use of a general aviation airport to move into a community because of its airport. Many business parks are built around general aviation airports in a community. This increase in business supports the local economy in many ways. It contributes money to the tax base in corporate tax and personal tax.

It also supports local business at the airport such as the fixed-base operations, food service, and aviation repair services. Other businesses in the area that benefit from general aviation include taxi service, rental car service, food service, and hotels. General aviation also supports tourism in an area where the airport is located, such as museums, theme parks, and historical and musical attractions.

Feeder Airport

General aviation airports serve as feeder airports to commercial airports. According to the Central Intelligence Agency *World Factbook* for 2011, there are 5,380 paved general aviation airports and 5,180 unpaved general aviation airports in the United States compared to 372 commercial airports. Without general aviation airports, the commercial airports would be overwhelmed with hundreds of general aviation aircraft flying in and out and taxiing on their tarmac. The general aviation aircraft would also require service, fuel, tie-down space, and hangar space. It would cause not only a space issue on the ground but also more congestion with air traffic control at commercial airports. The general aviation feeder airports reduce the risk of accidents at commercial airports by reducing the congestion at the commercial airport on the ground and in the airspace.

General aviation airports are also critical staging areas close to each community in time of calamity due to extreme weather, natural disasters, or terrorist activity. General aviation airports are critical to the national security and defense of the United States by providing an infrastructure of small airports in all areas within fifty states, including urban, suburban, and rural areas.

Promotion of Aviation and Education

Promotion of aeronautics and flight training is critical to ensure that there will be new pilots and aviation professionals into the future. One of the best places to create an interest in aviation is at the local general aviation airport. Airplane rides and open houses catch the dreams of many. The general aviation airports and aircraft have been the start for numerous individuals who have gone into the aeronautics field as a profession as flight instructor, commercial pilots, or as those who service the nation and their local communities as military, law enforcement, and public safety pilots.

Most general aviation airports offer flight training. This is a great start for many individuals who later go on to higher education in aeronautics, such as at Embry-Riddle Aeronautical University, to train and obtain certification and a degree in aviation so that they can become a commercial carrier and transport airline pilot or a military pilot or to advance their flying and aviation career.

General aviation airports are a great place to start for new flight instructors to build time in the different type of aircraft and to build time as a flight instructor. They can then go on to work for airlines or even into airport and airline management positions.

General aviation airports also support the education of children and young adults with open houses and tours for school groups. These activities create an interest in aviation as a profession.

Some general aviation airports will host a Civil Air Patrol cadet squadron or Boy Scout viation Eagle Scout troop. This can facilitate the teaching of aeronautics to children and young adults. There is also the Experimental Aircraft Association (EAA) Young Eagles program that is hosted at general aviation airports. The EAA Young Eagles program provides an opportunity for children to experience the wonders of flight firsthand.

Figure 1.8 The author's previous Cessna C-150, Reigle Airport, Palmyra, Pennsylvania. (Photo by Daniel J. Benny.)

Personal Use

One of the most enjoyable activities for many individuals is the pleasure of flight. It opens up a new and exciting world of fun, adventure, and achievement. It provides the pilot the opportunity to soar beyond the boundaries of Earth and congestion of traffic so he or she can travel and enjoy the satisfaction of flight.

Many pilots will purchase their own aircraft so that they can fly for pleasure and business at their leisure. For those who do not own an aircraft, general aviation airports offer small planes to rent by the hour or day. General aviation aircraft such as the single-engine Cessnas, Pipers, and Grummans, the most popular for personal use, can be found at all most general aviation airports. Most personal use aircraft are based at a small general aviation airport (Figure 1.8).

THE THREAT FROM GENERAL AVIATION

After the events of the devastating terrorist attack against the United States on September 11, 2001, the initial focus from the U.S. government, media, and the public was on security at commercial airports and aboard commercial airlines. This focus was due to the nature of the terrorist attack:

Perpetrators boarded commercial aircraft at commercial airports and used them as a weapon of mass destruction in New York City, Washington, D.C., and Pennsylvania to murder over 3,000 individuals.

As the identity of the terrorist hijackers became known, along with their activities in the United States in making preparations for the attack, there was the revelation that the terrorists who flew the aircraft received flight training at flight schools operating out of general aviation airports in the United States.

Mohamed Atta, who hijacked American Airline Flight 11, attended flight instruction in Venice, Florida.

Marwan al Shehhi, who hijacked United Airlines Flight 175, attended flight instruction in Venice, Florida.

Hani Hanjour, who hijacked American Airlines Flight 77, attended flight instruction in Arizona. He obtained both his private pilot's license and commercial pilot rating.

Ziad Jarrah, who hijacked United Airlines Flight 93, attended flight instruction in Venice, Florida.

Based on intelligence and learning that the terrorists obtained flight instruction at general aviation airports in the United States and utilized general aviation aircraft operating out of general aviation airports, the government, media, and the general public became focused on general aviation security. Speculation on the potential threat to the United States from terrorists utilizing general aviation became rampant.

Fears of this threat were heightened 4 months after the commercial aviation terrorism disasters in New York City, Washington, D.C., and Pennsylvania when, on January 5, 2002, a student, Charles J. Bishop, taking lessons in Tampa, Florida, from a flight school at a general aviation airport, stole a Cessna C-172, a general aviation aircraft, and flew it into a high-rise building in Tampa. A note was found on Bishop's body that stated that the student flew the Cessna C-172 into the building as an act of terrorism in support of Osama Bin Laden. Fortunately, there was no loss of life in this incident other than Bishop. There was the loss of a new Cessna C-712 and damage to the building.

After this incident, there was a huge outcry by the media and many within the government to mandate security regulations for general aviation airports, aircraft, and flight schools. While the use of a general aviation aircraft in Tampa to strike a building is tragic and a threat not to be taken lightly, one needs to look at the history of the use of general aviation

13

aircraft in the United States for such acts of terrorism to place the threat from general aviation aircraft in perspective.

There was only one incident in the United States where a general aviation aircraft was use as a weapon before the Tampa incident. There has been only one such incident since the 2002 attack in Tampa.

On September 13, 1994, before the Tampa incident, Frank Eugene Corder flew a stolen Cessna from a Maryland general aviation airport into the White House in Washington, D.C. This act was done in an attempted assassination of then president of the United States, Bill Clinton. There were no injuries or fatalities other than Corder, who flew the aircraft into the White House and died on impact. There was no damage to the White House.

The third documented use of a general aviation aircraft in an act of terrorism occurring on February 18, 2010. On that date, Joseph Andrew Stack flew his own aircraft into the Internal Revenue Service building in Austin, Texas. It is unfortunate that there was one other fatality in addition to Stack. who died on impact.

While these three incidents that resulted in the tragic loss of life and injuries are deplorable, it is obvious that, based on the history, there has been no significant terrorist threat from the use of general aviation aircraft flying from general aviation airports. This does not mean that the general aviation community should be complacent; on the contrary, it is an indicator that it can happen and that it could happen again. Security of general aviation aircraft, airports, hangars, fixed-base operators, and flight schools must continue to be a priority in the aviation profession to reduce the threat of loss of life by using general aviation aircraft as a weapon.

BIBLIOGRAPHY

Aircraft Owners and Pilots Association. (2003). *AOPA Airport Watch*. Frederick, MD: AOPA.

Central Intelligence Agency. (2011). *World Fact Book*. Washington, DC: Government Printing Office.

Fischer, R.J., & Green, G. (2004). *Introduction to security* (7th ed.). Burlington, MA: Elsevier.

Moore, K.C. (2000). *Airport, aircraft and airline security*. Burlington, MA: Elsevier Butterworth-Heinemann.

National Counter Terrorism Security Office. (2012). *Counter terrorism protective security advice for general aviation*. London: National Counter Terrorism Security Office.

Price, J.C., & Forrest, J.S. (2009). *Practical aviation security*. Burlington, MA: Elsevier Butterworth-Heinemann.

Sweet, K.M. (2009). *Aviation and airport security*. Upper Saddle River, NJ: Pearson/Prentice Hall.

Transportation Security Administration. (2011). Retrieved from http://www.tsa.gov/

Turney, A.M., Bishop, J.C., & Fitzgerald, P.C. (2004). Measuring the importance of recent airport security interventions [Electronic version]. *Journal of Air Transportation*, 9, 3.

Wiencek, D. (2005). Open skies? *Journal of Counterterrorism and Homeland Security International* 11, 12–24.

2

The Security Threat to General Aviation

SECURITY THREATS AGAINST INDIVIDUALS IN THE AVIATION ENVIRONMENT

The security threat to individuals in the aviation environment located at general aviation airports can be the same as a threat to an individual at most any public location. These threats could include harassment, stalking, assault, robbery, sexual assault, and even homicide. Most often, violent crimes against an individual are committed by a known person and are not related to the general aviation location.

The threat against an individual at a general aviation airport could be related to a threat against the actual airport property such as a robbery at the fixed-base operator or terrorist incident directed toward the aviation facility.

SECURITY THREATS AGAINST AIRCRAFT

The security threats against the aircraft would include its theft, destruction, hijacking, and vandalism. It also includes the theft of the aircraft avionics or property located inside the aircraft.

Theft of the aircraft may occur for several reasons. The aircraft could be stolen with the intention of using it for a joyride and then returned to the home base airport or left at some other location. The aircraft could be stolen so that it can be utilized in criminal activity. The criminal activity might include smuggling of drugs, weapons, or other contraband. Theft of the aircraft may be to convert the aircraft to personal long-term use. It may be taken for aircraft parts, which would be sold for profit or personal use. The theft of an aircraft may be so that it can be utilized in an act of terrorism to be used as weapon.

Destruction of an aircraft could occur with insurance fraud as a motive; the owner of the aircraft burns or destroys the aircraft in some manner for the insurance money. The destruction could be for revenge against a private aircraft owner, fixed-base operator, or flight school that may own the aircraft; this could lead to the crime of arson or the use of an explosive device. The destruction could be an act of terrorism. Terrorists most often will use an explosive device as a method of operations and as a weapon.

Hijacking of a general aviation aircraft would occur as a pilot performs the exterior preflight checklist or at the time the pilot is entering the aircraft to begin the flight. The motive in this type of situation is most often to force the pilot to take the perpetrator to a specified destination or to use the pilot and aircraft in the commission of some criminal activity or in the commission of a terrorist act, such as using the general aviation aircraft as a weapon.

One of the most common threats to a general aviation aircraft is vandalism. The vandalism could damage the aircraft hull with scratches and dents. The aircraft control surfaces could be damaged or bent. Windscreens and windows can be scratched or broken. Tires may be punctured. In some cases, the interior of the aircraft could be damaged by cutting the seats and causing damage to the flight instruments by smashing them. Accidental vandalism may occur by individuals hanging on or moving the flight control surfaces and not realizing how sensitive they are to damage.

General aviation aircraft are equipped with avionics that are used in the communication and navigation of the aircraft. This equipment is expensive and is often the target in crimes against an aircraft. The equipment is stolen for personal use and to sell for profit. There is not only the loss of the avionics but also often extensive damage to the aircraft in gaining access and the removal of the avionics from the instrument panel.

SECURITY THREATS AGAINST GENERAL AVIATION AIRPORTS

There are many security threats against the general aviation airport. The most obvious threat is accessing the airport property to commit crimes against individuals, aircraft, hangars, the fixed-base operator, and the flight school. The security concerns of each of these targets of crime are be addressed separately.

The threats to the airport property itself would include vandalism of fencing and gates surrounding the airport. There can also be vandalism or the theft of signs, general lighting, runway lighting, visual approach slope indicator (VASI) lighting, beacon light, wind socks, and wind vans.

Other areas to consider would be navigation and communication equipment antennas, weather collection equipment, and airport vehicles such as trucks, cars, tractors and snow plows. One of the most critical threats is to the fueling operation area of the general aviation airport.

Aerial work general aviation aircraft, such as crop dusters or firefighting aircraft that operate from the airport, need special security attention. These aircraft have tanks that are installed on the aircraft to hold pesticides or fire suppression chemicals. The aircraft must be protected from theft. They must also be protected due to safety issues related to the contents of the tanks. The aircraft and tanks must be secured from sabotage by terrorist organizations, which could insert chemical or biological agents into the storage tanks so they would be unknowingly disbursed on crops or during firefighting operations.

The motive of these threats could be to damage property, an act of vandalism, or revenge against the airport. It could also be an act of terrorism. Removal and theft of airport property might be to convert the items for personal use. The property might be sold for profit.

SECURITY THREATS AGAINST HANGARS

Security threats will be based on an attempt to steal or vandalize the aircraft stored in the hangars. It might also be related to the theft of avionics and property stored in the aircraft that is kept in the hangar.

In some cases, the goal may be just to destroy the hangar by arson or use of explosives regardless of whether there is an aircraft or property in the hangar. This could be a means of revenge, insurance fraud, or an act of terrorism.

SECURITY THREATS AGAINST
THE FIXED-BASE OPERATION

The threats against the fixed-base operator facility could be the theft or burglary of property such as office equipment, pilot supplies, computers, information, and communications equipment. The goal may be the theft of airport vehicles or keys to hangars or aircraft kept in the fixed-base operator facility. The stolen keys would be used for stealing such property or gaining access for other criminal intent.

The threat may also be to obtain information with regard to the airport, employees or aircraft owners, and the aircraft. This can be accomplished through burglary and obtaining the information from paper records. Hacking into the organization's computer system to retrieve such information is a serious threat.

SECURITY THREATS AGAINST THE FLIGHT SCHOOL

The threats against the flight school are very similar to the threats to the fixed-base operator. The flight school may be housed in the same building as the fixed-base operator. The threats include the theft or burglary of property such as office equipment, pilot supplies, personal computers, and communications equipment. The hangars and aircraft keys kept in the flight school can be taken for the purpose of stealing such property or gaining access to the hangar for other criminal intent.

The threat may also be to obtain information with regard to the flight school staff, students' records, and the aircraft. This could be achieved through burglary and obtaining the information from paper records. It can also include hacking into the flight school computer system to retrieve such information.

SECURITY THREAT FROM TERRORISTS
USING GENERAL AVIATION AIRCRAFT

When exploring the security risk posed by general aviation aircraft that could be used to carry out a terrorist attack, there are several concerns that have been raised. They would include the use of a general aviation aircraft to carry conventional explosives. There is a concern that a general aviation aircraft could be used as a platform for a chemical, biological, or radiological release over a populated area. The final scenario would be to use a general aviation aircraft to crash into a nuclear, chemical, oil, or gas facility, thus causing the release of radioactivity or dangerous chemicals or resulting in an explosion and fire based on the type of facility that was targeted.

To evaluate the risk of a general aviation aircraft being used to carry conventional explosives, one needs to look at the aircraft weight, payload capacity with full fuel tanks, range, and speed. General aviation aircraft such a Cessna-172, one of the most common types of aircraft found at a general aviation airport, have limited payload capabilities with one passenger and a full load of fuel. The range is about 4 hours at 120 miles an hour based on head- or tailwinds. This would allow for less than 800 pounds of useful payload. That size payload to carry explosives would not compare to the 1,300-pound device used for the first bombing of the World Trade Center or the 5,000 pound device that took down the federal building in Oklahoma City. There are many security professionals who feel that general aviation aircraft would be used to defeat vehicle barriers at secure facilities because they can fly over the physical security barriers. Based on capabilities of the payload, the threat of a general aviation aircraft being used by a terrorist organization with conventional explosives is remote.

The use of a general aviation aircraft as a platform for a chemical, biological, or radiological release over a populated area poses a more significant threat. General aviation aircraft can carry such material and, because they can fly low and slow, could be effective in the release of chemical, biological, or radiological material. Some general aviation aircraft that are used for aerial spraying of crops are already equipped to facilitate such an operation.

When one looks at the reality of such an attack, the risk diminishes. The aircraft would need to be loaded with such an agent. That process could cause suspicion at the general aviation airport, especially if there is an active security program to include one as effective as the Aircraft Owners and Pilots Association Airport Watch Program. The Aircraft Owners and Pilots Association Airport Watch Program is discussed in detail further in this book.

The payload of the agent would be small and most likely would become ineffective because of the low concentration when mixed with the atmosphere when disbursed. It must be noted that under the right conditions, there could be numerous casualities by such a release using a general aviation aircraft.

The release of such agents can be easily detected by law enforcement, public safety, and emergency management organizations on the ground, which would allow for immediate countermeasures. Because general aviation aircraft do fly low and slow, they would also be an easy target for law enforcement or military aircraft to eliminate the airborne threat.

Should a terrorist organization obtain a nuclear explosive device to load on a general aviation aircraft, the result would be significant. It would, however, be just as easy—if not easier—for a terrorist group to use a ground vehicle for such an attack.

Another concern is the use of a general aviation aircraft to crash into a nuclear, chemical, oil, or gas facility. Most nuclear facilities could withstand the strike of a general aviation aircraft. Some nuclear facilities, such as Three Mile Island in Middletown, Pennsylvania, near Harrisburg, can withstand the strike of a commercial aircraft (Figure 2.1). Commercial aircraft fly out of Harrisburg International Airport.

A general aviation aircraft flown into a chemical, oil, or gas facility could be destructive based on the construction of the facility and where the general aviation aircraft struck. The weight and speed of the aircraft would also be a determining factor in such an incident.

While there are risks that a terrorist organization may attempt to use a general aviation aircraft as a platform for destruction, there are many

Figure 2.1 Three Mile Island, nuclear facility, Middletown, Pennsylvania. (Photo by Daniel J. Benny.)

variables that would affect the outcome or success of such a strike. The key is to know and understand the risk and put measures in place as described in this book to prevent or minimize the effect of such an incident.

TERRORISM AND COUNTERTERRORISM

To understand and counter the threat from terrorism, it is important to have a grasp of the strategies and tactics employed by terrorist organizations. It is also important to understand why they are such a threat.

Terrorism

You may have heard the words, "One man's terrorist is another man's freedom fighter." It may be hard to agree on what a freedom fighter is, but a group of individuals who specifically target civilians are not freedom fighters. They are terrorists and are practicing terrorism on innocents. While it is often not always so cut and dried, to my mind, a dead terrorist is a good terrorist.

There are many different definitions of terrorism. The most direct definition is the use or threat of violence to obtain specific goals. What are the goals of terrorist organizations? There are four: political, ideological, religious, and violence for effect.

Political Goals: A political goal is to change the leadership or political structure of a country. An example of this would be the conflict between the United Kingdom and Ireland over the control of Northern Ireland. While often both sides had different religious affiliations, the real issue was political.

Ideological Goals: Ideological goals would include the goal of terrorist groups to stop a certain practice. These groups may include animal rights, environmental, or antiabortion groups who take part in criminal acts in support of their ideological cause.

Religious Goals: Some terrorist organizations base their action on religious views, such Islamic jihadists. Their goal is to convert those on the earth to Islam by force if necessary. Islamic jihadists' goals are also political and ideological because Islam is a way of life and is their political and judicial system.

Violence for Effect: The ultimate goal of violence for effect is to influence an audience beyond the immediate victims. These individuals want to attract attention to the cause, demonstrate power,

exact revenge, obtain logistical support to carry out terrorist operations, and if possible cause government overreaction to gain support of the masses and media.

Terrorist Categories

There are three specific categories of terrorists: state directed, state supported, and non-state supported. For state-directed terrorists, a country
uses terrorism as a matter of national policy, such as Iran. For the state-
supported category, a country provides aid to terrorism in the form of
money, weapons, or harboring terrorists, as was the case in Iraq. Non-
state supported terrorists are groups who operate independently with no
assistance from a nation. This could include domestic groups such as the
Ku Klux Klan or Black Panthers.

There are two broad categories of terrorist organizations. National
terrorists operate within the boundaries of a single nation to affect issues
related to that nation. Transnational terrorists operate in a region or worldwide to affect issues that have an impact on numerous nations or regions
or have global impact.

Typical Profile of a Terrorist

While a terrorist can be anyone, there are some typical profiles that have
emerged over the years. Generally, they have been male, between the ages
of 22 and 28, unmarried, of urban origin, and university-level educated.
They have been upper middle class in their society and are often recruited
from universities, religious groups, and prison.

Most foreign terrorists to the United States are Marxist or Islamic
jihadists. Most domestic terrorists in the United States are antigovernment, Marxist, Islamic jihadists, or racist groups.

Organizational Structure of Terrorist Groups

While each terrorist group could be organized differently, there are some
common structures. Hardcore leadership is the management of the organization. Individuals or groups of individuals may control a particular
terrorist organization.

The active cadre is the individuals in a terrorist organization who
carry out the terrorist acts and collect intelligence for target selection.
They will also be involved in gathering logistic support in the field, such
as vehicles, weapons, and safe houses. The structure of the active cadre
is that of small cells made up of four to six individuals. This is done for
security reasons. The cells are organized by function, such intelligence,

which conducts intelligence missions for target selection. There are the logistics cells that secure weapons, explosives, vehicles, and safe houses. The tactical cell carries out the terrorist activity.

Active supporters are individuals who provide behind-the-scenes support for the terrorist organization. It may include legal support, laundering of money, medical support, or political support.

Passive supporters are those who donate money, conduct fund-raising, or take part in public demonstrations in support of their cause.

Operational Tactics

Operational tactics are how the terrorist acts are carried out or the method of operation. The most common tactic is the use of explosives. The group makes a simple or complex explosive, based on the funds and capabilities of the group members. There are numerous methods of activating an explosive device, such as a timer, altimeter, light sensor, radio frequencies, pressure, or trip wire and suicide bombing. The last allows the terrorist to escape capture or to die for the cause.

Assassinations are used to take out a specific target. This may be a political leader, law enforcement member, or any selected target. This may be enacted by hijacking an aircraft or other mode of transportation or taking a group hostage in a structure. Kidnapping, armed assault, robberies, burglaries, and fraud are used to obtain money or weapons. Street action is used to infiltrate demonstrations and cause unrest. The most effective tactic is the element of surprise.

Target Selection

Target selection involves picking and indentifying an individual, group of individuals, or a structure to strike. The terrorist groups seek a target that is soft, visible, or has high-impact value. A soft target is one that does not have a high level of security. General aviation airports or aircraft are considered soft targets. A visible target is one that is well known, such as the World Trade Center or a national monument. A high-impact target is one that will cause much damage or loss of life and will obtain the most media attention.

U.S. Domestic Terrorist Threat

There is a variety of domestic threats within the United States. Such groups may be politically left wing or right wing. The agenda of these groups also may be antigovernment, environmental, animal rights, antiabortion, religious, or racism.

U.S. Foreign Terrorist Threat

There are many international terror organizations, but the most dangerous to the United States are the Islamic jihadist groups. They are a serious threat because their cause is tied to their religion, which makes it a very strong cause that many are willing to die for. The goal of the Islamic jihadist is to reform and convert those on earth by force if necessary. Money is no object to support the cause, and they have transnational capabilities. It allows them the ability to unite followers through a militant and violent interpretation of Islam.

Counterterrorism

General aviation airports, fixed-base operators, flight schools, pilots, aircraft owners, and corporate flight departments must be proactive to counter the threat of terrorism. As part of the airport risk and threat analysis, the threat from terrorism must be calculated into that equation.

Intelligence is the key in assessing the threat from terrorism and developing counterterrorism measures. Sources of intelligence for the general aviation airport would include the news and current events, liaison with local law enforcement agencies, the Transportation Security Administration, and security consultants.

Participation in the Aircraft Owners and Pilots Association Airport Watch Program includes physical security measures, security awareness and training, and possible use of security forces, based on the threat.

Use of Profiling for Counterterrorism

Profiling is not new to the law enforcement, intelligence, and security agencies and is a part of the investigative and intelligence process. It has been utilized in efforts to identify and apprehend individuals involved in various types of criminal activity, such as those involved with serial murders, organized crime, the drug cartel and crimes related to illegal drugs, espionage, hate groups, and terrorist organizations.

When utilizing profiling as an investigative tool, it is vital that law enforcement, intelligence, and security agencies base it on the facts of the case and not on bias or stereotyping. It needs to be based on objective data with numerous descriptive variables so that the range of offenders can be narrowed down. This has led to the term *criminal profiling* to be swapped for *behavioral profiling*. This profiling uses the behaviors of observed characteristics and their interactions with others, including law enforcement agents, to determine when something (or things) are amiss and suspicious and unusual behavior is occurring.

It is important that law enforcement, intelligence, and security agencies not be restricted in performing their duties in identifying a suspect in terrorism because of political correctness. Behavioral profiling is an accepted tool and should never be disregarded because of political correctness or because someone is offended. Certainly, interactions, searches, pat downs, or other actions must be done in a professional manner.

Racial profiling is often confused with criminal profiling, and in the minds of some, it is one and the same. Racial profiling can be defined as investigating an individual or taking a law enforcement or security action against that individual based on the individual's race, national origin, religion, ethnicity, or sexual orientation.

Often, what some would say is racial profiling is nothing more than the perception that it is occurring when in fact it was a clear case of the proper use of behavioral profiling. In any event, some might say perceptions are everything. In the matter of offended feelings and misguided perceptions, they are not a justifiable reason to prohibit the law enforcement, intelligence, and security community from performing their duties effectively in providing protection from terrorism through behavioral profiling.

To counter terrorism, criminal profiling can be a viable tool when properly utilized.

Signs of Terrorism
To counter terrorism, it is important to be alert to what is occurring at or around the general aviation airports. There are some distinctive signs of possible terrorist activity against a general aviation airport, including

- Surveillance
- Elicitation
- Tests of security
- Acquiring supplies
- Suspicious people who do not belong
- Dry runs
- Deploying assets/getting into position

Surveillance
When terrorists have chosen a specific target, that area will be observed during the planning phase of the operation to gather intelligence. The goal

is to determine the strengths, weaknesses, and number of personnel that may respond to an incident. Routes to and from the target are established during the surveillance phase. It is important to take note of someone recording or monitoring activities, drawing diagrams on or annotating maps, using vision-enhancing devices, or having in one's possession floor plans or blueprints of hangars, the fixed-base operator, flight school, and runway and roadway configurations. Any of these surveillance-type acts are indicators that something is not right.

Elicitation

The second sign is elicitation. An individual is attempting to gain information about an airport, person, or tenant operations at the airport. An example is someone attempting to gain knowledge about type of aircraft, fuel storage, or hours of staffing. The person may also attempt to place key people in sensitive work locations by obtaining part-time or full-time positions on the airport property.

Tests of Security

Tests of security are another area in which terrorists would attempt to gather information and intelligence about the general aviation airport. These are conducted by driving by the target, moving into sensitive areas, and observing airport security or law enforcement response. Terrorists would be interested in the time it takes to respond to an incident or the routes taken to a specific location. They may also try to penetrate physical security barriers or procedures to assess strengths and weaknesses. They often gain legitimate employment at key locations to monitor day-to-day activities. In any event, they may try to gain this knowledge to make their mission or scheme more effective.

Acquiring Supplies

Another sign of terrorism is anyone acquiring supplies. For instance, someone is purchasing or stealing explosives, weapons, or ammunition. It could also be someone storing harmful chemicals or chemical equipment. Terrorists would also find it useful to have in their possession law enforcement equipment and identification, military uniforms and decals, flight passes, badges, or even flight manuals. If they cannot find the opportunity to steal these types of things, they may try to photocopy IDs or attempt to make passports or other forms of identification by counterfeiting. Possessing any of these would make it easier for one to gain entrance into secured or usually prohibited areas. Such items could be stored by the terrorist in a hangar or aircraft at a general aviation airport.

Suspicious People Who Do Not Belong

A fifth preincident indicator is observing suspicious people who just do not belong. This does not mean we should profile individuals; rather, it means we should profile behaviors. It may mean having someone at the airport or tenant activity who does not fit in because of their demeanor, their language usage, or asking unusual questions.

Dry Runs

Another sign to watch for is dry runs. Before execution of the final operation or plan, a practice session will be conducted to work out the flaws and unanticipated problems. A dry run may very well be the heart of a planning stage of a terrorist act. If you find someone monitoring an airport and police radio frequency and recording emergency response times, you may very well be observing a dry run. Another element of this activity could include mapping routes and determining the timing of aircraft or vehicle traffic. This stage is the best chance to intercept and stop an attack. Multiple dry runs are normally conducted at or near the target area.

Deploying Assets/Getting into Position

The final sign to look for is someone deploying assets or getting into position. This is the last opportunity to alert authorities before the terrorist act occurs. It is also important to remember that preincident indicators may come months or even years apart. It is extremely important to document all information received no matter how insignificant it may appear and forward this information to the Aircraft Owners and Pilots Association hotline and airport manager.

International Terrorist Organizations

The most serious terrorist threat is from international foreign terrorist groups. These terrorist groups can operate directly in the United States or recruit individuals currently living in the United States.

The list of international terrorist organizations identified and provided by the U.S. Department of State, provided in Appendix A, represents international terrorist organizations that have been active in the last 5 years.

BIBLIOGRAPHY

Aircraft Owners and Pilots Association. (2003). *AOPA Airport Watch*. Frederick, MD: AOPA.

Bragdon, C.R. (2008). *Transportation security*. Burlington, MA: Elsevier Butterworth-Heinemann.

Carter, D. (2002). *The police and the community*. Upper Saddle River, NJ: Prentice Hall.

Fischer, R.J., & Green, G. (2004). *Introduction to security* (7th ed.). Burlington, MA: Elsevier.

Moore, K.C. (2000). *Airport, aircraft and airline security*. Burlington, MA: Elsevier Butterworth-Heinemann.

National Counter Terrorism Security Office. (2012). *Counter terrorism protective security advice for general aviation*. London: National Counter Terrorism Security Office.

9/11 Commission. (2004). *The 9/11 Commission report: Final report of the National Commission on Terrorist Attacks Upon the United States*. New York: Norton.

Price, J.C., and Forrest, J.S. (2009). *Practical aviation security*. Burlington, MA: Elsevier Butterworth-Heinemann.

Swanson, C., Territo, L., & Taylor, R. (2005). *Police administration*. Upper Saddle River, NJ: Prentice Hall.

Sperry, P. (2005). *Infiltration*. Nashville, TN: Nelson Current.

Sweet, K.M. (2008). *Transportation security*. Upper Saddle River, NJ: Pearson/Prentice Hall.

Sweet, K.M. (2009). *Aviation and airport security*. Upper Saddle River, NJ: Pearson/Prentice Hall.

Transportation Security Administration. (2004). *Security guideline for general aviation airports*. Washington, DC: Transportation Security Administration.

Transportation Security Administration. (2011). Retrieved from http://www.tsa.gov/

Turvey, B. (2001). *Criminal profiling an introduction to behavioral evidence analysis*. San Diego, CA: Elsevier Academic Press.

U.S. Department of State international terrorist organizations. Retrieved from http://www.cdi.org/terrorism/terrorist-groups.cfm.

Wiencek, D. (2005). Open skies? *Journal of Counterterrorism and Homeland Security International* 11, 12–24.

3

Physical Security for the Aviation Environment

INTRODUCTION

Physical security measures will be utilized as part of a comprehensive security program at general aviation airports. Physical security aid the protection of life and the protection of aircraft, airport property, hangars, the fixed-base operation, and the flight school.

The goals of physical security are to deter entry, delay entry, and detect entry.

Deter Entry

The use of signs, intrusion detection systems, barriers, locks, access control, and security cameras can deter an individual from taking part in criminal activity at the protected airport.

Delay Entry

By utilizing various physical security measures, should an individual not be deterred and attempt to take part in criminal activity on the airport property, the physical security measures put in place can delay the perpetrator. During this period of delay, the perpetrator may be observed by airport staff, a pilot or aircraft owner, security, or local law enforcement, and the crime can be averted.

Detect Entry

With the use of physical security devices, should an individual attempt to take part in criminal activity on the airport property, the individual's presence and actions will be detected. This could result in the perpetrator stopping the criminal activity and leaving the airport. It could result in the detection by airport staff or security personnel or detection and apprehension by law enforcement. If a crime is detected, then the individuals in charge of airport security know that there has been a threat, and they can evaluate the adequacy of the current physical security system to prevent future threats.

Physical security also controls the movement of people, such as employees, pilots, aircraft owners, visitors, customers, and vendors. Physical security measures can control access to enter and leave the airport property or gain access to the runway, fueling area, fixed-base operator, and flight school. Physical security also controls the movement of vehicles entering the property. They may be vehicles owned or driven by employees, pilots, aircraft owners, customers, visitors, or vendors. Physical security can also control the movement of aircraft at the general aviation airport.

Physical security controls the movement of airport, fixed-base operator, flight school, and pilots' property. It aids in ensuring that property is not removed and stays on the airport premises.

INTRUSION DETECTIONS SYSTEM

An intrusion detection system is designed to provide notice of someone entering a protected area of the airport or any of the buildings, such as hangars, fixed-base operator, or flight school. This is accomplished by a system of sensors that sends a notification to the computer base's monitoring stations or to a local sound-producing device when the sensor is activated. The intrusion detection system can be a proprietary central station in which it is monitored by the airport or fixed-base operator. It can also be a contract central station. The contract central station is a contract security-monitoring service not located or associated with the airport being protected. The contract central station receives the alarm and then notifies police, fire, emergency medical services, and the airport management based on the type of alarm that is received.

The most common sensors that are utilized include those that involve electromagnetic contacts, photoelectrics, lasers, glass breakage, pressure, vibration, audio, ultrasonics, microwaves, passive infrared, capacitance proximity, integrated fire protection, natural gas or carbon monoxide, and water flow.

Electromagnetic Contacts

Electromagnetic contacts are used to provide protection for doors and windows on hangars, the fixed-base operator, or the flight school (Figure 3.1). Contacts are place on the door and door frame or the window and window sash. When the door or window is closed, the contacts match. When the alarm system is activated, a current passes through the matching contacts. When the door or window is opened while the alarm is activated, it breaks the circuit and the alarm is activated.

Figure 3.1 Electromagnetic door contact sensor. (Photo by Daniel J. Benny.)

Photoelectrics

The photoelectric sensor is utilized to provide protection for doors and passageways based on use of a light beam. When the light beam is broken by an individual, the alarm is activated. The photoelectric cell can also be used to activate security lighting automatically during periods of darkness.

Lasers

The laser sensors can provide protection for doors and passageways and are based on use of a laser light beam. When the laser beam is broken, the alarm is activated. It can also be used to activate security lighting automatically during periods of darkness.

Glass Breakage

The glass breakage sensor is used on glass windows or door areas with glass to detect attempted entry through the breaking of glass. The sensor is mounted on the glass itself or near the glass window or door glass area and detects the vibration of the breaking glass.

Pressure

The pressure sensor is used to detect a person walking on a surface in the interior of a structure or the exterior grounds. The pressure-sensitive sensor is placed under a carpet inside a structure. If used outdoors, it is buried under the surface of the ground. The alarm is activated when an individual walks over the surface where the sensor is concealed. This is often used in the fixed-base operator or flight school buildings to provide customer service in addition to security by alerting staff that someone has entered the facility.

Vibration

Vibration is used to provide protection in utility ports large enough for an individual to access. It could be a hangar, fixed-base operation, or flight school. When a perpetrator attempts to access an area protected by this sensor and touches the vibration sensor, it will activate the alarm.

Audio

The audio sensor is a microphone, in most cases a series of microphones, placed inside the facility to be protected. Should there be unauthorized access into the structure, the microphones are activated. The microphones can transmit all that is heard to a central station monitored by airport staff or, in most cases, a security officer at a contract central station. The security officer can then dispatch whatever is needed in response to the airport and notify the local police.

Ultrasonics

Ultrasonic sensors are used for interior protection of a facility when not occupied. The sensor transceiver sends out sonar waves across the room that traverse back to the transceiver in a timed sequence. Should an individual enter the protected area, the sonar waves are interrupted, and the alarm is activated. It is not recommended for hangars because the air movement that can occur in a hangar can set off the alarm.

Microwaves

A microwave sensor transceiver is used for interior protection of a facility when not occupied. The sensor transceiver sends out microwaves across the room that traverse back to the transceiver in a timed sequence. Should an individual enter the protected area, the microwaves are interrupted, and the alarm is activated. This sensor should not be used in a room with large areas of glass, which are common in a fixed-base operator facility, as it will penetrate the glass and could result in false alarms.

Passive Infrared

The passive infrared sensor is the best motion transceiver for use in interior protection of a facility when not occupied (Figure 3.2). The sensor transceiver sends out light energy that detects body heat. Should an individual enter the protected area, the passive infrared detects the heat of the person and the heat in the protected area, and the alarm is activated. This sensor is recommended for hangars, fixed-base operator facilities, and flight schools. It can also be utilized inside an aircraft.

Figure 3.2   Passive infrared sensor. (Photo by Daniel J. Benny.)

Capacitance Proximity

The capacitance proximity sensor is used to protect metal safes and metal security containers. Once the sensor is attached to the metal safe or metal security container, a magnetic field around the protected item is established. The magnetic field will extend one foot around the protected safe or container. When a person walks into that space or touches the safe or container, the person's body will draw in the magnetism. This will cause a drop in the magnetic field protecting the safe or security container and activate the alarm. This could be used for a safe or steel aircraft key security container.

Integrated Fire Protection Sensors

Almost all protection systems now include intrusion detection and fire safety in one integrated system. The fire protection system can be activated manually by use of a pull station should one smell or see smoke and fire. The pull station will activate the audible and visual strobe fire protection enunciators in the building and notify the central station or emergency dispatch for the fire department. In addition to the manual pull station, there is a fire protection sensor that can be placed in the protected facility that will send an automatic signal to the central station or emergency dispatch for the fire department and activate a set of the audible and visual strobe fire protection enunciators.

The following fire protection sensors will be utilized: dual-chamber smoke detector and rate-of-rise heat detector.

Duel-Chamber Smoke Detector

The dual-chamber smoke detector sensor will provide early detection of smoke. It is used primarily for the protection of life, but early detection of a fire can also save property and aircraft if used in a hangar by providing early detection of fire.

Rate-of-Rise Heat Detector

The rate-of-rise heat detector sensor is used in area where a smoke detector cannot be used. This would include bathrooms and cooking areas at a fixed-base operator or flight school and any aircraft repair shops on the airport property where the normal activity in those areas would set off a smoke detector. The rate-of-rise heat detector will sense a rapid increase of the heat in an area due to a fire and will than activate the alarm system.

Natural Gas and Carbon Monoxide Detectors

The natural gas and carbon monoxide detectors are used to detect deadly gases that may build up in a facility. These sensors will provide early warning for evacuation.

Water Flow

For facilities that have fire protection sprinkler systems, the water flow sensor will detect the drop in water pressure when the sprinkler is activated during a fire. This will result in an alarm being activated. A sprinkler system could be used in a fixed-base operator or flight school. Do not use a water sprinkler system in a hangar with an aircraft.

SECURITY CAMERAS

The use of security camera surveillance at an airport, in or around a hangar, at the fixed-base operator, or at a flight school is effective in the prevention of crime. It also allows the documentation of events and provides evidence for an investigation should a crime occur. Security cameras can be utilized to provide protection from both external and internal theft.

An airport may install security cameras at any location on the exterior of its property and in almost all interior areas. The areas a security camera may not be utilized are in restrooms and locker rooms at the airport, fixed-base operators, or flight school. Other than those locations, there is no expectation of privacy in the workplace or at the airport.

The components of a security camera system include the lens/camera, transmission of the signal, monitoring, and recording.

Lens/Camera

An effective security camera will require a low-light, variable lens so that it is adaptable to low-light situations. This will allow effective operations during both day and night hours. It should be color rather than black and white to identify color, which is critical in security applications. It should be housed in a protective cover and have the ability to be operated remotely to allow for zoom, pan, and tilt.

Transmission of the Signal

Methods of transmitting the signal include the use of coaxial cable, fiber optics, the Ethernet, microwaves, radio-frequency (RF) radio, and lasers. The best connection would be from coaxial cable, fiber optics, or the Ethernet. In situations where a direct line cannot be used due to distance and other factors, microwaves, RF radio, and lasers can be used. These methods must be installed so they do not interfere with aviation navigation systems at the airport.

Monitoring

The camera image can be viewed on a traditional television screen, which should have a resolution of no less than 491-512 pixels with 580 lines. It can also be viewed on a desktop or laptop computer screen.

Digital Recording

Digital recording can be accomplished using a digital recording system. Digital recording allows for the ability to store more information for a longer period of time depending on the server capacity. It also allows

Figure 3.3 Security camera at General Aviation Airport. (Photo by Daniel J. Benny.)

obtaining stills from the video and enhancing and enlarging them for identification and to share with law enforcement agencies. Another important feature of digital recording is that a time frame in the video can be searched by typing in the date and time period. This makes retrieving and reviewing an important time event fast and easy.

Motion Detection

Security cameras (Figure 3.3) can be equipped to work in conjunction with motion detection sensors that would activate the recording of the viewer of the camera only during the time of the activation by the motion sensor. The advantage of this is to save on the amount of recorded time on a VHS tape when using the analog system or space on the server when using the digital system. It is most often used during the investigation of internal theft when the security department only needs to view an area when the sensor has been activated rather than going through hours of recording.

DETERMINING TOTAL SYSTEM COST OF THE SECURITY SYSTEM

When determining the total security system cost, there are several categories that must be explored. These include the system design cost, system installation cost, system operational cost, maintenance cost, and the replacement cost of the security system in part or in its entirety at some point in the future.

System Design Cost

Initially, there is the cost to develop the specifications for the project. This would include the type of security system that is required and the various components of the system. Included in this assessment should be the intrusion detection system central station server, computer and monitors, security and fire sensors, access controls, and security cameras that will be integrated into the total system.

The system design cost will also include development of the drawings and blueprints of the system that is to be constructed and installed. There are, of course, the consultant fees for the individual or firm hired to design the security system and create the drawing and blueprints of the project.

There are many aspects of the system design cost that must be taken into account. This will be important when submitting a budget for such a project. The life cycle of the security system should also be a consideration for long-term budget projection.

System Installation Cost

One of the most expensive aspects of the entire security system project will be the system installation cost. This includes the cost of the products or components of the security system, including the server, computer, monitors, control panel, wiring, metal conduit, security cameras, camera brackets, and housing. There is also the expense of the various sensors integrated into the system, such as door and window contacts, motion sensors, and fire protection sensors. If access control is part of the system, then there is the cost of the readers and cards to be used with the product.

Once the products have been identified and purchased, there will be the shipping cost to transport the system components to the installation site. This could include fees for rail and truck transport of large parts and the cost of local carriers for smaller products associated with the security system.

Labor costs for the individuals installing the system can be sizable based on the local union or nonunion wages in the local area. This would include electricians, and if other construction is needed to support the security system, it may also include masons, carpenters, and painters.

Permits will be required in most cases for the new construction and electrical installations. The cost of the permits will vary based on the requirement of the local government of the location of the security system project. Based on the nature of the product, there may also be state or Environmental Protection Agency permit fees to pay.

System Operational Cost

Once the system is installed, there will be initial and ongoing system operational costs. To ensure the proper function of the system, current policies, such as the airport security plan, will need to be rewritten, and new policies with regard to the operation of the security system will need to be written.

Since all new security systems are computer based, there will be significant initial and ongoing support from the organization's information technology (IT) department. This includes integrating the security system into the company's IT system, the development of IT security procedures, and software to protect the system.

The increase in cost for electrical power is also part of the system's operating cost.

In the event of a power loss, the security system must function, so an emergency backup generator must be included in the ongoing cost.

Maintenance Cost

Keeping the system operating will require an investment in ongoing maintenance. This would include routine costs to keep the system hardware running and upgrades to the software. It will also require updates to the physical components of the system, such as wiring and mechanical functions.

Replacement Cost

All things must pass, and that is true of security systems that become inoperable or antiquated. When designing and installing a new system, it is important to determine the life of the system. The manufacturer can most often advise on the life cycle of the system and potential future changes that may occur along with a time frame for such changes. Based on the life expectancy projection, a long-term budget should be established so that there are funds for the replacement of the security system at the anticipated replacement time.

LOCKS AND KEY CONTROL

The use of locks is one of the oldest forms of security and is still utilized in airports, hangars, fixed-base operators, and flight schools. There are two general categories of locks: those that operate on mechanical concepts and those that use electricity to operate mechanical components of the locking system. Locks, along with their keys, are used to secure personal doors, hangar doors, aircraft doors, prop and throttle locks, windows, utility ports, gates, file cabinets, and security containers for the protection of people, aircraft, property, and information.

In addition to preventing access based on security concerns, locks can prevent access to areas for safety-related issues. This might include securing hazardous materials storage areas and electrical rooms and locking equipment on/off switches.

Mechanical Locks

A mechanical lock utilizes physical moving parts and barriers to prevent the opening of the latch and includes the following: The latch or bolt holds the door or window to the frame. The strike is the part into which the latch is inserted. The barrier is a tumbler array that must be passed by use of a key to operate the latch. The key is used to pass through the tumbler array and operate the latch or bolt.

Wafer Tumbler Lock

The wafer tumbler lock utilizes flat metal tumblers that function inside the shell of the lock housing that creates a shear line. Spring tension keeps each wafer locked into the shell until lifted out by the key. The shell is matched by varying bit depths on the key.

Dial Combination Lock

The dial combination lock is used on security containers, safes, and vaults and is opened by dialing in a set combination. By eliminating a keyway, it provides a higher level of security. While they do not utilize a key, these locks work on the same principle as the lever lock. By aligning gates on tumblers to allow insertion of the fence in the bolt, the lock can be opened by dialing in the assigned combination. The number of tumblers in the lock will determine the numbers to be used to open the combination lock.

Figure 3.4 Dead-bolt lock. (Photo by Daniel J. Benny.)

High-Security Dead-Bolt Lock

The dead-bolt lock is utilized for securing exterior and interior doors (Figure 3.4). The elements of a high-security dead-bolt lock are the use of a restricted keyway so the key cannot be easily duplicated, a 1-inch latch with ceramic inserts so the latch cannot be forced open or cut, and tapered and rotating cylinder guards so that a wrench cannot be used to remove the lock.

Card Access Electrified Locks

Electrified locks permit doors to be locked and unlocked in a remote manner (Figure 3.5). They can be a simple push button near the lock or at a security central station or work as part of a card reader system or digital keypad. This system allows for the use of traditional electric latches or can be used with an electric high-security dead-bolt system.

Exit Locks

Exit locks or panic bars are used on doors designed as emergency exits from a building. They are locked from the outside but can be opened to exit the building by pushing on a bar that disengages the lock. Emergency doors are never to be locked from the inside in any manner that would not allow for immediate exit from the building or hangar.

Figure 3.5 Proximity card access. (Photo by Daniel J. Benny.)

Master Locking System

When establishing a master locking system, it must be designed to meet the security needs of the airport, fixed-based operator, and flight school. Without planning, the locking system will usually degrade to a system that is only providing privacy but not effective security. The goal is to make the locking system effective and user friendly so that the functions of the airport can continue unimpeded.

The following design criteria need to be considered in the development of a master locking system:

Number of locks: This includes the total number of locks that will be installed in the airport on exterior and interior doors.

Categories of the locking system: The categories of a locking system would include exterior airport gates on the perimeter of the airport, exterior doors entering the building or hangars on the property, interior doors, high-security areas, combination locks for security containers and safes, and desk, computer, and file cabinet locks.

Control of Keys and Locking Devices

The security department, if there is one, or the airport manager should control all keys and locking devices. This would include responsibility for the installation and repair of all locks, as well as maintaining the records of all keys made, issued, and collected.

Master Key
The master key, a single key that fits all locks in the airport, must be controlled and secured by the security department or manager and should not be removed from the property. This key may be signed out to members of the staff. It should only be issued each day and needs to be signed for and returned at the end of the shift when the security staff or top management leave the airport for the day. Sub-master keys that allow access to specific areas of the airport may be issued for the term of employment to top management or security staff. The security department should keep a duplicate of all keys to the facility, desk, and file cabinets and access numbers to combination locks on security containers.

Duplication of Keys
The duplication of airport, hangar, fixed-base operator, flight school, and aircraft company keys must be controlled. No key should be duplicated by the authorized locksmith without the authorization of the management or the security department.

Lost Keys
Lost or misplaced keys are to be reported at once. An investigation regarding the circumstances related to the loss or misplacement of keys must be conducted.

Disposition of Employee Keys on Transfer or Termination
On the transfer of an employee within the airport or the termination of an employee, all keys that were issued must be returned and accounted for. This would include door, desk, file cabinet, hangar, and aircraft keys that were issued to the employee.

Security Containers
When protecting the airport, fixed-base operator, and flight school, records and aircraft key security containers meeting the approval of the U.S. General Services Administration (GSA) are recommended. All security containers that are approved by the GSA will bear a GSA Approved Security Container label affixed to the front of the security container and are assigned six classes, discussed next,

Class 1
The class 1 security container is insulated for fire protection, and the protection provided is

30 man-minutes against surreptitious entry
10 man-minutes against forced entry
1 hour against fire damage to contents
20 man-hours against manipulation of the lock
20 man-hours against radiological attack

Class 2

The class 2 security container is insulated for fire protection, and the protection provided is

20 man-minutes against surreptitious entry
1 hour against fire damage to contents
5 man-minutes against forced entry
20 man-hours against manipulation of the lock
20 man-hours against radiological attack

Class 3

The class 3 security container is uninsulated, and the protection provided is

20 man-minutes against surreptitious entry
20 man-hours against manipulation of the lock
20 man-hours against radiological attack

There is no forced entry requirement.

Class 4

The class 4 security container is uninsulated, and the protection provided is

20 man-minutes against surreptitious entry
5 man-minutes against forced entry
20 man-hours against manipulation of the lock
20 man-hours against radiological attack

Class 5

The class 5 security container is uninsulated, and the protection provided is

20 man-hours against surreptitious entry (increased from 30 man-minutes on containers produced after March 1991)
10 man-minutes against forced entry
20 man-hours against manipulation of the lock
20 man-hours against radiological attack
30 man-minutes against covert entry

Class 6

The class 6 security container is uninsulated, and the protection provided is

20 man-hours against surreptitious entry
20 man-hours against manipulation of the lock
20 man-hours against radiological attack
30 man-minutes against covert entry

There is no forced entry test requirement.

Security Filing Cabinets

There is a variety of security filing cabinets manufactured to meet the standards of the class 5 and class 6 security containers. Security filing cabinets are available in a variety of styles, including those with single, two, four, and five drawers and in both letter-size and legal-size models.

SECURITY BARRIERS AND FENCING

A security barrier can be anything that prevents vehicle or pedestrian access to the airport. It may be a natural barrier such as water, trees, or a rock formation. These natural barriers may already be in place or can be placed on the airport property to provide a natural barrier. This is one of the aspects of what is known as crime prevention through environmental design (CPTED).

One of the most cost-effective security barriers to secure the perimeter of an airport or high-risk area such as the location of fueling tanks is a chain-link fence. Chain-link fence is relatively low cost and provides the flexibility to move it as needed. It also allows visibility beyond the property line by security, staff, and security cameras.

The security industry height for the fence is 6 feet with a 1-foot top guard mounted on a 45° angle facing away from the property and constructed of barbed wire or razor ribbon. The fence must be secured in the ground by metal posts with a bracing bar across the top and bottom of the fence. The opening in the fence wire should be no more than 2 inches.

With any fencing that is utilized around the airport, there should be at least two points of access in the event that one access is closed due to an emergency. Gates that are not used on a regular basis need to be secured with a high-security padlock. The locked gate should also be equipped with a numbered security seal. This seal needs to be checked each day by security or airport staff to ensure the numbered seal is intact and matches the numbered seal placed on the gate. This is to ensure that an unauthorized key is not being used so that a person can enter and exit the gate. It is also used to ensure that the original padlock on the gate was not was cut off and replaced with a different lock and then used by a perpetrator for continued unauthorized access into the airport or secure area.

Access to the airport through the gate access can be controlled by the use of a proximity access card and electric locking system on the gate. This can be used for vehicles or individuals.

SECURITY LIGHTING

Security lighting is used to illuminate the perimeter of the airport, gate access area, the vehicle parking area, the fueling area, as well as the fixed-base operation and flight school. Lighting must be situated so that it does not interfere with airport runway and taxiway lighting. The most effective security lighting is the sodium vapor.

Lighting fixtures need to be placed in a security housing to prevent damage. The light can be mounted on posts, buildings, and hangars. Lights can be activated using a photoelectric cell that will automatically turn the light on at dusk and turn it off at dawn. This is more efficient than manually turning lights on and off each day.

All light fixtures should be numbered and identified on the airport layout document for easy identification. This will be of value when reporting lights that are not working to ensure that they are repaired as quickly as possible.

These types of lighting devices include the following:

- Incandescent
- New fluorescent (to replace the incandescent)
- Quartz
- Mercury vapor
- Sodium vapor

Incandescent

The incandescent light is what is known as the common lightbulb or floodlight; it is being phased out. It has been used to provide illumination at doorways and to direct light to a building at night. It is suitable for security for a single building but is not considered for security lighting of large facilities. This is due to the high energy cost and low illumination that it provides.

New Fluorescent (to Replace the Incandescent)

The new fluorescent lights are used to provide illumination at doorways and to direct light to a building at night and are replacing the incandescent bulbs. They are suitable for security for a single building but are not considered for security lighting of large facilities. This is due to the low illumination they provide.

Quartz

The quartz light provides better illumination the incandescent or new fluorescent light and emits a white light. It is activated instantaneously when turned on and has been used to light parking areas. It does have a high energy cost.

Mercury Vapor

The mercury vapor light provides good illumination and emits a white light. It does require a warm-up time and cannot be activated instantaneously when turned on. It is used to light parking areas and roadways. It has a lower energy cost than fluorescent or quartz light.

Sodium Vapor

The sodium vapor light is considered the best for security. It will light instantaneously and has a lower energy cost than all other lighting. It has excellent penetration at night and in fog due to the amber light. The amber light can distort color on security cameras and on viewing objects by security officers or airport staff.

WINDOW SECURITY

At a general aviation airport, there are many buildings that will have windows that will require protection. These structures may include the fixed-base operator building or airport manager's facility. It could include a flight school or other tenant locations. Many hangars with doors will have windows for natural lighting.

The first security consideration for window protection is the window itself or what is called *glazing*. This is the type of glass or plastic that is used as a window. The more security that is required, the stronger the glazing should be. The stronger the glazing is, the more expensive it will be. What is used will be based on the threat assessment and if there are any interior intrusion detection systems used in the structure.

Window areas can be made of glass, acrylic, or what is known as Lexan®. The following is a list of the glass, acrylic, and Lexan products that can be used for non-bullet-resistance protection:

- Annealed glass
- Wire-reinforced glass
- Tempered glass
- Laminated glass
- Annealed glass with security film
- Acrylic
- Lexan

There is also bullet-resistant material.

Annealed Glass

Annealed glass also known as windowpane glass; it breaks easily and provides the least amount of protection of all of the glazing materials. It breaks into shards of glass that are sharp and can be used as a weapon. These shards can cause injury to individuals in the area if the glazing material is broken by a perpetrator or explosive blast.

Wire-Reinforced Glass

Wire-reinforced glass is annealed glass with wire embedded into the glazing. While it looks as if it adds security, it does not and is easily broken. The one advantage is that the glass will not break in large shards as the wire will hold the broken glass together.

Tempered Glass

Tempered glass is a stronger material than annealed glass but can be defeated easily. When broken, it breaks into small pieces of glass that are relatively harmless. This glass was used in older vehicle windscreens.

Laminated Glass

Laminated glass is coated with a plastic. It also can be defeated easily. When broken, the glass holds together in large harmless sheets. This is what is used in vehicle windscreens.

Annealed Glass with Security Film

Annealed glass with security film has a layer of acrylic between two layers of glass. It is difficult to break through this glazing and is the best of the glass products for security protection when bullet resistance is not a requirement.

Acrylic

Acrylic is a plastic and offers little protection. It also breaks into large shards if broken. It can be scratched easily and will discolor over time due to sunlight.

Lexan

Lexan is a trademarked name of a glazing that is impregnable to breakage and is the best of all the security glazing when bullet resistance is not a requirement.

Bullet-Resistant Material

Where bullet resistance is required due to a high threat of robbery or terrorist attack by firearm or explosive devices, the following bullet-resistant material can be utilized:

- Bullet-resistant glass
- Bullet-resistant acrylic
- Lexgard®

Bullet-Resistant Glass

Bullet-resistant glass is a glass glazing that can be from a quarter inch to 1 inch in thickness. The thicker the glass is, the more protection it provides from small arms weapons. It will stop most bullets, but it does cause spalling. Spalling is when the bullet is trapped in the glass; a small particle of glass will break off and fly in the direction away from where the bullet was fired. This can cause injury to anyone near the bullet-resistant glass.

Bullet-Resistant Acrylic
Bullet-resistant acrylic is an acrylic glazing that can be from a quarter inch to 1 inch in thickness. The thicker the glazing is, the more protection it provides from small arms weapons. It will stop most bullets, but it does cause spalling.

Lexgard
Lexgard is the trademarked name of an acrylic glazing (Figure 3.6). The glazing at 1-inch thickness is the best protection from firearms and explosive devices and will stop bullets from all small arms weapons and most rifles. With Lexgard, there will be no spalling. This a product that one would find on the presidential limousines used by the U.S. Secret Service.

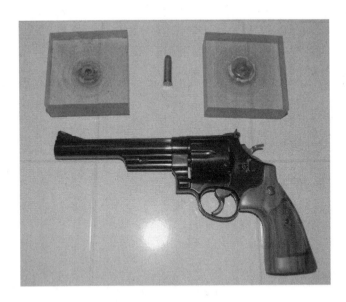

Figure 3.6 Lexgard that has stopped a .44 Magnum bullet. (Photo by Daniel J. Benny.)

Other Window Security

Window protection can also be provided by the use of security bars or steel screening placed over the windows. The bars and screens should be securely mounted into the window frame. It is important to make sure that the use of bars and steel screens on the windows will not impede emergency access out of the structure in the event of an emergency evacuation.

BIBLIOGRAPHY

Baker, P., & Benny, D.J. (2012). *Complete guide to physical security.* Boca Raton, FL: CRC Press.

Elias, B. (2005). *CRS report for Congress securing general aviation.* Washington, DC: U.S. Government Printing Office.

Fischer, R.J., & Green, G. (2008). *Introduction to security* (8th ed.). Burlington, MA: Elsevier.

Transportation Security Administration. (2011). Retrieved from http://www.tsa.gov/

4

Airport/Corporate Aviation Security Force

INTRODUCTION

Based on the threat to the general aviation airport and the operational and payroll budget, the establishment of a security force may be a consideration. For corporations that have their own corporate general aviation aircraft and hangar facilities, there may be a need to provide security force coverage for the hangar and aircraft.

The security force coverage for the general aviation airport or corporate aviation department could be proprietary security; the security officers are employees of the airport or corporate flight department. Or, it may use security officers from a licensed contract security firm.

CHIEF SECURITY OFFICER

When establishing a general aviation airport or corporate aviation department security force, hiring or contracting a security or chief security officer is the first priority. The selection of this individual is critical to the success of the operation of the security department. The chief security officer should report to the airport manager or chief executive officer of the corporation. The individual selected should have at minimum a bachelor's degree from an accredited university or college in security administration or criminal justice, with a master's degree preferred.

A security professional with professional security certification should also be considered. There are two security-related certifications that would be of value to the director of security of a general aviation airport. The first is offered by the American Society for Industrial Security International (ASIS International). ASIS International has developed a professional security certification, the Certified Protection Processional (CPP) that is accepted nationally and internationally by the security profession as well as the U.S. Homeland Security and Transportation Security Administration.

The CPP has been established for individuals working in security supervision and management. On successful completion of the comprehensive examination covering all aspects of the security management profession, such as management methods, security force management, legal issues, investigations, physical security, protective service, terrorism, and budgeting, the designation of CPP is bestowed.

Another professional security certification related to airports is the Airport Certified Employee-Security (ACE) designation. This is offered by the American Association of Airport Executives (AAAE). The 3-day course covers all aspects of airport security and culminates with a final examination. When the course is completed and the final examine is passed, the individual is then bestowed the designation of ACE.

DETERMINING THE SIZE OF THE SECURITY FORCE

Once the chief security officer is hired, that individual must work with the airport manager or corporate chief executive officer to make a determination with regard to the size of the security force that will be required. The need for a security force must be established and will be based on several factors.

These factors include a physical security survey of the general aviation airport to be protected by the security force or the airport and hangar facility for the corporate aviation program. The duties and functions of the security force at the airport, the size of the airport, hours of operation, and number of employees, visitors, and flights are taken into account. The final consideration is the security threat to the general aviation airport.

The physical security survey and the physical security measures to be utilized at the airport will have an impact on the number of security officers required to provide adequate protection for the fixed-base operator, hangars, ramp area runway, aircraft, and public roads and parking areas at the airport.

The use of intrusion detection systems, security cameras, security lights, fire protection systems, and access control such as proximity card readers may reduce the number of security officers required to patrol the airport. If there are no or limited physical security measures, there will be a requirement to establish a larger security force to secure the airport effectively. The use of more physical security measures may allow for the reduction of the size of the force. Regardless of the level of physical security protection, there will in almost all cases be a need for security officers to monitor the intrusion, fire, access control, and camera systems. There is also the requirement for security officers to be able to respond to the various alarms or activity observed on security cameras.

For each security post to be covered 24 hours a day, the airport would need to hire four security officers to account for days off, holidays, and vacations. So, if a general aviation airport would require two security officers on duty 24 hours a day, the airport would need to hire eight security officers.

MISSION OF THE SECURITY FORCE

In determining the size of the security force, the mission and duties of the security force must be determined. The primary duty of a security force is to provide proactive patrols of the airport to protect life and prevent losses, respond to emergencies, and provide assistance to staff, pilots, aircraft owners, and visitors. They must also enforce airport security and safety regulations.

The airport or corporate aviation facility security patrols may be conducted by numerous methods, including foot patrol and the use of vehicles such as automobiles, all-wheel-drive vehicles, bicycles, Segways, or other special-use modes of transportation. This will depend on the terrain, weather, and other geographical features of the airport and the state where it is located.

The security force may also be utilized to control access to the property. The access control may begin at the perimeter of the airport and at vehicle entrances. The security force would be responsible for obtaining identification of drivers and may also conduct inspections of vehicles entering the facility if necessary. Access control points required to be covered by security officers may also include pedestrian entrances and entrances to the high-risk areas on the airport property, such as fuel storage and other designated restricted areas.

Escorts into restricted areas are often provided by the security force at airports. These escorts could also be for the transportation of money, high-value items, or airport confidential information. These escorts may take place on the airport's property or off the airport in the case of a money escort to a banking facility. Providing security escorts to employee parking areas for employees leaving work during hours of darkness may also be a service that is provided by the security force.

Inspections of the airport or corporate aviation department facility for security threats, safety, and loss hazards are a function that should be performed. Depending on the size of the airport and property and the number of building and hangars, this may be a duty that would be performed by security officers on patrol.

Investigations of losses, safety issues, accidents, violations of airport regulations, and employee misconduct will require the attention of investigators if there is a significant case load based on the size and population of the airport. In most cases, this function at a general aviation airport would be conducted by the security director.

Protective service may be a function of the security department for airport management or if dignitaries frequent or have a private or corporate aircraft based at the airport. For a corporate aviation department, protective service may be required for the chief executive officer and family when at the airport and flying on the corporate aircraft.

Special events must also be considered in determining the size of the security force. If the airport has numerous special high-profile events during the year, there will be a need for additional security during those periods of time.

Monitoring of intrusion detection and fire safety systems, security cameras, and access control points is an import function of security. The establishment of a proprietary security communications and monitoring center to dispatch security staff, answer security-related calls, and monitor the security, fire safety, cameras, and access control points will require the hiring of additional security officers to perform these vital functions. These positions should be staffed by trained security officers who can be rotated between patrol functions and monitoring duties. This is critical since a trained security officer will be more effective at responding to security calls and situations arising while monitoring the security and safety systems than a person hired only to work in the proprietary airport communications center. It is also important not to have an individual monitor such systems for more than 2 hours. A security officer will become less effective at monitoring a security camera if the assignment lasts more than 2 hours. By having security officers working in the communications center, they can be rotated to the patrol function of the airport after 2 hours in the communications center.

The final function to consider is the administrative duties associated with a security department. These duties will include securing security department records, processing of internal violations such as partaking tickets, and preparing correspondence, monthly reports, and any other administrative duties that may be required. These positions may be in the role of secretary to the director and administrative clerks.

Based on a review of all the possible duties and functions of a security department that have been described, a final determination will be made of which services and duties the security department will perform.

AIRPORT PROFILE AND SECURITY THREAT

A review of the profile of the airport to be protected or where the corporate aviation aircraft and facility are based is necessary when determining the size of the security force. The type of airport with regard to services offered, its size, hours of operation, and number of employees, visitors, and aircraft based at the airport as well as security threats are key elements that must be considered to make a determination about the size of the security force.

The security threat to the general airport will be based on numerous factors, including the type of service, type and number of aircraft based there, its size, hours of operation, and the location of the airport in relation to a large population area and terrorist targets. The local crime rate and previous crime and losses against the airport must also be evaluated to determine the current risk to people, aircraft, and the airport.

Size of the Airport

The size of the airport, including the square footage of buildings, the number of floors in the buildings, the total number of hangars, and number of based aircraft to be protected must be calculated in determining the number of security officers required to provide adequate protection.

Hours of Operation

Hours of operation will have an impact on security force coverage. If the airport is only open 8 hours a day and then the buildings and hangars are secured with an intrusion detection system, it obviously will require less security force coverage than a 24-hour operation. As hours of operation lessen or expand based on the specific situation, the level of security coverage will also need to be adjusted to meet the need of the airport.

Number of Employees, Visitors, Pilots, Aircraft

The number of employees, pilots, and based aircraft as well as air traffic at the airport will have an impact on the size of the security force, depending on the services offered to the staff.

PROPRIETARY SECURITY FORCE

A proprietary security force is one in which the security officers are employees of the airport or the corporate aviation department. A proprietary security force may be full time, part time, or a combination of full- or part-time positions. Based on the type of position, the force members may qualify for full or limited company benefits, such as medical coverage, insurance, vacation, and sick leave.

The advantages of a proprietary security force include control of who is hired by establishing standards and qualifications for the positions and conducting an extensive preemployment background investigation. With a proprietary security force, there is more opportunity to provide professional and effective training to the staff. Also, a proprietary security force will have more loyalty to the organization because they are employees and because of the benefit and training packages offered. This leads to a more loyal employee and a reduction in high turnover of the security force. Long-term security officers, because of their experience, will be an asset to the organization.

The disadvantages of a proprietary security force include that it takes longer to hire staff and costs more as the airport must place advertisements for recruitment, conduct preemployment background investigations, and supply uniforms and equipment. There is also the cost of a complete benefits package.

Another disadvantage is that once the security officer makes it past the probationary period, it is more difficult to terminate an officer. To do so, all actions must be documented, and progressive disciplinary action must be utilized unless the offenses are serious enough to warrant immediate termination.

CONTRACT SECURITY FORCE

A contract security force is one that is made up of security officers working as employees of a licensed security or investigative firm that provides security service on a contract basis and who are not on the payroll of the organization utilizing their service. In most all states, contract security providers must be licensed, so it is important to select a firm that meets this legal requirement.

The advantage of utilizing a contract security force is that there is the flexibility to hire full- or part-time security or a combination of both for whatever length of time required. The airport utilizing the contract security officer does not need to place ads to recruit, interview, or hire the officers. It is less expensive because the licensed contractor firm pays for the benefits, training, equipment, and uniforms of the security officers. Another advantage is that contract security officers are easy to terminate. If an officer is not performing well, the security contractor can remove the officer from the airport property and replace him or her with another security officer.

Some of the disadvantages include a lack of loyalty by the contract security officer to the airport where they are assigned as their loyalty in most cases will be with the licensed contract agency. Based on the training provided by the contact agency, it may not be at the level of a proprietary security force. There may also be a high turnover rate due to the lower pay received by contract security officers, or they may be pulled from one work location to another by the contract security firm to meet various client schedule demands.

There are advantages and disadvantages to both proprietary and contract security. The airport needs to make a determination regarding which is best for its requirements and budget. The airport can utilize full-time proprietary security officers, full-time contractor security officers, or a combination of both.

SECURITY FORCE UNIFORMS

Traditionally, security officers wear a uniform. A uniform is a symbol of authority and allows the security officer to be easily identified during an emergency or when assistance is required by staff or visitors to an organization. The most common security uniform is slacks and a short- and long-sleeve police-/military-style shirt with a security patch, name tag, and a badge where authorized by state or local laws. Utility belts are often worn to carry security and protective equipment such as keys, radios, flashlight, OC (oleoresin capsicum; pepper spray) spray, baton, or firearms. During colder weather, there is a variety of light- and heavyweight water-resistant jackets and coats that can be utilized. Patches, name tags, and badges are also placed on the outer garment for ease of identification. Headwear is also part of the security uniform and can be a more formal eight-point cap, trooper hat, or ball cap style with badge or security insignia placed on the front of the headwear.

The appearance of the security officer, especially when in uniform, is critical in presenting a professional and authoritative image. In a corporate aviation department setting, the security attire may be business dress or business casual.

SECURITY FORCE IDENTIFICATION

Just as the security uniform provides a symbol, so does security force identification. Badges, where authorized by state and local law, are a universally recognized symbol of authority. Shoulder patches also add to the authority of the security officer and identify the airport or contract agency of their employment. The most important aspect of security identification is a photo identification card to be worn on the uniform or carried in a case to provide positive identification of the security officer and the airport for which the officer works.

This professional image begins by wearing the assigned uniform in a proper manner. Security officers should only wear the uniform items issued and should not be permitted to customize it by adding or deleting aspects of the issued uniform. If this takes place, the security officers are no longer "uniformed," and it is unprofessional. The security uniform must also be clean and pressed at all times when the security officer reports for duty.

There should be grooming standards for a security officer who is wearing a uniform. These grooming standards should relate to hair length and style, facial hair such as beards, and the wearing of jewelry, earrings, and other piercings visible when wearing the security uniform. Proper hygiene should also be addressed in the standards.

The demeanor of the security officer in uniform is also important. Exhibiting good posture and professional attitude will project a professional image for the airport and the security profession.

Security uniforms and identification allow the security officer to be identified as an authority figure, but uniforms and identification alone do not provide the security officer with such authority. The authority must come from legal codes that apply to the security officer, depending on the state where they operate. The authority also comes from the airport for which they are employed with regard the security officers' ability to enforce airport regulations on the airport's property. This legitimacy must also be based on the proper use of such authority.

SECURITY FORCE PROTECTIVE EQUIPMENT

Where authorized by law, protective equipment may be considered for the security force. The type of protective equipment utilized will be based on the threat level, location, and mission of the security force and may range from handcuffs to the carrying of firearms. Many states require specialized training before authorization to carry various types of protective equipment. In Pennsylvania, for example, security officers who carry a baton or firearm must complete what is known as the Lethal Weapons Act 235 Course. To attend the 40-hour course, the student must submit to a criminal background check and medical and psychology evaluations. The 40-hour course covers the legal aspects of carrying a weapon, the authority of a security officer, use of force considerations, and the Pennsylvania Crimes Code. Students must pass a written test and qualify on the firing range to become certified under the Lethal Weapons Act. It is important to know the requirements with regard to carrying a weapon in the state where security officers are operating to ensure compliance with the laws of the state.

Handcuffs are important should the security officer be required to make a citizen's arrest in the performance of duties. Handcuffs provide a means to secure an individual who becomes violent either before or after a citizen's arrest. The use of handcuffs in such situations provides for the safety of the security officer and the public. Handcuffs should be of good quality and have the capability of being double locked. The double-locking mechanism prevents the handcuffs from being tightened on the suspect by accident or by the suspect, which may lead to an injury claim from their use.

Oleoresin capsicum or OC spray is a lachrymatory irritant agent that can be carried by security officers. It provides a nonlethal method of self-defense for the security officer and is effective in most situations. Security officers should be certified by the manufacturer of the oleoresin capsicum product to ensure proper use and for liability purposes.

Batons have been carried by security for over 100 years, and they can be used as both defensive and offensive protective tools. When used offensively, they are considered a deadly weapon. Batons come in various styles, including the traditional striated baton, the collapsible ASP baton, and the PR-24 full-size or collapsible model. Certification should be obtained by the manufacturer of the particular baton that is carried for proper use and liability protection.

Firearms may be carried by the security force based on the legal requirement of the state and threat and mission of the security force at a particular airport where they are operating. A revolver or semiautomatic firearm may be carried, and in some situations security officers may also carry a shotgun. In addition to state legal requirements for qualification and certification to carry a firearm, security officers should be trained and qualify at least once a year with the weapons and ammunition they carry. Many security departments require such training and qualification twice and up to four times a year.

SECURITY FORCE TRAINING

One of the most important aspects in the management of a security force is to ensure that the security officers are effectively trained to meet any state regulatory requirements as well as security industry standards of training. Such training will promote professionalism within the security force and reduce the liability risk. Security force training can be accomplished by on-the-job experience and training and through the use of various formal educational methods.

On-the-job experience and training are comprised of a structured and documented approach in instructing the new security officer with regard to the day-to-day duties as a security officer. Each new security officer should be assigned to a mentor. The mentor may be a supervisor, lead officer, or training officer who will guide the new officer through the daily activities, providing instruction on how to perform these duties. As each new task is learned, it should be documented in a written training record for each security officer.

As the security officer accumulates time in the profession and the various security assignments, the officer will gain knowledge and proficiency in the profession. Other on-the-job educational tools may include having the security officer take part in organizational meetings and committees to expand professional knowledge. This may include being part of the airport's security and safety committee or attending meetings related to special events that might be scheduled.

In addition to on-the-job training, more formal educational methods should be applied. This may include company assistance for the security officer to obtain a college degree in security or criminal justice. In-service training can also be used; the security officer is provided with information in a classroom environment covering security procedures, report writing, patrol methods, or court testimony. In-service training can also be used to provide the security officer with various certifications, such as first aid and cardiopulmonary resuscitation (CPR), handcuff use, or OC or baton certification.

Another option for education is to have the security officer take part in self-study by online proprietary training or via a Web site offering free training, such as the Homeland Security Federal Emergency Management Agency Academy and Transportation Security Administration. Organizations such as the Aircraft Owners and Pilots Association also offer an online general aviation security course. Time for such online training can be provided during the work schedule, or training can be accomplished off duty. Directed reading is another source of education; articles or documents related to security are made available in the security office; the security officers are required to read and sign off on the document that it has been read.

To ensure that the security force is professionally trained, a security training program needs to be established, and mandatory training needs to be provided to all security officers. All state regulatory training requirements, where applicable, must be completed. It is important that all training completed by each security officer be documented in the security officer's training file. This will allow for the tracking of the training to ensure that it has been completed and such documentation as required by regulatory agencies or related to liability issues has been submitted.

PROFESSIONAL SECURITY CERTIFICATIONS

Professional security certification can be obtained and are of value to those in the security profession. As previously discussed, the ASIS International has developed several professional security certifications that are for individuals working in security supervision and management. They also have two certification courses for the nonmanagement security professional. The Professional Certified Investigator (PCI) was established for the security investigator or private investigators. On successful completion of the examination that covers all aspects of security and private investigation, including investigative methods, legal consideration, and interview methods, the designation of PCI is bestowed.

The Physical Security Professional (PSP) designation is designed for those in security who have responsibility for physical security within their organization, such as an airport. The examination covers intrusion detection systems, barriers, security cameras, locks, and access control. On successful completion of the examination, the designation of PSP is bestowed.

The ACE certification is also of value to security officers working at the airport.

SECURITY FORCE RECRUITMENT AND SUPERVISION

The first step in the recruitment of a security force is to establish a position description identifying the required duties and responsibilities of the position, as discussed previously in this chapter. Experience, education, and physical ability requirements also need to be established, not only to ensure that the best individuals for the positions are hired but also to comply with the Americans with Disabilities Act. Recruitment of security officers should come from outside the airport and not from current employees in other departments. Hiring from within the organization can create conflict of interest with former coworkers and departments where they worked in the past.

The background investigation of the final candidates is critical to ensure the individuals meet all the requirements of the position and that they are qualified, ethical, and trustworthy. Previous employment, education, criminal history, credit reports, driving history, military history, and references should all be part of the background investigation.

When making the final selection, also investigate the person's motives for applying for the position. Examine the person's ability to deal effectively with other employees and visitors to the airport as it relates to security issues.

Security officers employed by the airport need direction regarding their duties and responsibilities. This is accomplished through the development of a security policies and procedures manual. This document provides the security officer with detailed guidelines with regard to their responsibilities and duties within the security department and at the airport. It also gives them the authority to perform such duties on behalf of the airport.

The security policies and procedures manual should be written in a brief, clear, and concise manner so that it can easily be understood. A written copy should be given to each security officer. The security officer should be required to sign for the receipt of the manual and then be tested on it. This will document not only that the officer received a copy, but also that he or she has read and understood the contents of the publication. This is vital with regard to liability issues and the discipline of security officers who fail to perform their duties in a proper manner.

The security policies and procedures manual needs to reviewed and updated a least once a year or more often when needed. This would include the changing of any security policies and procedures.

Always keep the manual current and never put anything in the security policies and procedures that cannot be accomplished by the department or security officers. Should there be civil action, the airport will be held to its own standards as established in this document. That is why it is important that what is written in the manual is and can be accomplished.

Within the security policies and procedures manual, a standard of conduct for the security officers needs to be established. This will be the basis of evaluating the security officer's conduct on the job. The goal is to inform the security officer of what is expected of him or her and the penalties for not adhering to the code of conduct.

Performance and conduct of the security officer need to be evaluated and dealt with through progressive disciplinary action. There will be some conduct offenses, such as theft, falsification of reports, and violent behavior, that may require termination, but for most conduct offenses and performance issues, correction of the problem is the best solution.

There are five steps in progressive disciplinary action that allow the organization to take corrective action and allow the security officer the opportunity to improve conduct or performance:

- Counseling. This is a process of advising the security officer of a problem with his or her performance or conduct and discussing with the officer what is required to correct the problem as well as determining why the failure occurred. A review of the policies and procedures and retraining are common solutions to correct the security officer's performance or conduct.
- Oral reprimand. If a security officer has a second offense with regard to conduct or performance, the next step is an oral reprimand. The organization has moved beyond the counseling and education phase and has placed the security officer on notice that he or she must correct the issues at hand.
- Written reprimand. For the third offense, the security officer's actions are formally documented in written form, advising the security officer of the seriousness of the situation. The security officer is to be advised that if he or she fails to correct personal performance or conduct, a suspension or termination from the position could take place.
- Suspension. The suspension step is a serious action; the security officer will lose pay and will be given one last chance to correct performances or conduct.
- Termination. Termination is the final step after all other steps have failed to correct the security officer's performance or conduct; the officer must now be removed from the position. When terminating the security officer, do not allow the officer to remain on the job site. Collect issued identification, keys, equipment, and uniforms and escort the individual off the airport property.

Progressive disciplinary action is an effective means of correcting issues with security officers and gives them the opportunity to improve and continue to be a part of the security force. It is also an excellent management tool to remove from the security force a security officer whose performance or conduct does not meet the department's standards.

BIBLIOGRAPHY

Fischer, R.J,. & Green, G. (2008). *Introduction to security* (8th ed.). Burlington, MA: Elsevier.

Kovacich, G.L., & Halibozek, E.P. (2004). *The manager's handbook for corporate security*. Burlington, MA: Elsevier.

Transportation Security Administration. (2011). Retrieved from http://www.tsa.gov/

5

Security of General Aviation Aircraft

AIRCRAFT THREAT ASSESSMENT AND SECURITY PLAN

All private or corporate aircraft owners should conduct a threat assessment and develop an aircraft security plan. This is not a legal requirement but will aid in the protection of individuals and the aircraft.

There are several principles that must be considered when conducting a threat assessment and security plan for general aviation aircraft. These include protection of the aircraft from theft and vandalism, protection of the aircraft crew and passengers from crime, and assurance that the aircraft is secure so that it cannot be used as a weapon. The aircraft could be used as a weapon by stealing or hijacking the aircraft and using it to fly into a target. A general aviation aircraft could be sabotaged by the unknowing placement of an explosive device on the aircraft.

Aerial work general aviation aircraft that perform crop-dusting services could be used to disseminate chemical or possibly biological agents on food and water supplies or the population. An aerial work general aviation aircraft could be sabotaged by the unknowing placement of toxic agents in aerial work aircraft dispersal tanks.

To develop an effective security plan for the protection of the aircraft, a threat assessment needs to be conducted so that the risk to the aircraft can be established. Once the threat and risk have been identified, you need to establish what needs to be protected. Next, determine the severity of the threat and probability of occurrence. This is accomplished by making an examination to determine the required security to prevent or reduce the threats.

Threat: Risk of threat = Severity of threat × Probability of occurrence

The next step is to identify the measures to be implemented to reduce the threat. Review the security measures and plans and rehearse. Make any changes as needed.

As an example, the threats to a general aviation aircraft as discussed previously would include using the aircraft as a weapon and instrument of terrorism. The risks would be based on the type, size, and operational capability of the aircraft. Would a terrorist want to use that aircraft to fly into a target? What are the possible terrorist targets in the area of the airport: military facility, power plant, large population, or major sporting event? If there are possible terrorist targets, then that would include the risk. If the aircraft were used in a terrorist operation, how much damage could it cause, and what is the probability of such an event occurring? This is the thinking process that must be used; think like a criminal, think like a terrorist with regard to the vulnerability and security of the aircraft.

The development of an aircraft security plan is vital in the protection of the aircraft, crew, and passengers. This aircraft security plan would detail the security measures to be implemented to protect the aircraft whether it is privately owned or corporate aircraft. The aircraft security plan would also cover security of the aircraft when in flight and when at other airports and hangar or tie-down facilities. To preserve the integrity of the plan, access to the written aviation security plan must be limited to those individuals who have an operational need to know.

The aviation security plan must be updated whenever there is change to the security program. The plan should be reviewed at least once a year to ensure that it is current. Security awareness training for flight and ground crew is vital to the success of the plan and needs to include a review of routine security and emergency procedures as set forth in the plan.

AIRCRAFT DOCUMENTATION

Information on the aircraft should be documented in the event that the aircraft is stolen, missing in flight, or damaged. This documentation will aid law enforcement or rescue agencies in identification and recovery.

Documentation of the aircraft will also aid with insurance claims should the aircraft be stolen, damaged, or destroyed.

The documentation of the aircraft should include color photographs of the exterior and interior. A copy of the aircraft registration and airworthiness certificate should be kept on file as part of the documentation of the aircraft. Copies of these papers will provide the aircraft type, make, model, year, registration (also known as the N number), serial number, and the owner of the aircraft.

AVIONICS DOCUMENTATION

All avionics utilized and installed in the aircraft should be documented (Figure 5.1). This would include color photographs of the equipment, writing down the model number or name, serial numbers, and other identifying marking or number engraved on the equipment.

Positive identification of each item is necessary to aid in the investigation and recovery of stolen items by law enforcement agencies. Having these records of the avionics will facilitate any insurance claims that need to be filed for damage or theft of the aircraft avionics.

Figure 5.1 Author's Cessna C-172 avionics, Reigle Airport, Palmyra, Pennsylvania. (Photo by Daniel J. Benny.)

AIRCRAFT KEY CONTROL AND LOCKING DEVICES

Positive key control is vital to controlling access to the aircraft. If the aircraft is not new and has been purchased from another party, the lock to the aircraft should be rekeyed. Due to the widespread unauthorized possession of master keys to manufacturer-installed locks in the aviation industry, the security of existing manufacturer-installed locking systems cannot be ensured. If the aircraft is purchased used, there is no way to account for previous issued or lost keys. All locking devices for the aircraft should be professionally rekeyed utilizing a restricted keyway system. Once you are assured of the integrity of the key system, strict control measures must be established. This will include the documentation of all keys issued or signed out. Documentation of keys that are returned is also vital to an effective key control system. This will include keys for the ignition, aircraft doors, luggage compartments, and any security control devices such as prop locks, throttle locks, and wheel security boots.

Keys that are returned and keys that are not in use must be secured in a locked key control container. Daily inventory of the keys is essential to ensure that they are all accounted for. The immediate investigation of an unreturned key or keys is critical to locate the missing keys.

Lost or misplaced keys must be reported immediately, and an investigation to determine the circumstance of the lost key or keys must take place.

An unattended aircraft, whether it is in or out of the hangar, may be protected with devices such as special antitampering tape on doors, windows, utility ports, inspection plates, and luggage compartments. The tape is made so that it cannot be removed under normal conditions. The tape is weatherproof and heat resistant and available with self-destroying slits that will enhance the tamper detection capability. The tape can prevent unauthorized access and can alert the aircraft owner that unauthorized access has occurred.

Locking devices are also available to prevent the theft of an aircraft. One method to prevent the starting of an aircraft is the use of a prop lock (Figure 5.2) to prevent the aircraft prop from rotating. If the prop cannot rotate, one cannot fly the aircraft. The prop lock includes a steel chain cover in a plastic sheath so the aircraft prop is not scratched. The security chain is wrapped around the aircraft prop and held in place with a high-security padlock.

Another method to prevent the starting of the aircraft is the use of a throttle lock. This is a steel cover that is placed over the throttle in the cockpit of the aircraft. It is then held in place with an integral high-security

Figure 5.2 Prop lock on the author's Cessna C-172, Reigle Airport, Palmyra, Pennsylvania. (Photo by Daniel J. Benny.)

lock. This prevents the operation of the throttle, which controls the fuel to the engine, and prevents the theft of the aircraft.

An additional method of preventing the theft of a general aviation aircraft is the use of a wheel security boot. The wheel security boot is a steel device with an integral high-security lock that fits over the wheel of the aircraft. This prevents the aircraft from moving and the theft of the aircraft.

AIRCRAFT INTRUSION DETECTION SYSTEMS

Permanently installed external and internal aircraft intrusion protection sensors may be utilized on all types of general aviation aircraft. Exterior protection includes the installation of sensor devices in the aircraft's exterior skin. This would include the use of omnidirectional, range-gated, pulsed, monostatic microwave devices. These sensors would be located in the aft sections of the aircraft as well as wingtips. Depending on the size of the aircraft, two to six sensors may be required for complete protection. This system establishes a protective zone of 15 feet surrounding the air-

75

craft. Movement inside the zone caused by wind blowing over the aircraft control surfaces would not activate the detection system.

Additional protection can be provided through the installation of interior electromagnetic sensors at aircraft openings such as cabin doors, baggage compartments, engine access panels, emergency window exits, ground power utility ports, wheel wells, radar domes, and refueling ports. These sensors detect the opening of the access points and activate the protection system. Interior protection can be utilized for cockpit, cabin, and baggage areas of the aircraft. The types of sensors utilized may include photoelectric or passive infrared. The alarm signal is transmitted through the intrusion system control panel located in the cockpit. This unit is powered by several small solar panels, which are placed on top of the aircraft instrument panel. Power can also be achieved from the aircraft battery system. Communication between the sensors, onboard control panel, and enunciator is accomplished using radio-frequency (RF) links. The enunciator can be a permanent tabletop model or a portable device about the size of a pager. The enunciator can be monitored by fixed-base operator staff or a commercial or proprietary central security station owner. The portable model can also be monitored by the aircraft owner or pilot in command.

AIRCRAFT ACCESS AND BAGGAGE CONTROL

As part of the aircraft security plan, it is critical that the aircraft owner or pilot in command ensures that all baggage loaded onboard the aircraft is known and identified and matches the passengers on board. Baggage must be in control of the owner until it is loaded onto the aircraft and not left unattended.

Any cargo to be transported should be verified as from a known source, with the contents known, and authorized for transport. It would be appropriate for the aircraft owner and pilot to request that all baggage and cargo be searched before loading it onto the aircraft or go through a screening process.

AIRCRAFT MAINTENANCE SECURITY

All routine work on the aircraft should be scheduled in advance. Ensure that only certified and authorized aircraft maintenance personnel work on the aircraft. A process should be established to be able to identify and document who will and who has worked on the aircraft.

All spare aircraft parts maintained by the aircraft owner should be secured in a locked storage area that is equipped with high-security locks and an intrusion detection system. This will prevent theft or tampering with the parts.

IN-FLIGHT SECURITY

In-flight security begins with a review of emergency aircraft and security procedures by the flight crew prior to departure. This would include emergency landing and hijacking procedures. In addition to the routine preflight inspection, flight crew should look for any evidence of tampering with the aircraft or the placement of foreign objects on or in the aircraft.

The pilot should file a flight plan and adhere to it. If changes are required, an in-flight change should be made detailing the reason for the change and notification of the changes communicated to flight service. Once arriving at the destination, fight service needs to be notified.

In the event of a hijacking, the pilot should, if possible, apply distress radiotelephone procedures relaying the aircraft "N" and type, present position, circumstances of the incident, and the number of crew, passengers, and hijackers. If unable to transmit over the radiotelephone, the correct transponder code 7,500 for a hijacking incident and other predesignated code words to alert air traffic controllers of the emergency should be utilized.

The pilot must also be familiar with law enforcement or U.S. military intercept flight procedures related to radio communication and aircraft single movements in the event of an emergency or hijacking situation related to terrorism.

REMAIN-OVERNIGHT SECURITY

When flying from the home fixed-base operator to a destination where the aircraft will remain overnight, it is important to plan ahead to ensure the security of the aircraft at the remain-overnight fixed-base operator. This process begins with a review of the destination airport and fixed-base operator where the aircraft will remain overnight. Contact the fixed-base operator to arrange secure accommodations for the aircraft and to arrange any other special security needs. The availability of fuel must also be a requirement. If possible, the aircraft should be kept in a hangar. Inquire regarding the availability of a hangar to secure the aircraft. If the hangar has doors that can be locked, that will provide minimal security for the aircraft. Determine if the locked hangar has an intrusion detection system and, if not, whether staff are on duty 24 hours a day for added aircraft security. If the hangar that is available is a T-hangar with an open front and no door, then there will only be protection from the weather and no security protection.

If hangars are not available, then the aircraft should be parked on a well-lit ramp area away from perimeter gates, fences, parking areas, and buildings. In this situation, as with a T-hangar, based on the security threat, a member of the aircrew may be required to remain with the aircraft at all times. If the aircraft is left unattended, all protective systems should be activated.

If maintenance is required, a member of the aircrew should be present. The key to the aircraft should not be given to the fixed-base operator. The key to the aircraft needs to be in the control of the pilot in command at all times. If the aircraft will be kept at the remain-overnight airport for several days unattended by a member of the flight crew, the aircraft should be inspected at least once each day. This should be done by a member of the flight crew. Prior to departing the remain-overnight airport, a complete security inspection must be conducted along with the required preflight safety checklist.

BIBLIOGRAPHY

Aircraft Owners and Pilots Association. (2003). *AOPA Airport Watch*. Frederick, MD: AOPA.

Bragdon, C. R. (2008). *Transportation security*. Burlington, MA: Elsevier Butterworth-Heinemann.

Elias, B. (2005). *CRS Report for Congress securing general aviation*. Washington, DC: U.S. Government Printing Office.

Fischer, R.J., & Green, G. (2008). *Introduction to security* (8th ed.). Burlington, MA: Elsevier.

Price, J.C., and Forrest, J.S. (2009). *Practical aviation security*. Burlington, MA: Elsevier Butterworth-Heinemann.

Sweet, K.M. (2009). *Aviation and airport security*. Upper Saddle River, NJ: Pearson/ Prentice Hall.

Transportation Security Administration. (2004). *Security guideline for general aviation airports*. Washington, DC: Transportation Security Administration.

Transportation Security Administration. (2011). Retrieved from http://www.tsa.gov/

6

Security of General Aviation Airports

GENERAL AVIATION AIRPORT THREAT ASSESSMENT AND SECURITY PLAN

While not a legal requirement, it is important that every general aviation airport conduct a threat assessment and develop a written airport security plan for the protection of the facility and for liability issues. Before the airport security plan can be developed, there must be a threat assessment conducted of the total airport facility. There are several principles that must be considered when conducting a threat assessment of the airport. These include protection of individuals on the airport property, the airport runway, hangars, aircraft, fuel storage, fixed-base operator, flight school, and other tenants that may be situated on the airport property from crimes such as assault, robbery, theft, vandalism, and arson. The threat assessment must also take into account risk of terrorism and an aircraft being used as a weapon.

Once the threat and risk have been identified, the next step is to determine what is required to protect the airport from those risks. This is accomplished by making an examination of the risk severity and probability of occurrence:

Threat: Risk of threat = Severity of threat × Probability of occurrence

Implement security measures to reduce the threat. A review of the security measures and plans should then be made and any changes made as needed.

After conducting the threat assessment, the next step is the development of a written general aviation airport security plan that details all of the security measures that are implemented. The airport should designate an individual to be the airport security coordinator, and an airport security committee should be established. The coordinator should take the lead in the development of the airport security plan with the assistance of the airport security committee. The individual may be the airport manager or fixed-base operator, depending on the ownership and organizational structure of the general aviation airport. It can be anyone the airport designates; the important factor is that the appointment be made to ensure the development and continued operation of an effective airport security plan. The committee should be made up of representatives of the airport owners/management, fixed-base operator, the flight school, a tenant, a pilot/aircraft owner, the local police chief, and the local fire chief.

The written general aviation security plan needs to cover all security aspects of the airport, including the protection of the perimeter of the airport, access on the airport, roadways, taxiways, runways, hangars, fueling area, aircraft, fixed-base operator, and flight school. If the airport, fixed-base operator, flight school, and other activities are all owned and operated by a single entity, this will make the writing of the plan much easier. If there are tenant activities such as a flight school or pilot shops, they should share a written security plan for their operation. That plan then can be included as an annex to the airport security plan.

The airport security plan will begin with a cover page identifying the airport name, designator, and location, such as Reigle Airport, 58° N, Palmyra, Pennsylvania. This would be followed by a table of contents. The next area would be the introduction; the purpose of the airport security plan is stated to show the airport community that security of the airport is important.

The fact that an airport security coordinator and airport security committee have been established should be addressed next with a listing of the titles of who will make up that committee. A list of important contacts should be next in this section of the airport security plan. It should include the airport manager and the airport security coordinator and may also include the members of the airport security committee.

The next area of the airport security plan would be the communications section. This will include all the nonemergency and emergency phone numbers, such as those of the airport manager, security coordinator, flight school, tenant activities, local police, fire department, and emergency agencies.

This part of the plan should also include the Aircraft Owners and Pilots Association (AOPA) suspicious activity hotline 1-866-GA-SECURE. Local Transportation Security Administration (TSA) and Federal Aviation Administration contacts should also be included. Some plans also include aircraft owners who have their aircraft hangared at the airport.

The next section of the airport security plan should provide physical information on the airport. This would include the number of runways and their length, the number of aircraft based at the airport, and any special use aircraft such as those for law enforcement, emergency medical, firefighting, Civil Air Patrol, or aerial crop spraying. The types of other aviation activity should also be listed to include flight school or charter activities.

Any possible terrorist targets in the area of the airport that could be attacked using a general aviation aircraft should be listed in this section of the airport security plan. This could include military facilities, national landmarks, governmental buildings, power plants, dams, power lines, pipelines, larger sports venues, or large population areas.

Other areas of security that need to be addressed in this area of the plan would include access control onto the airport and around the hangars and aircraft located on the airport.

Security lighting, airport information, and security signage should also be addressed in the security plan. Special areas such as the fueling area must also be addressed in the security plan.

An airport layout or sketch showing the perimeter boundary, runways, taxiways, roadways, hangars, and buildings should be placed in the airport security plan. This will allow a visual reference of the airport.

The next part of the airport security plan should cover security and law enforcement support of the airport. The security may be provided by airport staff as a collateral duty. The security may also be professional proprietary security officers hired by the airport or contracted through a licensed contact security agency.

A review of the AOPA Airport Watch Program, and the aspect of that program that has been implemented at the airport should be covered in this area of the airport security plan.

A description of the law enforcement coverage should also be listed. In almost all cases, this would include drive-bys during the day or evening hours and response to emergencies.

The final area of the airport security plan should cover the identification of suspicious activity that may be observed at the airport that would warrant reporting. The reporting protocols should be addressed in this area. The reporting and response to emergency situations will be the final topic addressed in this area of the airport security plan.

The airport security plan is not a legal requirement, so the airport can write into the plan what that airport feels is important to that aviation facility. For liability reasons and professional credibility, never write anything in the airport security plan that you are not doing or cannot accomplish.

The aviation security plan must be updated whenever there is a change to the security program. The plan should be reviewed at least once a year to ensure that it is current, and the required review and updating should be documented in writing.

The sample airport security plan found in Appendix C can be used as a template in the development of an airport security plan. Each plan will vary in complexity based on the size of the airport, activities at the airport, and surrounding area.

SECURITY AWARENESS AND TRAINING

Security awareness is the first line of defense in the protection of general aviation airports. For it to be effective, the entire airport community must be involved. Adopt the AOPA Airport Watch Program. In March 2003, the AOPA developed the Airport Watch Program. The goals of the Airport Watch Program were to enhance security at general aviation airports, to aid in the prevention and reduction of crime in the general aviation community, and to prevent mandated security regulations from the TSA. The AOPA Airport Watch Program encompasses two concepts related to security: physical security and security awareness. As it relates to physical security, the program recommends and encourages general aviation airport managers, aircraft owners, and pilots to utilize physical security practices to prevent and reduce crime.

The security awareness aspect of the program focuses on making general aviation airport owners and employees, as well as aircraft owners and pilots, aware of their surroundings. This includes being aware of what is considered normal activity at the general aviation airports and what is not.

To involve the airport community, hold periodic security awareness meetings and training programs. Promote security by the use of AOPA Airport Watch signs (Figure 6.1).

Figure 6.1 AOPA airport watch sign, Capital City Airport, New Cumberland, Pennsylvania. (Photo by Daniel J. Benny.)

The AOPA Airport Watch handouts and DVD are free and are excellent educational tools for security awareness at general aviation airports. Provide training to airport staff, pilots, and aircraft owners on recognizing suspicious activity and effective response tactics. The AOPA offers a free general aviation security course online that should be taken by all airport and flight school staff. It is also recommended for pilots and aircraft owners.

If the airport has a Web site, that would be an excellent location to address security awareness. It can also be used to link to other aviation-related Web sites, such as that of the AOPA and TSA.

Awareness training should also include a review of the signs of suspicious or possible criminal activity. It would include the following:

1. Any aircraft with unusual or unauthorized modifications
2. Persons or vehicles loitering for extended periods in the vicinity of the airport, especially people in the airport operations area
3. Pilots who appear to be under the control of other persons
4. Persons with above-average interest in aircraft and their performance capabilities and asking question about the airport or aircraft
5. Persons wishing to obtain a rental aircraft without presenting proper credentials

6. Persons who present apparently valid credentials but do not have a corresponding level of aviation knowledge
7. Anything that does not look right or does not fit the pattern of lawful, normal activity at your airport

Communication procedures should also be covered as part of the training, including calling 911 for an obvious criminal act or emergency. Airport management and the AOPA hotline 1-866-GA-SECURE should be called for suspicious activity at the airport.

AIRPORT PERIMETER SECURITY

The perimeter security of the general aviation airport begins with the property line of the airport. This is the first line of defense in a layered or security in-depth approach to the protection of a general aviation airport or any property or structure. The goal is to put in place many layers of security as part of an integrated security program for the maximum effect in deterring and detecting criminal activity and terrorism at the airport.

Based on the location of the general aviation airport, the threat assessment, and funding, the decision will be made to utilize only natural security barriers or to construct security barriers to secure the airport. For the most effective security of the airport and for safety and liability issues, it is always recommended that security barriers be constructed. This, of course, is an airport management decision that each general aviation airport must make based on the threat, crime history, safety concerns, and availability of funding.

The goal of perimeter security barriers, natural or constructed, is to deter, delay, or detect access onto the airport proper in the area of the airport perimeter other than through the directed access control points such as roadways or pedestrian walkways. Those access points can then be utilized for general observation of who is entering the airport property or for positive control of who enters the airport. The positive control is exemplified by the use of card access or the monitoring of the access points by a security officer or designated airport staff.

The use of natural security barriers, also known as crime prevention through environmental design (CPTED), is most effective in the control of vehicle access to the general aviation airport property. Natural barriers such as streams, lakes, wetlands, rocks, trees, high-density undergrowth areas, and natural trenching in most situations will deter or prevent access by vehicles onto the airport property other than by the designated access areas. It could deter some individuals, but anyone wanting to walk onto the airport property will not be stopped by natural barriers.

The most cost-effective constructed security barrier that can be used to protect the perimeter of an airport is a chain-link fence. Chain link fencing is relatively low in cost compared to the construction of masonry walls. The chain-link fence provides the flexibility to move it as needed. Because one can see through the chain-link fence, it allows visibility beyond the airport property line by security, airport personnel, pilots, or aircraft owners based at the general aviation airport. This visibility provides early warning to unauthorized access attempts onto the airport property and can result in the prevention of such attempts to breach security at the airport.

With the visibility afforded beyond the airport property line by chain-link fences, other physical security measures can be integrated into the perimeter barrier. Use of security signage is easily accomplished by posting the signs on the security fence. Security lighting can light up the area not only at the fence but also beyond the airport property line for visibility at night.

Security cameras can be used on the perimeter of the airport and can see beyond the fence line, thus providing a deterrent and early warning of unauthorized access. Should access occur, the security cameras can record the incident for future identification and prosecution of the perpetrator of the incident.

Any security fencing installed on the perimeter of the airport property should meet the security industry standards for such fencing. Heavy-gauge fencing needs to be used with an opening no larger than 2 inches. The height of the fence should be at least 6 feet with a 1-foot top guard mounted on a 45° angle facing away from the property. The top guard is utilized to prevent an individual from climbing over the fence. The top guard needs to be constructed of barbed wire or razor ribbon.

The fence must be secured in the ground by metal posts with metal bracing bars or wire across the top and bottom of the fence. This is used to prevent the fencing from being pulled down or lifted up for access over the top or under the barrier (Figure 6.2).

The perimeter fence should be inspected daily for any signs of unauthorized entry, damage to the fence, or erosion under the fencing or around the fence post. To ensure visibility around the perimeter fencing and to prevent damage to the fence, a clear zone of 15 to 20 feet needs to

Figure 6.2 Chain-link fencing protection of runway, Daytona Beach, Florida. (Photo by Daniel J. Benny.)

be established on either side of the fence. The growth of trees close to the fence could be used as access portals over the top of the perimeter fencing.

Many general aviation airports with fencing will provide a perimeter road, either stone or paved, along the fence line. This allows for the easy inspection of the perimeter fence each day for security purposes. It also allows easy access for any groundskeeping in the clear zone or repair of the fence or other physical security devices integrated into the perimeter fence line.

AIRPORT ACCESS AND KEY CONTROL

As previously stated, access control points such as roadways or pedestrian walkways allow for the general observation of who is entering the airport property. Parking areas, the fixed-base, and the operation building will be open to the public and tenants. This could include the fixed-base operator and other airport tenants, such as a flight school, restaurant, or Civil Air Patrol unit operating at the airport.

Access control points can be utilized to facilitate positive control by the use of card access or monitoring by security cameras, a security officer, or designated airport staff in areas of the airport that require higher security. This would include access to the runway, taxiways, aircraft tie-downs, the ramp areas, hangars, aircraft, area chemical storage, and fueling pumps, trucks, or storage.

When fencing is used at the airport pedestrian gates to control access to and from the ramp areas, the tie-down area, hangars, and aircraft for pilots, passengers, and airport staff who need access, the gate or gates can be controlled using a proximity access card and keys. It can also be controlled by remote access with the integration of security camera monitoring by security or airport staff.

Access cards or keys to these areas need to be secured when not in use. They should only be issued to authorized individuals. This may include airport staff and aircraft owners.

Gates will also be required when fencing is used at general aviation airports to allow authorized vehicle access into the secure area of the airport. These vehicles many include those of aircraft owners and pilots, authorized vendors, airport or tenant staff, and emergency vehicles such as those of law enforcement, firefighters, or emergency medical service. Only airport-owned vehicles should have access to the runway, taxiways, ramps, and service roads. Pilots and aircraft owners should only have vehicle access to the hangar areas. Airport vehicle access for visitors needs to be controlled and limited to the parking area of the general aviation airport.

Access of vehicles at the access points with gates is best accomplished using a proximity access card. Remote access can be used with the integration of security camera monitoring by security or airport staff. This would limit the number of access cards or keys that are issued. The vehicle access points should also be covered by security cameras to monitor and record the activity. The security cameras should be monitored by airport security or staff.

If the airport perimeter is fenced, there need to be at least two entrance points even if both are not used each day. It is important to have a secondary point of access should there be an emergency and access through the primary gate is denied.

Gates that are not used on a regular basis need to be secured with a high-security padlock. The locked gate should also be equipped with a numbered security seal. This security seal needs to be checked each day by security or airport staff to ensure the numbered seal is intact and matches the numbered seal placed on the gate. The use of a security seal and the daily inspection of the security seal will ensure that an unauthorized key is not being used so that a person can enter and exit the gate without detection. It is also used to ensure that the original padlock on the gate was not cut off and replaced with a different lock and then used by a perpetrator for continued unauthorized access into the airport or secure area.

Airport Security Signage

Signage is used at the general aviation airport to provide information. The information provided by signs may include services offered at the airport and driving and parking directions to control traffic. Signs can also be used to provide directions to locate airport facilities, tenant activity, hangars, and airport operations areas. These signs, while not directly security related, do contribute to the security of the airport. This is because the signs begin the process of directing individuals and vehicles to areas of the airport where they are authorized. This would include the proper roadways to drive on, where to park a vehicle, and where an individual may walk on the airport property to visit the fixed-base operator, flight school, or other tenant activity.

Other nonsecurity signage would include pilot information for operating on the ramps, taxiways, and runways. There are of course the required Federal Aviation Administration marking and signage related to air operations. Other signage related to the air operations could be directions to the ramp and fueling areas. Clearly marked hangars and directions to the fixed-base operator and tenant activity for the ramp, tie-down, or hangar areas can also be part of the general aviation airport signage.

General aviation airports should use signage to promote safety. This would include vehicle speed limit and traffic control signs. All vehicle traffic control signs on private property should meet U.S. and local state department of transportation requirements. This is to ensure they are understood by the driver for the safety of all and for liability reasons. Other safety signs might related to no smoking areas and directions to fire extinguishers. Safety-related signs may also be posted around the fueling pumps and air operations area. Inside structures and hangars, emergency exit signs will need to be installed.

The most important signs are those related to security. Security signage provides security information and warnings to those entering the airport property. Security signage needs to begin on the airport perimeter. If there is perimeter fencing, then the fence would be the best area to post security signs. If there is no fencing, then signs can be posted on sign poles around the perimeter of the property. These security signs should indicate no trespassing areas to deter individuals from entering the air operations area, such as the runway, ramps, tie-down, and hangar areas. The posting of such signs can prevent unauthorized access and, if it does occur, can aid in the prosecution of the perpetrator for trespassing since it was legally posted. If the area is protected by security cameras, intrusion detections systems, or security patrols, that information can also be posted on a security sign as a preventive measure. Never post regarding a security protection system that you do not have. The professional criminals and many amateurs will know that there is no protective equipment. It will only provide those at the airport with a false sense of security.

An examples of a sign would be as follows:

AIRPORT
PROPERTY
NO TRESPASSING
VIOLATORS WILL BE PROSECUTED

Security signage should include the AOPA Airport Watch signs to show participation in the program. These signs also include the TSA/AOPA 1-866-GA-SECURE number.

Other locations for signs would be at the entrance to the airport and access points to the air operations, hangar, and fueling areas (Figures 6.3–6.5). These signs should state that authorized individuals and vehicles only are permitted into the area. The AOPA Airport Watch signs should also be posted at these locations.

Examples of signs for these areas would be as follows:

AIRPORT
AIR OPERATIONS AREA
NO UNAUTHORIZED PERSON
BEYOND THIS POINT
AIRPORT
RESTRICTED AREA
KEEP OUT
AVIATION FUEL
STORAGE FACILITY

Figure 6.3 Airport security sign, Chester County Airport, Coatesville, Pennsylvania. (Photo by Daniel J. Benny.)

Figure 6.4 Airport security sign, Capital City Airport, New Cumberland, Pennsylvania. (Photo by Daniel J. Benny.)

Figure 6.5 Airport security sign, Capital City Airport, New Cumberland, Pennsylvania. (Photo by Daniel J. Benny.)

Signs should be prominent and large at vehicle access points and around the perimeter of the airport. Smaller signs can be used in areas with only pedestrian access.

Signs with emergency contact information should include phone numbers of the nearest responding law enforcement agency, 911, or TSA/APOA's 1-866-GA-SECURE and the airport or fixed-base operator manager, whichever is appropriate. These signs are appropriate at vehicle and pedestrian access points. Additional posting might be included in fixed-base operations, in pilot lounges, or near hangars, flight schools, and other tenant activities.

Airport Security Lighting

Security lighting takes away the sense of privacy of perpetrators who may consider entering the airport property at night. Security lighting also allows for better visibility with the use of security cameras and security patrols of the airport by security officers, airport staff, or drive-by law enforcement officers. Even aircraft owners going to and from their hangar and aircraft may be able to detect an unauthorized individual at the airport at night because of the security lighting. Security lighting at the general aviation airport is a deterrent to crime. The lighting also provides for a safer and more inviting environment to visitors, vendors, pilots, and aircraft owners.

Security lighting should be utilized on the perimeter of the airport to illuminate the boundary and fencing, if fencing is utilized. Security lighting needs to be used on all airport roadways, vehicle and pedestrian access points, and vehicle parking areas.

Buildings such as the fixed-base operator, flight school, or vendor facilities need to be illuminated. Entryways and doors should have effective lighting. Hangar areas can have lights placed on the exterior wall to light the area around the hangars.

The use of security lighting in the deterrence of crime against aircraft will also be part of the airport security lighting program. This would include aircraft in T-hangars, long-term aircraft tie-down areas, and remain-overnight aircraft parking locations.

Fuel storage areas where fuel pumps, storage tanks, or fueling trucks are located need to be well lit at night. This would also include chemical storage areas for working aircraft that may be based at the general aviation airport.

It is recommended that all security lighting be activated using solar photo cells so that the lights will activate automatically at night or during periods of low visibility due to fog or storms that may occur during daylight hours. This method of activation ensures that the security lighting is operating when it is needed.

All light units should be placed in a protective housing to prevent damage (Figure 6.6). The lighting can be mounted on posts or the side of buildings and hangars. The lights should be spaced so that if one light is out, they are close enough to still illuminate the area until the light is operational. Each light should be numbered so it can be easily identified and located on the airport security plan if they become inoperable. It is important to inspect the lights each night to ensure that they are all operating. Any inoperable light should be made operational as soon as possible.

Emergency lights need be installed within the buildings that are occupied by individuals for easy egress during an emergency. A backup battery or fuel-powered generator power source is recommended to ensure that emergency lighting continues to work during a power outage. Critical security lighting can also be part of the emergency lighting backup system.

Figure 6.6 Security and emergency lighting mounted on an airport building. (Photo by Daniel J. Benny.)

Airport Security Cameras

Security cameras aid in taking away the privacy of perpetrators who may consider entering the airport property. Security cameras allow for surveillance of the entire airport property or, based on the threat level and funding, provide security coverage for specific high-risk areas, such as aircraft, hangars, the fixed-base operator, or fuel storage. The security cameras provide a safer and more inviting environment for visitors, vendors, pilots, and aircraft owners.

The use of security cameras can supplement the use of airport security patrols by security officers, airport staff, or drive-by law enforcement officers. Security cameras at the general aviation airport are a deterrent to crime. In addition to capturing events live, they can record the activity for future use in the identification and apprehension of criminal suspects and for security modification to the general aviation airport security program.

Security cameras should be utilized on the perimeter of the airport to provide early warning of unauthorized access and to act as a deterrent to criminal or terrorist activity. Security cameras can also be utilized on airport roadways, vehicle and pedestrian access points, and vehicle parking areas.

Buildings such as the fixed-base operator, flight school, or vendor facilities should have security camera coverage. Hangar areas need to be included in the security camera coverage. This would include aircraft in T-hangars, long-term aircraft tie-down areas, and transit remain-overnight aircraft parking locations.

Fuel storage areas where fuel pumps, storage tanks, or fueling trucks are located and chemical storage areas for working aircraft that may be based at the general aviation airport are important areas to place security cameras. This is not only for security but also for safety and fire protection issues.

All security cameras should be placed in a protective housing to prevent damage and provide protection from the weather. The security cameras can be mounted on posts or the sides of buildings and hangars. They should be spaced so that if one is out, they are close enough to still provide security in the area until the other camera is made operational. Each security camera should be numbered so it can be easily identified and located on the airport security plan by the camera operator. This is also helpful for locating the cameras if they become inoperable. It is important to inspect the security cameras each day to ensure that they are all operating. Any inoperable security cameras should be made operational as soon as possible.

RUNWAY SECURITY

All access points from the airport property and fixed-base operator to the aircraft ramp and runway should be secure and monitored. These entry points should be accessible only to airport or fixed-base operator employees or other authorized individuals, such as pilots and aircraft owners.

Only authorized vehicles that have been properly identified and approved by the airport or fixed-base operator should be permitted onto the ramp area and runway. This would include passenger transport vehicles driven by pilots and aircraft owners and cleared limousines, rental cars, and service vehicles. Taxicabs and other vendors should never be permitted to enter the ramp under any circumstance. The airport or fixed-base operator should require authorized airport vehicles accessing the ramp or runway area to be driven by properly trained and credentialed individuals. They should be wearing a valid airport security badge that authorizes their presence within that area of the airport.

Physical security is the key to protecting the runway. The use of chain-link security fencing is the best method of securing the runway. The use of security signs posted on the fencing will reinforce the security protection. All gates to the runway must be locked when not in use; a card access

Figure 6.7 Reigle Airport runway, Palmyra, Pennsylvania. (Photo by Daniel J. Benny.)

system or padlocks can be used for less frequently utilized access points. Strict key control needs to be in place for all access cards and keys that are issued to authorized individuals.

Security cameras and at high-risk airports intrusion detection systems such as ground sensors or microwaves may also be used to secure the runway. As previously discussed, security lighting at the perimeter of the runway will play a significant role as part of the total physical security program.

Observation of the runway can also be provided by airport staff as they perform their day-to-day duties. Pilots and aircraft owners can also be observant. Based on the threat, the general aviation facility may utilize proprietary or contract security to patrol, including the ramps and runway area. Local law enforcement may also assist by periodic patrols of the airport and runway area (Figure 6.7).

AIRCRAFT TIE-DOWN AND RAMP AREA SECURITY

Aircraft tie-down and ramp areas or grass areas are used for the placement of transit aircraft or for short-term airport-based aircraft. In some cases, when hangar space is not available or if there are no hangars at the general aviation airport, then these tie-down and ramp areas would also be used for long-term placement of airport-based aircraft (Figure 6.8).

As in all flight operations and hangar areas of the general aviation airport, access to the tie-down and ramp areas must be controlled. The area needs to be secured and limited to only authorized individuals. This would include the pilots, aircraft owners, and airport or fixed-base operator staff. The tie-down areas also need to be secured to control access of unauthorized vehicle near the aircraft.

Only authorized vehicles that have been properly identified and approved by the fixed-base operator or airport manager should be permitted into the tie-down area. This would include passenger transport vehicles driven by pilots and aircraft owners and cleared limousines, rental cars, and service vehicles.

Taxicabs and other vendors should never be permitted to enter the tie-down area under any circumstance. The fixed-base operator or airport manager should require authorized airport vehicles accessing the ramp to be driven by properly trained and credentialed individuals. They should be wearing a valid airport security badge that authorizes their presence within that area of the airport.

The physical security measures to be utilized will be based on the threat level. These may include the use of natural barriers or security signs restricting access to the area.

Perimeter fencing, security lighting, and security cameras should also be considered to secure the area.

The fixed-base operator should encourage all aircraft pilots and owners to use auxiliary locking mechanisms to further protect aircraft from unauthorized use. Commercially available options for auxiliary locking mechanisms include locks for propellers, throttles, and tie-downs.

FUEL STORAGE SECURITY

Fueling facilities at general aviation airports are operated by the fixed-base operator. The aviation fuel may be disbursed from a fuel truck operated by the fixed-base operator. When using the fixed-base operator fuel truck method of fuel distribution, there will be aboveground or underground aviation fuel storage tanks that are utilized to keep the fueling truck full. Based on the type of fuel available at the general aviation airport fixed-base operator (aviation fuel or jet fuel), there will be several

Figure 6.8 Airport tie-down area, Reigle Airport, Palmyra, Pennsylvania. (Photo by Daniel J. Benny.)

tanks and in some cases more than one fueling truck used by the fixed-base operator.

At smaller general aviation airports, fuel may be disbursed by self-service fuel pumps with in-ground fuel tanks. By this method, the pilot and aircraft owner will fuel the aircraft they are flying with no assistance from the fixed-base operator.

When the aviation fueling operation is controlled by the fixed-base operator through the use of a fueling truck or when the fixed-base operator fuels aircraft at a fuel pump, it provides more security and safety for the fueling area. Utilizing the self-service method reduces the security of the fueling area. If self-service is made available in hours that the fixed-base operator is closed, it further lessens security of the fueling operation at the airport.

Fixed-base operator fuel facilities including aboveground and underground storage, fueling trucks, and fuel pumps need to be secured. The fuel pump will be inside the air operations area. The air operations areas should be fenced with access control, with signage designating it as a restricted area. Additional security measures including access control, security lighting, and security cameras should be utilized to provide security for the air operations area. At the fuel pump, signs related to safety operation should be posted. The fuel pump area needs to be well lit, and there should be security camera coverage.

If the fuel pumps are used for self-service, aviation fuel security controls must be in place at the pumps. Keys can be signed out for the pilot to fuel the aircraft and then return the keys to the fixed-base operator. Keys to the fuel pump should not be permanently assigned to pilots. Card readers could be utilized for pilots to obtain fuel through the self-service method, especially if the fixed-base operator wants to make fuel available to airport base pilots when the fixed-base operator is closed.

It is recommended that the fixed-base operator operate the aviation fuel pumps and if that is not possible, then have the pilot sign out a key to unlock the pumps and return it after fueling of the aircraft is completed.

When the fixed-base operator is closed, the nozzle of the fuel pump should be locked in place with a padlock. The fuel pump should also have an electric cutoff switch to turn off power to the fuel pump. This will prevent theft of fuel and decrease safety and fire hazards at the fuel pump.

If fueling trucks are used, when not in use the doors should be locked at all times, and the keys need to be secured inside the fixed-base operator facility. All access ports to the fuel in the fueling truck also need to be locked. The fueling truck should be kept in a locked fenced area when not in use. The fueling truck storage area should also have access-controlled gates, security signage, lighting, and security cameras. Only authorized individuals should be permitted to enter the secure area where the fueling truck is kept.

If fuel is kept in aboveground thanks at the airport, they should be secured inside a fenced area. The fuel tank storage area should also have access-controlled gates, security signage, lighting, and security cameras (Figure 6.9). Only authorized individuals should be permitted to enter the secure area where the fueling tanks are located. All access ports on the fueling tank need to be locked.

AERIAL WORKING CHEMICAL STORAGE SECURITY

Aerial working aircraft used for agricultural or firefighting operations may be based at a general aviation airport. The owner/operator of aerial working aircraft must take appropriate steps to secure the aircraft when unattended. This includes the locking of aircraft doors, throttle locks, propeller locks, and hidden ignition switches. The aircraft should also be stored in a hangar with steel doors that are locked with an intrusion detection system.

Figure 6.9 Airport fuel truck, Capital City Airport, New Cumberland, Pennsylvania. (Photo by Daniel J. Benny.)

Chemicals associated with the operation should be stored in locked facilities. They can also be stored in a fenced area that includes access-controlled gates, security signage, lighting, and security cameras. Only authorized individuals should be permitted to enter the secure area where the chemical storage tanks are located. All access ports to the chemical storage tanks need to be locked.

Agriculture and firefighting aircraft operations pose a significant terrorism threat since the aircraft could be utilized for a chemical or biological attack. Any suspicious behavior in or around agricultural aircraft should be reported immediately to local law enforcement and airport management.

INTERNET SECURITY

With the widespread use of the Internet in the aviation community and at general aviation airports, an entire new area for criminal activity and misuse has been created. To know how to protect your airport's assets, it is vital that you have an understanding of the threat.

Protection of the Internet and the information that can be retrieved, manipulated, or removed is complex. There are loose rules and regulations for the systems worldwide; therefore, security is the end-system user's responsibility. The threat to your system at a general aviation airport, fixed-base operation, or flight school and information that can be stolen can come from hackers, competitors, customers or clients, contractors, or employees. They can wreak havoc on the Internet through the destruction or modification of your data; copying or stealing your data; denial of service or compromising valuable resources; counterfeiting of checks or credit cards; destructive manipulation using trojan horses, logic bombs, or viruses; and the transmission of contraband. Such activity is considered computer crime, which is any crime in which a computer is used as primary or secondary in the commission of a crime.

While most states have laws relating to computer crime, it is also a federal offense and falls under Title 18, Section 1030, and Title 18, Section 2701. The Federal Bureau of Investigation has primary jurisdiction over all traditional investigations related to national defense, foreign relations, or any restricted data that can be used to cause damage to the United States. The U.S. Secret Service has primary jurisdiction over criminal acts involving consumer reporting or U.S. Treasury computers. The Federal Bureau of Investigation and the U.S. Secret Service have concurrent jurisdiction over financial institution fraud.

As in developing a security program to protect the aircraft, hangars, and airport, you must conduct a risk assessment based on the projected use of the Internet and possible risk. Develop your airport Internet security policy based on the greatest risk and implement controls to enforce the policy. As part of your security controls, have at least two levels of protection for your most sensitive information and treat your infrastructure and applications as two distinct but mutually dependent areas. As always and in keeping with the words of the security consultant who coined the phrase "loss prevention" in the 1960s, Sal Astor's fifth law of loss prevention says that "any loss prevention control fails only upon audit." Ensure that there are strict monitoring and reporting procedures to support your security policy. Issues to consider are what services are allowed, what services or sites will be blocked, and the enforcement of employee e-mail.

As part of the protection plan, minimize the number of connections to the Internet at the airport and control them. Increase the security of each connected computer and strengthen the network perimeter. The key is to keep outsiders out but allow insiders to roam freely without doing any damage.

To allow insiders to roam freely and still provide protection for information, you must restrict access to key sensitive assets and minimize the impact of a penetration as most penetrations are from insiders or hackers masquerading as insiders. Provide access control on servers and only allow authorized users access to sensitive information.

Segregate functions and areas using firewalls, which are hardware/software systems that regulate communication between networks. The firewall philosophy should be that which is not expressly permitted is prohibited. Firewalls can filter network traffic based on your security policy and can detect potential hackers before they break in. While firewalls can provide protection, remember that 80% of all penetrations are from insiders, and 30% occur after a firewall has been installed. A firewall will not automatically detect an attempted break-in, and it may be incorrectly configured. Intruders can go into a network directly, bypassing the firewall altogether with an end-run.

The key factors in the protection of your airport assets through the Internet are the development of a sound security policy and the use of proxy firewalls when possible. Ensure that your firewall software is up to date and examine the security of modem connections to avoid end-runs. Conduct inspections and use penetration testing software against your system. Programs such as McAfee that are available for sale or free programs such as Spybot can detect and eliminate threats to your airport computer.

By following these guidelines, you can reduce the threat of loss through the Internet at your airport, fixed-based operation, or flight school. See Appendix B for a sample generic aviation airport security plan.

BIBLIOGRAPHY

Aircraft Owners and Pilots Association. (2003). *AOPA Airport Watch*. Frederick, MD: AOPA.

Bragdon, C.R. (2008). *Transportation security*. Burlington, MA: Elsevier Butterworth-Heinemann.

Elias, B. (2005). *CRS report for Congress securing general aviation*. Washington, DC: U.S. Government Printing Office.

Fischer, R.J., & Green, G. (2008). *Introduction to security* (8th ed.). Burlington, MA: Elsevier.

Oklahoma Aeronautics Commission. (2007). *Security plan for the airport*. Altus, OK: Oklahoma Aeronautics Commission.

Price, J.C., and Forrest, J.S. (2009). *Practical aviation security*. Burlington, MA: Elsevier Butterworth-Heinemann.

Sweet, K.M. (2008). *Transportation security.* Upper Saddle River, NJ: Pearson/ Prentice Hall.

Sweet, K.M. (2009). *Aviation and airport security.* Upper Saddle River, NJ: Pearson/ Prentice Hall.

Transportation Security Administration. (2004). *Security guideline for general aviation airports.* Washington, DC: Transportation Security Administration.

Transportation Security Administration. (2011). Retrieved from http://www.tsa.gov/

7

Airport Safety

INTRODUCTION

The information presented in this chapter is not all inclusive of a safety program. It is provided as an overview of the most important aspects that should be incorporated into safety and emergency response programs at your airport. Consult the Occupational Safety and Health Administration (OSHA) and your state and local laws to determine what requirements are applicable to your airport based on the size of the staff and activities that take place there.

GENERAL AVIATION SAFETY POLICY

It is important at the general aviation airport to ensure the safety of the staff, visitors, pilots, and aircraft owners. It is the responsibility of the airport manager or fixed-base operator, depending on the organizational structure of the airport and ownership, to establish an effective safety program. The safety program must meet the requirements of OSHA and state and local safety and fire codes. The safety fire protection program should also meet the standards of the National Fire Protection Association.

In pursuit of an effective safety program, an aggressive safety strategy must be incorporated into all activities. Safety is also an individual responsibility. All airport personnel must be held accountable for fulfilling their responsibilities under the airport safety program. Compliance with this policy will be part of the annual performance appraisal process.

SAFETY CULTURE

A safety culture is the airport's perceptions and behaviors with respect to safety. Airport management's fostering of a positive safety culture is critical to any effective safety program. The following concepts are vital in fostering a positive safety culture:

Commitment to safety as a behavioral pattern and pervasive way of life

Clear, easily understood operating and safety procedures

A clear system of communications for collecting, analyzing, and exchanging safety data

System for tracking incident and accident data, analysis of trends, and feedback of results

SAFETY PROGRAM

The safety program consists of the following components:

- A formal accident prevention program
- Employee safety and accident prevention education and training
- An internal reporting system for incidents and recognized hazards
- An internal assessment program to monitor the effectiveness of the safety program

Safety Coordinator

The airport should assign an individual as the safety coordinator to coordinate professional safety training for airport staff.

Safety and Fire Inspections

To maintain a safe environment, the airport must be inspected annually to identify safety and fire hazards and recommend corrective action for noted deficiencies. If hazards are observed, immediate corrective action should be taken if possible.

GENERAL AVIATION AIRCRAFT GROUND SAFETY

Members of the airport staff should be provided with safety training and protective equipment when operating around general aviation aircraft. As part of their job, they may be marshalling aircraft, towing aircraft, fueling the aircraft, and providing other services. It is important that ground crew at the airport or fixed-base operator understand safety issues with regard to general aviation aircraft. This would include the safety approach angles, such as staying away from a turning aircraft propeller as well as aircraft jet intake and exhaust, which should be addressed in training. Ensure that the aircraft is not running and the battery switch is turned off before servicing or moving the aircraft. When fueling, make certain the ground clamp is attached to the aircraft, the wheels are chocked, and the nozzle of the fuel pump is touching the rim of the filler cap to prevent static electricity.

Airport staff should be provided with protective safety equipment. It must be mandatory that ground crew working for the airport or fixed-base operator wear the protective equipment they have been issued at all times when operating around aircraft.

The following protective safety equipment should be issued to ground crew:

- Reflective vest and clothing
- Safety shoes
- Gloves
- Ear protection
- Eye protection
- Reflective or lighted batons for use at night

FIRE PROTECTION EQUIPMENT

The following fire protection equipment is utilized at the airport as part of the fire protection program:

- Manual and automated fire alarm system
- Fire alarm enunciator panel located in safety and security office
- Smoke detectors
- Sprinklers
- Standpipes (interior and exterior)
- Water flow alarms
- Fire hydrants

Table 7.1   Classes of Fire Extinguishers

Class	Material	Fire Extinguisher Type
A	Combustible materials (paper, wood, cloth, and some rubber and plastic)	Water, foam, loaded stream, or multipurpose dry chemical
B	Flammable or combustible liquids, flammable gases, and some rubber and plastic	Halon 1301, Halon 1211, carbon dioxide, dry chemicals, foam, and loaded stream
C	Energized electrical equipment	Halon 1301, Halon 1211, carbon dioxide, and dry chemical

- Suppression systems (food service areas)
- Fire extinguishers (Table 7.1)

Routine maintenance and inspection of these systems are critical to the safety of the airport. Any problems should be corrected immediately. Examples may include missing fire extinguishers, blocked hydrants, or broken smoke detectors or sprinkler heads.

FIRE EVACUATION PLANS AND DRILLS

Current evacuation plans must be posted in prominent areas of all rooms in every building and hangar at the airport. The purpose of the plans is to provide guidance to staff and visitors regarding the location of the nearest emergency exit. Any missing or damaged plans should be reported so that they can be replaced. Fire evacuation drills should be conducted at least once each year. The fire drill may be held with the help of the local fire department.

RIGHT-TO-KNOW WORKERS PROTECTION ACT

The airport management or fixed-base operator must administer the Right-to-Know/Worker Protection Act program. In accordance with the act, the following actions will be taken: hazardous chemical inventory, maintenance of Material Safety Data Sheets (MSDSs), marking of containers, and training in hazardous communications and the Right-to-Know program.

Hazardous Chemical Inventory

An inventory of all hazardous chemicals will be maintained, utilizing the Hazardous Substance Survey Form. A master inventory will be maintained for the airport. Each department will maintain an inventory for its area of responsibility.

Material Safety Data Sheets

The MSDSs will be maintained for all hazardous chemicals inventoried. A master copy of all of the MSDSs will be maintained for the entire airport by management, with each department maintaining MSDSs for its particular area.

Container Marking

All containers for hazardous materials will be marked utilizing the symbols designated in National Fire Protection Association 49.

Hazardous Communications/Right-to-Know Training

Airport management must provide training in hazardous communications and the Right-to-Know program for all staff exposed to hazardous chemicals. First responder training must be provided to all staff who act as first responders under the Worker Protection Act.

BLOODBORNE PATHOGENS ACT

The intent of the Bloodborne Pathogens Act is to set forth procedures for employees of the general aviation airport to provide for their health and safety and to comply with the requirements of OSHA regulations for preventing occupational exposure to hepatitis B virus (HBV) and human immunodeficiency virus (HIV).

Workers at risk are those whose work may involve exposure to blood or other potentially infectious materials. At airports, all staff who may come into contact with blood or other infectious materials and who are assigned the responsibility of cleaning up blood or other potentially infectious materials must fall under this program.

Bloodborne Pathogens Policy

The policy must be designed to reduce worker risk by establishing guidelines for exposure to blood and other infectious materials. The main components of the policy include general program management, exposure determination, universal precautions, engineering controls, the utilization of personal protective equipment, housekeeping practices, labels and signs, employee training, hepatitis B vaccination, and postexposure evaluation and follow-up.

Each affected department will be responsible for designating staff members to provide assistance in the cleanup and removal of potentially infectious materials. All departments falling under the requirements of this policy will ensure adherence to the guidelines set forth in this document.

There are four major categories of responsibility that are central to the effective implementation of the bloodborne pathogens policy. These responsible persons are

1. Exposure control officer
2. Managers and supervisors
3. Education/training instructors
4. Employees

Exposure Control Officer

The exposure control officer may be the airport manager or a designated person and will be responsible for overall management and support of the bloodborne pathogens policy. Activities that are delegated to the exposure control officer include, but are not limited to,

Overall responsibility for implementing the policy.

Developing and administering any additional bloodborne pathogen-related policies and practices needed to support the effective implementation of this policy.

Collecting and maintaining a suitable reference library on the Bloodborne Pathogens Standard and bloodborne pathogens safety and health information

- Knowing current legal requirements concerning bloodborne pathogens
- Acting as airport liaison during OSHA inspections
- Conducting periodic audits to maintain an up-to-date bloodborne pathogens policy

Airport or Department Managers and Supervisors

Airport or department managers and supervisors are responsible for exposure control in their respective areas. They will work directly with the exposure control officer to ensure that proper exposure control procedures are followed.

Education/Training Coordinator

The education/training coordinator could be the airport manager or designated person who will be responsible for providing information and assistance in the training of employees who have the potential for exposure to bloodborne pathogens. Activities falling under the direction of this position include

- Maintaining an up-to-date list of personnel requiring training
- Developing and scheduling suitable education/training programs
- Maintaining documentation of those employees receiving training

Employees

Employees of the airport have an important role in the bloodborne pathogen compliance program. Their responsibilities include

- Knowing what tasks they perform that have occupational exposure
- Attending the bloodborne pathogens training program
- Planning and conducting all operations in accordance with work practices
- Developing good personal hygiene habits

Availability of the Bloodborne Pathogens Policy to Employees

The bloodborne pathogens policy must be available for review by all employees. Copies of the policy will be kept on file by the airport manager.

Review and Update of the Policy

To ensure that the policy is kept current, it must be reviewed and updated at least annually, whenever new applicable tasks and procedures are implemented, and whenever new functional positions that may involve exposure are created.

Exposure Determination

To implement the bloodborne pathogens policy successfully, employees who may be exposed to bloodborne pathogens will be identified by job classification, tasks, and procedures. The list will be reviewed annually by the airport manager or designated individual.

Universal Precautions and Engineering Controls

A key aspect of the bloodborne pathogens policy is the use of universal precautions and engineering controls to eliminate or minimize employee exposure to bloodborne pathogens. Employees use cleaning, maintenance, and other equipment that is designed to prevent contact with blood or other potentially infectious materials.

Universal precautions and engineering controls include

- Rubber gloves
- Protective clothing, such as gowns, aprons, masks, and goggles
- One-way cardiopulmonary resuscitation (CPR) masks for first aid procedures
- Infectious waste cleaning kits and containers
- Hand-washing facilities
- Leakproof specimen containers with biohazard warning labels
- Personal hygiene practices, including washing of hands following contact with potentially infectious material
- Restrictions on eating or drinking in work areas containing potentially infectious material

Hepatitis B Vaccination Program

Even with good adherence to exposure prevention practices, exposure incidents can occur. As a result, a hepatitis B vaccination program and established procedures for postexposure evaluation and follow-up should exposure to bloodborne pathogens occur must be developed.

To protect employees from the possibility of hepatitis B infection, the airport must implement a vaccination program. This program must be available, at no cost, to all employees who are at risk of occupational exposure to bloodborne pathogens.

The vaccination program consists of a series of three inoculations over a 6-month period. As part of their bloodborne pathogens training, employees receive information regarding hepatitis vaccination, including its safety and effectiveness.

Vaccinations are performed under the supervision of a licensed physician or other health care professional. A list is maintained of employees taking part in the vaccination program. Employees who decline to take part in the program must sign a vaccination declination form.

Postexposure Evaluation and Follow-Up

Should an employee of the airport be involved in a possible exposure to bloodborne pathogen incident, the following actions will be taken:

- Investigate the circumstances surrounding the incident, including when and where it occurred, what potentially infectious materials were involved, the source of the material, the circumstances under which the incident occurred, personal protective equipment being used at the time, and actions taken as a result of the incident. A detailed report will be written, including recommendations for avoiding similar incidents in the future.
- The employee will receive medical consultation and treatment as expeditiously as possible.

Information Provided to the Health Care Professional

To assist the health care professional, the following information will be forwarded to them:

- A copy of the bloodborne pathogens policy
- A description of the exposure incident
- The exposed employee's relevant medical records
- Other pertinent information

Health Care Professional's Written Evaluation

Following the consultation, the health care professional will provide the airport with a written evaluation of the exposed employee's situation. The airport will furnish a copy of this report to the exposed employee. To maintain confidentiality, the evaluation will contain only the following information:

- Whether hepatitis B vaccination is indicated for the employee.
- Whether the employee has received the hepatitis B vaccination.

- Confirmation that the employee has been informed of the results of the evaluation.
- Confirmation that the employee has been told about any medical conditions resulting from the exposure incident that require further evaluation or treatment.
- All other findings or diagnoses remain confidential and are not included in the written report.

Medical Record Keeping

The airport must maintain comprehensive medical reports on all employees, which include the following information:

- Name and Social Security number of the employee.
- A copy of the employee's hepatitis B vaccination status, including dates of vaccinations and medical records relative to the employee's ability to receive vaccination.
- Copies of the results of examinations, medical testing, and follow-up procedures that took place as a result of the employee's exposure to bloodborne pathogens.
- A copy of the information provided to the consulting health care professional as a result of any exposure to bloodborne pathogens.
- As with all information in these areas, this information will be kept confidential. Information will not be disclosed to anyone without the employee's written consent, except as required by law.

Labels and Signs

The airport must implement a comprehensive biohazard warning system, using red "color-coded" containers with the bio hazard logo on it. The following items must be labeled:

- Containers of regulated waste.
- Refrigerators/freezers containing blood or other potentially infectious materials.
- Sharps disposal containers.
- Other containers used to store, transport, or ship blood and other potentially infectious materials.
- Laundry bags, containers, and contaminated equipment.
- On labels affixed to equipment, the portions of the equipment that are contaminated are to be indicated.

Information and Training

Having well-informed and educated employees is vital when attempting to eliminate or minimize employee exposure to bloodborne pathogens. Because of this, all employees who have the potential for exposure to bloodborne pathogens should receive comprehensive training and be furnished with as much information as possible on this issue. Employee training should be provided to all new employees and to any employees who change jobs or functions. Employees should be retrained at least annually to keep their knowledge current.

Training Topics

The topics covered in the training program will include, but are not limited to, the following:

- The bloodborne pathogens policy itself
- The epidemiology, symptoms, and modes of transmission of bloodborne diseases
- A review of the use and limitations of methods that will prevent or reduce exposure
- The selection, use, and disposal of personal protective equipment
- Biohazard warning labels and containers
- Information on the hepatitis B vaccination program
- Procedures to be followed if an exposure incident occurs and information on postexposure evaluation and follow-up

Record Keeping

To facilitate the training of employees and to document the training process, the airport must maintain training records containing the following information:

- Dates of all training sessions
- Name of instructor
- Names and job titles of employees attending

HAZARDOUS WASTE MANAGEMENT

To ensure the safe handling of hazardous materials, the following guidelines are to be used in the storage, handling, and removal of hazardous material and waste:

- All hazardous materials and biohazards are to be stored in safe containers and properly marked to identify the contents in a designated storage area at the airport. Proper safety precautions and protective equipment such as gloves, eye shields, and aprons should be used during the handling of hazardous and biohazard material.
- Hazardous and biohazard waste will be removed from the airport by certified contractors at regular intervals. To have this waste removed, the department will be responsible in ensuring that the waste is placed in a safe container and is properly marked.

BIBLIOGRAPHY

Bragdon, C.R. (2008). *Transportation security.* Burlington, MA: Elsevier Butterworth-Heinemann.

Fischer, R.J., & Green, G. (2008). *Introduction to security* (8th ed.). Burlington, MA: Elsevier.

Moore, K.C. (2000). *Airport, aircraft and airline security.* Burlington, MA: Elsevier Butterworth-Heinemann.

Price, J.C., and Forrest, J.S. (2009). *Practical aviation security.* Burlington, MA: Elsevier Butterworth-Heinemann.

Sweet, K.M. (2008). *Transportation security.* Upper Saddle River, NJ: Pearson/Prentice Hall.

Sweet, K.M. (2009). *Aviation and airport security.* Upper Saddle River, NJ: Pearson/Prentice Hall.

Transportation Security Administration. (2011). Retrieved from http://www.tsa.gov/

Wood, R. (2003). *Aviation safety programs.* Tabemash, CO: Jeppesen.

8

Emergency Response

INTRODUCTION

An emergency could occur at a general aviation airport, and it is important for the airport to be prepared to handle such situations. This chapter discusses some of the more common emergencies that may occur at an airport.

RESPONSE TO A GENERAL AVIATION AIRCRAFT ACCIDENT

Aircraft accidents may occur at general aviation airports that do not house any professional airport firefighters. The first responders to such an accident in most cases will be the airport, fixed-base operator, or flight school staff, followed by local police, fire, and emergency medical support. The first responder to a general aviation aircraft accident could save lives and affect the outcome of the crash investigation by knowing what to do.

The role of the first responder is to save lives and secure the scene until further help arrives. Since aircraft accidents are handled and investigated differently from other types of accidents, the following procedures will provide for an effective response to best save lives, prevent further injury, protect property, and preserve valuable evidence. The role of the first responder is to

- Rescue
- Report
- Secure

Rescue

Use caution in approaching the wreckage by vehicle or on foot, particularly if the approach is along the crash path as survivors may have been thrown from the aircraft, and valuable evidence could be destroyed. Provide standard first aid to survivors until you are relieved by medical personnel. If there is a postcrash fire or indications of the possibility of fire or explosion from fuel vapor, move survivors a safe distance away; otherwise, do not disturb them except as necessary for first aid, but always ensure that medical assistance is in route.

For safety from electrical or fire danger, turn off the aircraft's master or battery switch. It is usually located within the pilot's reach on the left bottom side of the instrument panel or the left bulkhead. The master switch is usually red and larger than the other switches. The battery switch may be a simple toggle switch. Other than these switches for safety, avoid moving any other instrument switches or the like as they will be critical to the accident investigation.

Beware of the propeller. Even if the master switch and magneto switches are off, the engine may start if the propeller is moved. Different types of aircraft pose different hazards. Agricultural aircraft will carry hazardous materials, and military aircraft should be considered armed. On military aircraft, do not touch anything in the cockpit. You could release the ejection seat or a weapon.

Some general aviation aircraft are equipped with ballistic parachutes. If the ballistic parachute has been deployed, this is not a danger, but if not, caution must be used. An explosive device is used to deploy the ballistic parachute that is located in the ceiling of the cabin above the pilot. Do not disturb the device.

Other explosive concerns would include general aviation aircraft with integral seat belt and harness airbags. They can be identified easily as the seat belt and shoulder harness will appear large and padded. The airbag is housed in the harness straps. Be cautious of pressurized containers that can explode. These would include oxygen bottles and fire extinguishers that may be carried onboard the aircraft.

Report

Contact the communications center by radio or cell phone. The emergency units that should respond would be additional police, medical, and fire personnel and the coroner should there be fatalities. Caution the coroner not to embalm any bodies. The Federal Aviation Administration (FAA) will provide a kit called a "tool box" for pathological and toxicological tests. Should it be a large-scale crash, then the Red Cross and other community service organizations will need to be notified.

The FAA local Flight Standards District Office (FSDO) must also be contacted. The FSDO will notify the National Transportation Safety Board (NTSB) and any other necessary federal agencies, such as the Federal Bureau of Investigation or the Environmental Protection Agency.

The FSDO (Figure 8.1) will need information about the aircraft. This will include the N number of the aircraft, accident location, a local contact, the number of injuries or fatalities, and when the accident was reported or discovered. Even if you do not have all of this information, you must still call the FSDO as soon as possible.

Figure 8.1 FSDO, New Cumberland, Pennsylvania. (Photo by Daniel J. Benny.)

Secure

The accident area must be secured and treated as a crime scene. Nothing should be moved or disturbed. No one is to be allowed inside the wreckage area other than those necessary for rescue and firefighting. It is also important to establish a no smoking area because of potential fire danger and to enforce it.

The only items that should be removed besides occupants are mail or other cargo to protect them from further damage. Logbooks and certificates can be removed if there is danger of damage before the FAA and NTSB investigators arrive. Anything removed must be protected as evidence and turned over to FAA or NTSB investigators. If it is necessary to disturb or move the aircraft or victims, take photographs or videotape or sketch their positions regarding where they were found. Be sure to indicate impact marks.

The key to safe and effective first response to an aircraft accident is to know the concepts of rescue, report, and secure, and you will be able to provide a professional, safe, and effective first response to the scene of an aircraft accident. This will preserve lives, property, and the accident site for the conducting of a proper investigation by FAA or NTSB investigators or other federal agencies.

This training should be provided to all airport, fixed-base operator, and flight school staff. Aircraft owners and pilots that are based at the general aviation airport should also have such training.

MEDICAL EMERGENCIES

Airport staff would be responsible for responding to medical emergencies that occur on airport property. The staff should have basic certification in cardiopulmonary resuscitation (CPR), first aid, and AED (automated external defibrillator) and will only treat victims at that level of certification.

Responding to Medical Emergencies

Airport staff should respond immediately to any medical emergency at the airport, taking with them the first aid kit. Response, whether it be on foot or in a vehicle, must be done in a safe manner. On arrival at the scene, they should assess the status of the victim. If any of the following conditions or injuries are evident, an ambulance will be immediately called:

- Injuries with severe bleeding
- Obvious fractured limbs
- Severe burns
- Serious eye injuries
- Unconscious victim or victim not breathing
- Serious respiratory injuries due to contact with hazardous materials
- Convulsing victim
- Severe chest pain or other signs of heart attack
- Airway blockage

The medical conditions or injuries must be assessed to determine if an ambulance should be dispatched. If the victim is conscious and the injuries are not severe or life threatening, the victim may make the decision regarding whether an ambulance should be called. If in doubt, have an ambulance dispatched.

If it is determined that an ambulance must be dispatched, call 911 to request an ambulance. The following information, if available, is to be provided: officer's name; location of victim; type of injury or illness; victim's name, sex, age, any known medical conditions or medications, and vital signs. Airport staff should remain with the victim until the ambulance arrives.

Treatment of the Victim

The airport staff must utilize protective equipment, such as gloves and one-way valves, when treating the victim. They must only treat the victim to the level of their certification. On the arrival of medical personnel, they will assume control of the victim. On completion of the treatment of the victim, all biohazardous material will be properly disposed, and all expended materials will be replaced so that they will be available for the next incident.

VEHICLE ACCIDENTS

On arrival at the scene of a vehicle accident on an airport roadway or in a parking area, the airport staff should determine if there are injuries and if medical, fire personnel, or local police are required. If so, call 911.

Response

Airport staff who respond to the area of the accident must evaluate the situation and request additional assistance as needed. The decision of whether to provide assistance to the victims of the accident should be at the discretion of the staff member, taking into consideration the staff member's own safety.

Should the staff member decide that it is safe to approach the vehicle, it will be done from the upwind side. Exercise caution and be alert to gasoline and gasoline fumes. If gasoline or its fumes are present, the staff member must call 911.

FIRES

In the event of a fire on the airport property, the airport staff should respond to the incident to evaluate if such a condition exists; to assist with evacuation of the building, hangar, or aircraft if safe to do so; and to secure the perimeter.

Notification of Fire

The airport staff could become aware of a smoke or fire condition or the activation of a fire alarm through direct observation, a phone call, or the activation of a manual or automatic fire protection system. On receiving notification of a fire, the staff should respond immediately to that location. When it has been determined that a fire or smoke condition exists, call 911 to request fire apparatus be dispatched.

Evacuation

Should a fire occur in a building or hangar, evacuation of the building or hangar is a requirement. If not already activated, activate the building's emergency alarm system, then assist with the evacuation. The following safety precautions should be utilized:

- Leave the building using the closest evacuation exit, as posted.
- Walk slowly; do not run.
- When leaving rooms, close doors and windows.

- Use emergency fire exits and stairwells, ensuring that doors are closed behind you.
- Never use an elevator.

Securing the Scene

Once the building or hangar has been evacuated, to secure the scene all persons are to remain at least 100 yards from the site.

Firefighting

While staff should have received training in use of fire extinguishers, they are not required to extinguish fires. If a fire is small enough to be extinguished or contained with a fire extinguisher and the airport staff member feels that he or she can attempt to extinguish the fire without endangering him- or herself, the staff member can attempt to do so.

Replacement of Extinguishers

Should a fire extinguisher be used, it needs to be pulled from service so that it may be refilled.

NATURAL GAS LEAKS

If natural gas is utilized at the airport and a gas leak occurs, there is a potential for serious injury or damage. Should there be a suspected or known gas leak, the following should occur:

- Notify the gas company.
- Notify the fire department.
- Evacuate the buildings or hangars and immediate area.
- Establish a safe perimeter around the threat area.
- Provide assistance to responding gas company and fire department personnel.

Important Safety Precautions

When evacuating a building or hangar for a gas leak, avoid any activity that could create a spark, including activating the fire alarm system, turning on or off electrical switches, and using two-way radios. If possible, open windows and doors to allow ventilation and turn off the source of the gas supply, if known.

SEVERE WEATHER AND NATURAL DISASTERS

Severe weather could cause possible danger to employees, visitors, aircraft, and property at the airport. This may include blizzards, hurricanes, tornadoes, thunderstorms, earthquakes, landslides, flooding, or natural fires.

Severe weather instances can usually be preannounced, and employees can be sent home in time to arrive safely. In the case of a tornado or other short-notice incident, the interior of the building or hangar will be the safest location. The site-specific evacuation plan should be consulted for the location of inside evacuation safe areas.

BOMB THREATS

A bomb threat could occur at your airport by a telephonic, e-mail, or written threat or by the discovery of a suspicious letter or package. Should a bomb threat occur, management will be immediately notified. The decision to evacuate and conduct a search for a bomb will be made by airport management if time allows. If a bomb threat is made that indicates that an explosive device will be activated within a short period of time, the buildings or hangars must be evacuated immediately.

Notification and Evacuation

Once a threat has occurred, local police and emergency personnel will be notified of the threat and will respond to the scene. The United States Army EOD (Explosive Ordnance Disposal) Unit or police bomb unit will be notified and placed on alert by local law enforcement but will only respond if a suspicious device or package is located. If time allows, based on the nature of the threat, prior to the evacuation of buildings and hangars, first examine all emergency exits and stairwells to ensure that no explosive devices are located in those areas.

After all exits have been cleared, occupants of the building or hangar should be advised in person by walking throughout the building or hangar that there has been a bomb threat and that they are being evacuated from the building. Prior to the occupants' departing their immediate area, they should be asked to observe if there are any unusual items in the area that do not belong there. They are to be instructed not to use any electronic equipment. Occupants can then be evacuated from the building or hangar using the emergency exits.

During the evacuation and while in the building or hangar:

- Two-way radio communications are not to be utilized, and radio equipment will be turned off as some explosive devices are activated by radio frequency.
- At no time will the emergency alarm system be activated or elevators be used.
- Do not turn on or off any light switches or electrical components.
- When leaving rooms and the building, leave all doors open to assist in venting.
- Once the building or hangar has been evacuated, all occupants must remain at least 100 yards from the building.
- Establish the perimeter and secure the area.

Bomb Search

After the building or hangar has been evacuated, a thorough search needs to be made with assistance from local law enforcement personnel. Utilizing the building or hangar floor plans, the search needs to be conducted beginning with the exterior of the building or hangar, working inward and upward by floor. In a hangar, each aircraft must also be searched. After a room has been searched, the search team will mark the entrance to the room with a piece of security tape, indicating that the room has been cleared.

Should a bomb or suspicious package be located, do not touch it. Evacuate the immediate area and wait for the bomb disposal unit. Even though a device or suspicious package is observed, the remainder of the building is to be searched as several devices may have been planted.

Notification of Bomb Disposal Unit

When a bomb or suspicious package has been located, the local law enforcement agency will notify the bomb disposal unit, which will respond and assume control of the scene.

Reentering

When it has been determined that no explosive device exists or the area has been cleared of any devices, the building or hangar may then be occupied.

HOSTAGE SITUATION

A hostage situation could occur due to a domestic violence incident, actions of a disgruntled employee, an attempted robbery, or a terrorist act.

1. Secure the scene and evacuate all persons from the building and secure the area.
2. Notify local police while the area is being secured.
3. Gather intelligence while waiting for the local police to arrive; obtain as much information as possible regarding the perpetrators, hostages, weapons, motive, and the layout of the area. This will assist the responding law enforcement agencies in dealing with the situation effectively.

BIBLIOGRAPHY

Fischer, R.J., & Green, G. (2008). *Introduction to security* (8th ed.). Burlington, MA: Elsevier.

Manley, A.D. (2009). *Security manager's guide to disasters: managing through emergencies, violence, and other workplace threats.* Boca Raton, FL: CRC Press.

Price, J.C., and Forrest, J.S. (2009). *Practical aviation security.* Burlington, MA: Elsevier Butterworth-Heinemann.

Sweet, K.M. (2008). *Transportation security.* Upper Saddle River, NJ: Pearson/Prentice Hall.

Transportation Security Administration. (2011). Retrieved from http://www.tsa.gov/

9

Security of General Aviation Hangars

HANGAR SECURITY AND SAFETY

There are three types of hangar most often found at general aviation airports:

- Community Hangars (Figure 9.1)
- Individual Door Hangars (Figure 9.2)
- Individual T-hangars (Figure 9.3)

Community hangars are large hangars operated by the airport or fixed-base operator in which numerous aircraft owned by different individuals or corporations are kept together. The aircraft are moved in and out of the hangar by the fixed-base operator. This is done to provide for the security and safety of all the aircraft and to prevent damage to aircraft when being moved. Most community hangars have doors and can be locked. Community hangars should also be protected by an intrusion detection and fire protection system. High-security locks, access control, security signage, security lighting, and security cameras are also recommended. The hangar should be designated as a restricted area with strict access control. Access control includes the use of identification cards, sign-in procedures, and passes and escorts for visitors.

Figure 9.1 Airport community hangar, Capital City Airport, New Cumberland, Pennsylvania. (Photo by Daniel J. Benny.)

Figure 9.2 Individual door hangar, Reigle Airport, Palmyra, Pennsylvania. (Photo by Daniel J. Benny.)

Figure 9.3 Author's Cessna C-172 in individual T-hangar, Reigle Airport, Palmyra, Pennsylvania. (Photo by Daniel J. Benny.)

Individual door hangars are hangars large enough to place one aircraft in them. Because they have doors, they can be locked. It is recommended that high-security locks, access control, security signage, security lighting, and security cameras be utilized to provide protection of the aircraft. If the fixed-base operator does not provide this protection, in many cases the operator would permit the aircraft owner to have such security measures installed at a cost to the aircraft owner renting the hangar space. The hangar should be designated as a restricted area with strict access control.

Individual T-hangars are hangars large enough to place one aircraft in them. They do not have a door in the front of the hangar. The hangar is only used to protect the aircraft from the weather. Because they do not have doors, they cannot be locked. It is recommended that security signage, security lighting, and security cameras be utilized to provide protection of the aircraft. If the fixed-base operator does not provide this protection, in many case the operator would permit the aircraft owner to have such security measures installed at a cost to the aircraft owner. The hangar should be designated as a restricted area. The aircraft owner renting the space can keeping the aircraft locked and use f prop locks and throttle locks.

FIRE PROTECTION

In addition to physical security considerations, fire protection of the hangar and aircraft located in the hangar should be part of the protection plan. Fire protection standards for aviation can be found in National Fire Protection Association Standards 408, Aircraft Hand Portable Fire Extinguishers, and 409, Aircraft Hangars. For fire protection purposes, hangars are divided into three groups.

1. Group I is a hangar with more than 28 feet of clear door height or over 40,000 square feet. A hangar housing an aircraft with a tail height over 28 feet would also fall into this group.
2. Group II hangars are those with 28 or less feet of clear door height and a square footage of 20,000 to 40,000.

Protection for hangars in Groups I and II includes the use of an automatic sprinkler system utilizing a foam-water combination. The availability of portable extinguishers and hand lines is also required.

3. Group III hangars, those with a clear door height of less than 28 feet and a square footage area between 15,000 and 40,000 are required to have only portable extinguishers.

A fire protection system should be installed to provide fire safety protection for the hangar and aircraft. The fire protection system should include smoke or rate-of-rise heat detectors based on the layout of the hangar and activities taking place in the hangar. The fire protection system needs to be monitored by the fixed-base operator, airport management, or a commercial central station during operating hours of the fixed-base operator. During hours when the fixed-base operation is closed, the fire protection system needs to be monitored by a commercial central station.

BIBLIOGRAPHY

Aircraft Owners and Pilots Association. (2003). *AOPA Airport Watch*. Frederick, MD: AOPA.

Bragdon, C.R. (2008). *Transportation security*. Burlington, MA: Elsevier Butterworth-Heinemann.

Elias, B. (2005). *CRS report for Congress securing general aviation*. Washington, DC: U.S. Government Printing Office.

Fischer, R.J., & Green, G. (2008). *Introduction to security* (8th ed.). Burlington, MA: Elsevier.

Price, J.C., and Forrest, J.S. (2009). *Practical aviation security*. Burlington, MA: Elsevier Butterworth-Heinemann.

Moore, K.C. (2000). *Airport, aircraft and airline security*. Burlington, MA: Elsevier Butterworth-Heinemann

NFPA. (2010). NFPA 408 Standard for Aircraft Hand Portable Fire Extinguisher. Quincy, MA: NFPR.

NFPA. (2011). NFPA Standards for Aircraft Hangars. Quincy, MA: NFPR.

Sweet, K.M. (2008). *Transportation security*. Upper Saddle River, NJ: Pearson/ Prentice Hall.

Sweet, K.M. (2009). *Aviation and airport security*. Upper Saddle River, NJ: Pearson/ Prentice Hall.

Transportation Security Administration. (2004). *Security guideline for general aviation airports*. Washington, DC: Transportation Security Administration.

Transportation Security Administration. (2011). Retrieved from http://www.tsa.gov/

10

Security of Fixed-Base Operation

INTRODUCTION

To ensure the safety and security of the general aviation fixed-base operator (Figure 10.1) calls for the utmost vigilance by not only general aviation aircraft operators but also the fixed-base operator aircraft support services. The primary security concerns for the fixed-base operator include

- General security measures
- Fixed-base operator security coordinator
- Fixed-base operator security coordinator training
- Aircraft security
- Aircraft rentals
- Transient pilots
- Reporting suspicious activity

GENERAL SECURITY MATTERS

Ramp Security Measures

All access doors and gates from the fixed-base operator to the aircraft ramp should be secure and monitored. These entry points should be accessible only to fixed-base operator employees or other authorized individuals, such as pilots and aircraft owners.

Figure 10.1 CYX Aviation fixed-base operator, Capital City Airport, New Cumberland, Pennsylvania. (Photo by Daniel J. Benny.)

Only authorized vehicles that have been properly identified and approved by the fixed-base operator should be permitted into the ramp area. This would include passenger transport vehicles driven by pilots and aircraft owners and cleared limousines, rental cars, and service vehicles. Taxicabs and other vendors should never be permitted to enter the ramp under any circumstance. The fixed-base operator should require authorized airport vehicles accessing the ramp to be driven by properly trained and credentialed individuals. They should be wearing a valid airport security badge that authorizes presence within that area of the airport.

Physical security is also important to the fixed-base operator and the operator's area of responsibility. The use of security signs, lighting, locks, security cameras, and intrusion detection systems for the fixed-base operator building is vital to the security of the fixed-base operator and the airport.

There must be adherence to strict key control of all aircraft owned by the fixed-base operator for rental or flight instruction. All aircraft keys need to be in a locked security container when not in use. When used, they must be signed out and back in when the flight is complete.

Areas to be protected should include the aircraft parking areas, hangar, fuel storage areas, and fuel trucks. If the fixed-base operator is responsible for the access points at the airport, the guidelines set forth under security of the airport in this book should be followed.

FIXED-BASE OPERATOR SECURITY COORDINATOR

Each fixed-base operator should designate a security coordinator and an alternate security coordinator. The duties of the primary and alternate fixed-base operator security coordinators should include acting as the fixed-base operator primary point of contact for airport management, airport security, and Transportation Security Administration personnel. They should also maintain communications with all members of the airport community, including fixed-base operator employees, airport and tenant activity staff, the flight school, pilots, and aircraft owners.

FIXED-BASE SECURITY COORDINATOR TRAINING

The fixed-base operator security coordinators should also complete the annual security awareness training provided online by the Aircraft Owners and Pilots Association and the Transportation Security Administration. It could also be a training program developed by the fixed-base operator to cover the recommended topics: recognizing suspicious activities and determining the seriousness of an occurrence; communication and coordination with airport security personnel (airport security coordinator, law enforcement, airport management); appropriate response procedures; and facility security.

AIRCRAFT SECURITY

The primary security goal of the fixed-base operator security program is to prevent the intentional misuse of general aviation aircraft for terrorist purposes. Properly securing an aircraft is critical in the prevention of the use of general aviation aircraft for terrorism. The fixed-base operator should secure its own aircraft if any are owned and should recommend to each aircraft operator using its facility to employ methods for securing these aircraft. Aircraft operators can employ multiple methods of securing their aircraft to prevent an unauthorized person from gaining access or to make it as difficult for an unauthorized person to gain access to the

133

general aviation aircraft. Some basic methods of securing a general aviation aircraft that can be recommended by the fixed-base operator include ensuring that door locks are consistently used to prevent unauthorized access or tampering with the aircraft; storing the aircraft in a hangar, if available, and locking hangar doors; ensuring that aircraft ignition keys are not stored inside the aircraft.

The fixed-base operator should encourage all aircraft pilots and owners to use auxiliary locking mechanisms to further protect aircraft from unauthorized use. Commercially available options for auxiliary locking mechanisms include locks for propellers, throttles, and tie-downs.

AIRCRAFT RENTALS

Aircraft rentals are an important aspect of the fixed-base operation business and a potential weak link in general aviation security. Fixed-base operators should validate the identity of an individual renting an aircraft by checking government-issued photo identification as well as the airman certificate and current medical certificate. In addition to any aircraft-specific operational and training check ride requirements, a first-time rental customer should be given a review of the airport operations and security procedures at that facility. Fixed-base operators renting aircraft should be attentive of suspicious activities. Individuals who inquire about an aircraft rental without possessing the necessary knowledge or certifications to operate such an aircraft should be reported to the Transportation Security Administration. Pilots' identification must now carry government-issued photo identification, such as a driver license with a picture along with their new Federal Aviation Administration (FAA) enhanced plastic airman certificate, which replaced the old paper airman certificate. The fixed-base operator should check this identification before renting hangars or tie-down space to aircraft owners and before renting aircraft to pilots. Transient pilots should be required to sign in and sign out when arriving or departing the airport.

TRANSIENT PILOTS

The fixed-base operator should have flight crew members check in and present appropriate credentials at the customer service counter on arrival at the fixed-base operator. As previously stated, pilots' identification must now carry government-issued photo identification such as a driver's license with a picture along with the new FAA enhanced plastic airman certificate.

The fixed-base operator should provide aircraft operators with local law enforcement contact information and the Aircraft Owners and Pilots Association Airport Watch materials and encourage them to adhere to its recommendations. At a minimum, the fixed-base operator should provide arriving and departing passengers and flight crew members a line-of-sight escort by a fixed-base operator employee to and from the aircraft. The fixed-base operator should also have a flight crew member identify and verify each passenger and his or her respective baggage before the passengers are permitted access to the aircraft ramp. The fixed-base operator should have its personnel clear and escort personal vehicles, containing passengers and baggage identified by the respective flight crew members, to and from the aircraft ramp.

REPORTING SUSPICIOUS ACTIVITY

The fixed-base operator should immediately report to the Transportation Security Operations Center (TSOC; recently renamed the Freedom Center) any threat information, as well as any suspicious incidents and activities that could affect the security of U.S. civil aviation, by calling the GA Secure hotline at 1-866-GA-SECURE (1-866-427-3287). This information could be related, for example, to suspected hijacking; bomb threats, both specific and nonspecific; information relating to the possible surveillance of an aircraft or airport facility; and correspondence that could indicate a potential threat to civil aviation by terrorist or criminal gangs.

As suggested by the Transportation Security Administration, the reports should include information on all threats, suspicious incidents, and suspicious activity provided to the fixed-base operator by

- A federal, state, or local government agency
- A foreign government
- An operator employee or authorized representative
- An airport operator
- A private individual
- An aircraft operator

Note: In the event of an immediate emergency, 911 or local law enforcement should be contacted first. The 1-866-GA-SECURE number should be contacted after initial notification to local authorities.

As suggested by the Transportation Security Administration, information reported to GA-SECURE should include

- The name of the reporting fixed-base operator
- The affected aircraft's flight number and tail number
- Departure/arrival airports
- Current location of the affected aircraft
- A description of the incident/activity
- The names, and other data, as available, of individuals involved in the threat, activity, or incident
- Aircraft with unusual or unauthorized modifications
- Unfamiliar persons loitering for extended periods in the vicinity of parked aircraft, in pilot lounges, or in other areas deemed inappropriate
- Pilots who appear to be under the control of another person
- Persons wishing to rent aircraft without presenting proper credentials or identification
- Persons who appear to be posing as pilots, security personnel, or emergency medical personnel or using uniforms or vehicles to gain access to the airport
- Persons presenting credentials that appear false or altered
- Persons who present apparently valid credentials but who do not display a corresponding level of aviation knowledge
- Any pilot who makes threats or statements inconsistent with normal uses of aircraft
- Events or circumstances that do not fit the pattern of lawful, normal activity at an airport

BIBLIOGRAPHY

Aircraft Owners and Pilots Association. (2003). *AOPA Airport Watch.* Frederick, MD: AOPA.

Bragdon, C.R. (2008). *Transportation security.* Burlington, MA: Elsevier Butterworth-Heinemann.

Elias, B. (2005). *CRS report for Congress securing general aviation.* Washington, DC: U.S. Government Printing Office.

Fischer, R.J., & Green, G. (2008). *Introduction to security* (8th ed.). Burlington, MA: Elsevier.

Moore, K.C. (2000). *Airport, aircraft and airline security.* Burlington, MA: Elsevier Butterworth-Heinemann.

Price, J.C., and Forrest, J.S (2009). *Practical aviation security.* Burlington, MA: Elsevier Butterworth-Heinemann.

Sweet, K.M. (2008). *Transportation security.* Upper Saddle River, NJ: Pearson/Prentice Hall.

Sweet, K.M. (2009). *Aviation and airport security.* Upper Saddle River, NJ: Pearson/Prentice Hall.

Transportation Security Administration. (2004). *Security guideline for general aviation airports.* Washington, DC: Transportation Security Administration.

Transportation Security Administration. (2011). Retrieved from http://www.tsa.gov/

11

Security of the Flight School

INTRODUCTION

The incident involving the September 11, 2011, hijackers who trained at general aviation flight schools in Florida and use of a Cessna-172 in Tampa, Florida, and its deliberate crash into a building by a student at that general aviation airport flight school raised alarm. The public, the media, and the government began to question the security of general aviation aircraft, airports, and flight schools. It demonstrated the need for flight schools, general aviation airports, and aircraft owners to do all they can to ensure the security of their aircraft.

This increased security is important for many reasons. It can aid in preventing the theft and use of aircraft as a terrorist weapon. Flight school security measures can also reduce the threat from traditional criminal activity and motives, such as the theft of aircraft for illegal drug trafficking, joy rides, and avionics.

Being a litigious society, the failure to provide adequate security of aircraft could lead to successful lawsuits against flight schools, fixed-base operators, airports, and aircraft owners. Security precautions will also assist in reducing or maintaining lower insurance rates for both liability and hull coverage of the aircraft.

In the past, during the period following the September 11, 2001, terrorist attacks, flight schools were unable to operate due to restrictions in airspace. To prevent this from occurring again and increased government restrictions and regulations on flight schools and general aviation, it is important for the general aviation flight schools to adhere to the Department of Homeland Security Transportation Security Administration guidelines established after the September 11, 2001, terror attacks. It is also important to go beyond the required security regulations and to establish additional voluntary security standards to ensure the security of the flight school, aircraft, and public. This gesture would go a long way in preventing additional mandated government restrictions and security procedures for flight schools.

The level of security that can be provided by a flight school depends on several factors. In the case of Reigle Aviation, located in Palmyra, Pennsylvania, where I base my Cessna-172, they own Reigle Airport, 58 N, and operate the fixed-base operation and flight school (Figure 11.1). In this situation, they have complete control over the entire airport facility and flight school-owned aircraft. Reigle Aviation is unlimited in the level of security measures it can implement. If the flight school is operating as a tenant at a general aviation airport, it will be limited in the security measures it can implement at the airport. Its focus will need to be the security of its flight school operations and flight school general aviation aircraft.

Figure 11.1 Reigle Aviation Flight School, Reigle Airport, Palmyra, Pennsylvania. (Photo by Daniel J. Benny.)

TRANSPORTATION SECURITY ADMINISTRATION SECURITY REQUIREMENT FOR FLIGHT SCHOOLS

While no measures can guarantee the security of aircraft, a flight school can establish security procedures to reduce the risk of their theft or misuse. Security begins with the hiring of staff and flight instructors. A thorough background investigation must be conducted on all applicants to verify their identity, work history, criminal history, emotional stability, and appropriate credentials for flight instructors. This can aid in preventing individuals with long-term terrorist or criminal goals from being able to insert themselves into a flight school operation in which they could have access to aircraft or be in a position to allow other potential unauthorized individuals to gain access to aircraft.

The next step is to establish written policies and procedures covering security of the flight school and to ensure that all staff members and instructors are trained in, understand, and follow the established procedures. The mere fact that written procedures have been established is of little value if they are not followed. These procedures should cover the screening of potential flight students, physical security of school aircraft, and control and access to the aircraft.

The screening of flight students is critical in the prevention of the misuse of aircraft and terrorist incidents. The flight school staff should interview all potential students and verify their identity. Students who are not of age to obtain a Federal Aviation Administration medical certificate should be required to obtain one from their own physician, indicating that they are physically and mentally cleared to participate in flight training activity. Flight schools should also initiate background checks of students, including a criminal check if authorized in their state, and reference checks.

The flight school or independent certified flight instructor must verify and record the citizenship of any student who applies for training for the following certificates or ratings only; the rationale behind this is that only these provide for the learning of a new skill:

- Recreational
- Light sport
- Private
- Instrument
- Multiengine

Citizenship can be verified by the student in one of the following two ways:

1. Provide an original birth certificate *and* a government-issued photo ID like a driver's license or
2. Provide a current passport

The record-keeping requirements can be satisfied in one of the following two ways:

1. Copy the documents used to verify citizenship and keep them on file for 5 years or
2. Make a logbook entry in both the student's and certified flight instructor's logbook, using the following wording:

> "I certify that (Student's Full Name) has presented to me a (description of document(s)) # _____ establishing that he/she is a U.S. citizen or national in accordance with CFR 49 Part 1552.3 (h)
>
> Date _____ Signature _____
>
> CFI # _____ Exp _____

The Transportation Security Administration prohibits a flight school from providing flight training to aliens and other individuals (candidates) designated by the Transportation Security Administration unless the flight school or the candidate submits certain information to the Transportation Security Administration. The candidate remits the specified fee to the Transportation Security Administration, and the Transportation Security Administration determines that the candidate is not a threat to aviation or national security.

Background checks of foreign nationals seeking instruction in aircraft 12,500 pounds or greater are required before flight instruction can take place. The Flight Training Candidate Checks Program allows candidates to apply online at https://www.flightschoolcandidates.gov. Flight instructors, flight schools, or training centers can obtain information about the requirements by contacting the Flight Training Candidate Checks Program.

Vision 100, the Federal Aviation Reauthorization bill, signed into law December 12, 2003, extended this to foreign national students for aircraft 12,500 pounds or less. Vision 100 also includes a provision that flight schools will be required to a conduct security awareness program for flight school employees to increase their awareness of suspicious circumstances and activities of individuals enrolling in or attending flight schools.

The alien student transportation security administration clearance process must be followed. If the prospective student is not a U.S. citizen or national, the following process must be completed prior to flight training: This is a process that is primarily for the purpose of verifying that the student has no criminal or other undesirable background. However, you must also be aware that the Transportation Security Administration will also review the immigration requirements for any applicant who requires a visa to enter the country for flight training. These requirements are best determined by U.S. Citizenship and Immigration Services at 1-800-375-5283 or http://www.uscis.gov or the State Department Consular Affairs Office for assistance. The Alien Flight Student Program (AFSP) will deny flight training requests from candidates who are present in the United States illegally or who do not have an appropriate visa for flight training. Any fees paid for denied applications are not refundable.

1. The flight school or independent certified flight instructor registers as a provider with the Transportation Security Administration through their Web site.
2. Candidate accesses https://www.flightschoolcandidates.gov and submits a flight training request online with AFSP. The training request includes background information submitted online and a scanned passport, also submitted online. During this process, the name of the training provider and the level of training is also specified as category 3, which pertains to flight training in aircraft less than 12,500 pounds. The course ID field must be completed with private, instrument, recreational, light sport, or multiengine as appropriate.
3. After AFSP accepts the application, an e-mail is sent to the provider requesting validation of the candidate via the AFSP Web site.
4. After the provider validates the student, the candidate is notified by e-mail and may then pay the $130 nonrefundable fingerprint processing fee.
5. After payment is confirmed, AFSP e-mails the candidate fingerprint instructions. The candidate then follows fingerprint instructions and mails AFSP the fingerprints. *Note:* Fingerprints must not be submitted before the fingerprint instructions are e-mailed or fingerprints will not be accepted. Fingerprint locations can be found at http://www.tsc-csc.com/printoffices/.

6. AFSP e-mails both provider and candidate a confirmation that fingerprints have been received, usually within 7 days of receiving them. Flight training for category 3 students may begin as soon as this confirmation is received.

7. A photograph must be taken of the foreign student before beginning flight training and uploaded to the https://www.flightschoolcandidates.gov Web site. A photo taken on the first day of training with a simple camera phone will suffice.

8. All training requests only stay active for 365 days from the date of approval, which means training must be completed by then. Students who receive security approval from the Transportation Security Administration are bound to complete their training with the same provider as in the original application. If the student wishes to switch providers, a new application process and fee are required. Any records required under 1552.3 must be retained for 5 years.

SECURITY AWARENESS AND TRAINING

The Transportation Security Administration requires flight schools to provide security awareness training to personnel, including the certified flight instructor, within 60 days of hire or beginning flight training; individuals must continue to complete this training annually in the same month as the initial training. The Transportation Security Administration training is available for free on its Web site. A certificate is provided on completion and includes the name and the date of the training. It is also required that a record is kept of the date and the training completed and whether it was recurrent or initial. The certified flight instructor's logbook is an excellent place to keep this record. Place the online certificate of completion in a safe place as the Federal Aviation Administration may ask for it when doing a review of certified flight instructor records.

The training will provide staff and the certified flight instructor with valuable information to look for. This would include possible indicators of terrorist intent, such as paying for training in large sums of cash or showing an interest or requesting training in only certain areas of flight to the exclusion of other areas that are critical to the full certification process. Other indicators are students who suddenly leave the program without explanation or act in any manner that appears suspicious or inconsistent with obtaining full flight certification. Potential students should also be observed and screened for any obvious mental or emotional conditions.

If any of these indicators appear during the course of flight training, the student should be reevaluated for suitability to continue.

ACCESS AND KEY CONTROL

Physical security and the control of access to flight school facility aircraft are important aspects of the overall security program. All keys to aircraft should be accounted for and maintained in a locked key cabinet when not in use. The aircraft N number should not be placed on the key or key ring. By doing this, if the key is lost, the aircraft the key is assigned to cannot be easily identified and used for unauthorized access and use.

It is recommended that the doors to the aircraft and the ignition be keyed separately. By having a separate key for the aircraft door and the ignition switch, this would allow a student to begin a preflight of the aircraft without the instructor present but would not permit the student to start the aircraft.

Aircraft, when not in use, especially when secured for the night, should be maintained in a locked hangar, with intrusion detection systems if possible. Other security measures could include prop cable locks, throttle locks, or wheel boots in addition to locking the doors and securing the windows of the aircraft. The use of signage indicating that access is restricted and that tampering with aircraft is a violation of the law, along with the use of adequate security lighting, should also be considered as part of the security program.

Student access to aircraft must be controlled. Students must be required to show a driver's license or other form of government photo identification. It is recommended that all students be given a flight school photo identification card on registering with the school. Students should check in with a staff member on arrival at the school and never be provided with a key to obtain access to an aircraft without the knowledge of their flight instructor. As mentioned, the aircraft door lock and ignition should be keyed separately. Students should sign for and only be given the door key to the aircraft if they are going to be doing a preflight check of the aircraft on their own. The flight instructor should then hand carry the ignition key to the aircraft before beginning dual flight instruction. Students permitted to conduct solo flights should sign for both door and ignition keys.

While there are no flight school security measures to prevent a solo student from misusing an aircraft when airborne, by following the recommended screening procedures and monitoring the student during the

145

dual instruction period, the risk of a student misusing an aircraft for terrorism or other unauthorized purpose will be greatly reduced. Should an unfortunate incident occur in spite of taking security measures, it would certainly provide insulation to the flight school with regard to liability and failure to provide adequate security of the aircraft.

There is a final consideration for flight schools that rent aircraft to certificate holders: Any individual wishing to rent an aircraft must be screened, including verification of identity by comparing the Federal Aviation Administration certificate with a photo driver's license. The inspection of a current medical certificate and a review of the pilot's logbook should also be part of the screening process.

Indications of any suspicious activity or motive for the rental of the aircraft should be noted. This may include paying in large sums of cash, asking questions about specific buildings or facilities in the area that could be potential terrorist targets, or any unusual luggage or packages to be taken aboard the aircraft.

Access control to the flight school facility must also be part of the total security program. Card access or the issuance of a key for the facility may be used. All access cards and keys must be accounted for. A sign-in procedure must be established for issuance of cards or keys.

SECURITY SIGNAGE

Security signs should be used to indicate any secure or restricted areas in or around the flight school. This may include the office area, parking area, and access to the flight school aircraft and airport ramp area.

SECURITY LIGHTING

Security lighting at the flight school would consist of lighting of the facility entrance and parking adjacent to the school. In most cases, the lighting around the flight school, hangar, and ramp area will be the responsibility of the airport.

SECURITY CAMERAS

The flight school can utilize security cameras on the exterior and interior of their facility. Areas to consider would include the entrance, parking area, aircraft ramp, and hangar areas. Other than locating cameras at the flight school facility, it would be the responsibility of the airport to provide additional security camera coverage on the ramp, hangar, and parking areas of the airport.

INTRUSION DETECTION SYSTEMS

The flight school facility should be protected by an intrusion detection system during periods when it is unattended. Due to the storage of aircraft keys, logbooks, and student records and personal information, the facility needs to be protected.

Electromagnetic door contact and passive infrared sensors would provide adequate protection in addition to locks, lights, and cameras.

It is vital that flight schools and general aviation airports and their community take the initiative to establish increased security at their facilities to ensure the safety and security of the United States and the continued support of general aviation by the public.

BIBLIOGRAPHY

Aircraft Owners and Pilots Association. (2003). *AOPA Airport Watch*. Frederick, MD: AOPA.

Bragdon, C.R. (2008). *Transportation security*. Burlington, MA: Elsevier Butterworth-Heinemann.

Elias, B. (2005). *CRS report for Congress securing general aviation*. Washington, DC: U.S. Government Printing Office.

Fischer, R.J., & Green, G. (2008). *Introduction to security* (8th ed.). Burlington, MA: Elsevier.

Moore, K.C. (2000). *Airport, aircraft and airline security*. Burlington, MA: Elsevier Butterworth-Heinemann.

Price, J.C., and Forrest, J.S. (2009). *Practical aviation security*. Burlington, MA: Elsevier Butterworth-Heinemann.

Sweet, K.M. (2008). *Transportation security*. Upper Saddle River, NJ: Pearson/Prentice Hall.

Sweet, K.M. (2009). *Aviation and airport security*. Upper Saddle River, NJ: Pearson/Prentice Hall.

Transportation Security Administration. (2004). *Security guideline for general aviation airports*. Washington, DC: Transportation Security Administration.

Transportation Security Administration. (2011). Retrieved from http://www.tsa.gov/

12

Corporate Aviation Security Department

INTRODUCTION

Many corporations own their own corporate aircraft. These aircraft are kept in corporate-owned hangars or in leased hangar space at a general aviation or commercial airport. If the organization has a corporate security department, then that department should be responsible for the protection of the corporate aircraft, hangar, executive, and staff when utilizing the corporate aircraft.

All of the relevant information in previous chapters of this book covering physical security, development of a security force, and aircraft and hangar security can be utilized for the protection of corporate aircraft, hangars, and staff. An overview of key security issues is addressed in this chapter, including a guide for executives and staff traveling in the corporate aircraft in the United States and overseas.

AIRCRAFT SECURITY

Corporate aircraft owners' corporate security department should conduct a threat assessment and develop an aircraft security plan. This will aid in the protection of individuals and the aircraft.

There are several considerations when conducting a threat assessment and security plan for the corporate aircraft. These include protection of the aircraft from theft and vandalism, protection of the aircraft crew and passengers from crime, and ensuring that the aircraft is secure so that it cannot be used as a weapon. The aircraft could be used as a weapon by stealing or hijacking it and using it to fly into a target. A general aviation aircraft could be sabotaged by the unknowing placement of an explosive device on the aircraft.

To develop an effective security plan for the protection of the corporate aircraft, a threat assessment needs to be conducted so that the risk to the aircraft can be established. When the threat and risk have been identified, you then establish what protection needs to be put in place. Determine the severity of the threat and probability of occurrence. This is accomplished by making an examination to determine the required security to prevent or reduce the threats.

The development of a corporate aircraft security plan is vital in the protection of the aircraft, crew, and passengers. This aircraft security plan would detail the security measures to be implemented to protect the aircraft. The aircraft security plan would also cover security of the aircraft when in flight and when at other airports and hangar or tie-down facilities. To preserve the integrity of the plan, access to the written aviation security plan must be limited to those individuals who have an operational need to know. The aviation security plan must be updated whenever there is change to the security program. The plan should be reviewed at least once a year to ensure that it is current and up to date.

Information on the aircraft and avionics should be documented in the event that the aircraft or avionics is stolen or the aircraft is missing in flight or damaged. This documentation will aid law enforcement agencies or rescue agencies in identification and recovery. Documentation of the aircraft will also aid with insurance claims should the aircraft be stolen, damaged, or destroyed.

It is critical that all baggage loaded onboard the aircraft is known and identified and matches the passengers onboard. Baggage must be in control of the owner until it is loaded onto the aircraft and not left unattended.

In-flight security begins with a review of emergency aircraft and security procedures by the flight crew prior to departure. This would include emergency landing and hijacking procedures. In addition to the routine preflight inspection, the flight crew should look for any evidence of tampering with the aircraft or the placement of foreign objects on or in the aircraft. Corporate security and the executive and other staff on the flight should also review all established security procedures. It must be noted that even if corporate security is onboard the flight, the pilot in command has the final say in all flight safety and security issues.

CORPORATE REMAIN-OVERNIGHT SECURITY

When flying from the corporate home fixed-base operator to a destination where the aircraft will remain overnight, it is import to plan ahead to ensure the security of the executives and staff as well as the aircraft at the remain-overnight fixed-base operator. This process begins with a review of the destination airport and fixed-base operator where the aircraft will remain overnight.

Contact the fixed-base operator to arrange secure accommodations for the aircraft and to arrange any other special security needs. The availability of fuel must also be a requirement. If possible, the aircraft should be kept in a hangar. Inquire regarding the availability of a hangar to secure the aircraft. If the hangar has doors that can be locked, that will provide minimal security for the aircraft. Determine if the locked hangar has an intrusion detection system and, if not, whether staff are on duty 24 hours a day as added security for the aircraft. If the hangar that is available is a T-hangar with an open front and no door, then there will only be protection from the weather and no security protection.

If hangars are not available, then the aircraft should be parked on a well-lit ramp area away from perimeter gates, fences, parking areas, and buildings. In this situation, as with a T-hangar, based on the security threat the aircraft may need to be protected by corporate security staff.

Security plans should also be developed for the transport of executives and staff from the corporate aircraft to their hotel or other designated location. Arrangements need to be made in advance for the transport service. Corporate security staff should accompany the executives to their destination.

EXECUTIVE AND STAFF TRAVEL SECURITY

For the executives, staff, and corporate flight crew traveling around the United States and overseas for business, vacations, or academic pursuits, it is important to follow security and safety precautions and have continuous awareness of one's environment. This is especially true if the traveler flies overseas and must adapt to new cultures, customs, and laws. Personal security and safety cannot be delegated to others; it is the responsibility of each traveler.

TRAVEL PREPARATIONS

Travel itinerary
- Leave a complete itinerary with your office and with family, including contact numbers if known.

Passport
- Check that your passport will be valid for the duration of the trip.
- Make three copies of the passport page containing your photograph. Place one in your carry-on bag, place one in your checked baggage, and leave one with your family.

Visas
- Make sure that you have the appropriate visas and that they are current.
- Visa application information must be accurate. False information may be grounds for incarceration.

Documents
- Take only credit cards you will need.
- Carry only the documents you will need in your wallet or purse.
- Realize that any document you carry may be subject to search, seizure, or copying.
- Carry a U.S. driver's license with a photo on it.
- Make two copies of the numbers of your credit cards and traveler's checks, airline tickets, and the telephone numbers to report a loss.

Health
- If you require prescription medications, carry a copy of your prescriptions and keep in original containers.
- If you wear corrective lenses, bring an extra pair and a copy of your eye prescriptions.

- Carry a list with your blood type, allergies, medical conditions, and special requirements.
- Keep personal affairs up to date. Arrange for power of attorney with family members.
- While traveling, eat moderately and drink plenty of water to avoid dehydration.
- Carry airsickness medication should it be required.
- On long flights, get up and walk around every hour to ensure proper blood circulation.
- Avoid a demanding schedule on arrival. Give yourself a chance to adjust to your surroundings.

SOURCES OF INFORMATION

United States Department of State Bureau of Consular Affairs
Washington, D.C.
1-202-647–5225
http://travel.state.gov/travel/cis_pa_tw/tw/tw_1764.html

Emergency Services to United States Citizens Abroad
http://travel.state.gov/travel/tips/emergencies/emergencies_1212.
html

Talk with people who have visited the country before.
The embassy of the country you plan to visit can provide information.

LUGGAGE

- Use a covered luggage tag to place your name on the outside of the luggage.
- Put your name and address on the inside of your luggage.
- Use sturdy luggage and do not overpack.
- Never leave your luggage unattended as it could be stolen or used by terrorists.
- Do not transport items for others. Any gifts received from a foreign contact should be thoroughly inspected before being placed in your luggage.

IN-FLIGHT SECURITY

- Control all personal baggage on the corporate aircraft.
- Keep your seat belt on at all times.
- Be alert to instructions by the corporate flight crew should an incident occur.

HOTEL SECURITY

Planning
- Use hotels recommended by your travel agent if possible.
- Make your own reservation and ensure that the room is guaranteed.
- Request information about hotel, parking, security, and fire safety.

Arriving at and departing from the hotel
- Disembark as close to the hotel entrance as possible and in a lighted area. Before exiting the vehicle, ensure that there are no suspicious persons and activities.
- Do not linger or wander in the parking lot or indoor garage.
- Watch for distractions that may be staged for criminal activity.
- Hand carry valuable papers and items to your room; do not give them to a bellman.

Check-in
- Keep control of your luggage during registration to prevent theft.
- In some countries, your passport may be held by the hotel for review by the police or other authorities. If so, retrieve it at the earliest possible time.
- Request a room between the second and seventh floor. Most fire departments do not have the capability to rescue above the seventh floor. Do not stay on the first floor as it is more accessible to theft and damage from an external bomb.
- Inquire how you will be notified during an emergency and locate all emergency exits, fire alarms, and fire extinguishers near your room.

- Review room security, such as the key and access control, auxiliary lock, window locks, and safes.
- Note how the hotel staff dresses and type of uniforms and identification badges. Verify hotel employees with the front desk before permitting entry into your room.

In the event of fire
- Keep calm; do not panic.
- Check your door for heat with the back of your hand or for smoke under it before you open it.
- If it is safe to exit, take your room key and stay low. Head for the fire exit and *never use the elevator.*
- If it is unsafe to exit your room, call the front desk to let them know you are there.
- Open a window for fresh air or to signal for assistance. Do not break the window as you may need to close it later if smoke begins to enter from the outside.
- Fill the tub and sink with water and soak towels and bedsheets. Use them to block air vents in the room and under the door.
- Cover your mouth and nose with a wet towel and wait for the fire department.

PERSONAL SECURITY IN A FOREIGN COUNTRY

Basics
- Assume that all hotel rooms could be bugged.
- Keep your hotel room key with you at all times.
- Keep your hotel room door locked at all times.
- At night, utilize a portable door alarm and secure your passport and other valuables.

Street smarts
- Use a corporate protective service team if possible.
- Invest in a good map of the city. Note the location of your hotel, police, U.S. Embassy, and hospital.
- Be aware of your surroundings at all times and try to blend in.

- Do not carry your passport or money in pockets accessible to pickpockets.
- Keep your passport with you at all times.
- Vary the time you leave and return to the hotel and avoid patterns.
- Avoid persons you do not know. Prostitutes, sex offenders, and other criminals—both men and women—take advantage of travelers through various ploys, including knockout drugs.

PERSONAL CONDUCT

- Do not do anything that might be misconstrued, reflect poorly on your personal judgment, or be embarrassing to you or your group.
- Do not carry, use, or purchase any narcotics, marijuana, or other abused drugs. Many countries have stringent laws related to drugs.
- Do not let a friendly ambiance and alcohol override your good sense and capacity when it comes to social drinking.
- Do not engage in black market activities.
- Do not carry any political or religious tracts or brochures likely to be offensive in the host country.
- Do not carry pornography or radical publications.
- Do not photograph anything that appears to be associated with military, internal security, or restricted areas.

ARRESTED

Foreign police and intelligence agencies detain persons for myriad reasons, including suspicion or curiosity. The best advice is to exercise good judgment and be professional in your demeanor.

- Ask to contact the U.S. Embassy or consulate. As a citizen of another country, you have this right, but that does not mean the host country will allow you to do so right away. Continue to make the request.
- Stay calm, maintain your dignity, and do not provoke the arresting officer.
- Admit nothing and volunteer nothing.

- Sign nothing.
- Accept no one at face value. Ask for identification.

By following these suggestions related to travel in the United States and overseas, the corporate security department can aid in making such travel safer and more enjoyable for the executives and staff.

BIBLIOGRAPHY

Bragdon, C.R. (2008). *Transportation security.* Burlington, MA: Elsevier Butterworth-Heinemann.

Fischer, R.J., & Green, G. (2008). *Introduction to security* (8th ed.). Burlington, MA: Elsevier.

National Counter Terrorism Security Office. (2012). *Counter terrorism protective security advice for general aviation.* London: National Counter Terrorism Security Office.

Price, J.C., and Forrest, J.S. (2009). *Practical aviation security.* Burlington, MA: Elsevier Butterworth-Heinemann.

Transportation Security Administration. (2011). Retrieved from http://www.tsa.gov/

13

Aircraft Owners and Pilots Association Airport Watch

OVERVIEW

In March 2003, the Aircraft Owners and Pilots Association (AOPA) developed the Airport Watch Program. The goals of the Airport Watch Program were to enhance security at general aviation airports, to aid in the prevention and reduction of crime in the general aviation community, and to prevent mandated security regulations from the Transportation Security Administration.

COMPONENTS OF THE AOPA AIRPORT WATCH

The Aircraft Owners and Pilots Association Airport Watch Program encompasses various concepts related to physical security and security awareness. As it relates to physical security, the program recommends and encourages general aviation airport managers, aircraft owners, and pilots to utilize physical security practices to prevent and reduce crime and terrorism at general aviation airports. This would include keeping the aircraft locked and the utilization of aircraft security devices such as wheel locks, a prop lock, or a throttle lock.

The locking of hangars with doors, lighting, and Aircraft Owners and Pilots Association Airport Watch signage is also recommended. Access control onto the airport and the use of locks and intrusion detection systems and the securing of all aircraft keys at the fixed-base operation or flight schools is also encouraged.

The security awareness aspect of the program focuses on making general aviation airport owners and employees, as well as aircraft owners and pilots, aware of their surroundings. This includes being aware of what is considered normal activity at the general aviation airports and what is not. If the activity is suspicious, the Aircraft Owners and Pilots Association Airport Watch phone number, 1-800-GA-SECURE, is to be utilized to report the suspicious activity. This phone number is a direct line to the Transportation Security Administration. The Transportation Security Administration, when notified, will document the information provided by a caller. It will then take the appropriate action based on the situation and information provided to investigate the circumstances of the report of suspicious activity.

If the activity is obviously criminal activity or may be an immediate threat, then the local police are to be notified by calling 911. The airport manager or fixed-base operator should also be notified of the suspicious activity and whether the police were called utilizing the 911 number.

The Aircraft Owners and Pilots Association has developed an Airport Watch handout and DVD that has been distributed free to general aviation airports and pilots and is available on request from the association. The organization also offers a free online training course through its Web site. The online training covers the concepts of their Airport Watch Program. On successful completion of the online course, the participant can print out a certificate of completion to document the training.

A STUDY OF THE AOPA AIRPORT WATCH

The following are the results of a study I conducted as part of my dissertation at Capella University.

Methodology

The research examined the relationship between the Aircraft Owners and Pilots Association Airport Watch program and the crime at the general aviation airports. The research was quantitative utilizing the ex post facto design because the data collected during the research were based on information and events from the past. The survey was the instrument that was to be used for the research. This method of research encompasses a measurement procedure that involved asking questions of the general aviation airports in the Commonwealth of Pennsylvania.

The data for the research were collected using a survey. The survey was reviewed by the Aircraft Owners and Pilots Association located in Frederick, Maryland, and the Federal Aviation Administration in Harrisburg, Pennsylvania, which are the premier professional organizations related to general aviation and comprised of general aviation experts. General aviation professionals associated with these two groups reviewed the survey questions and provided a professional opinion regarding the validity of the survey related to the study of crime and the impact of the Aircraft Owners and Pilots Association Airport Watch Program at general aviation airports in the Commonwealth of Pennsylvania.

The first step in the process was to obtain current information on the general aviation airports in the Commonwealth of Pennsylvania. This included the following information on these airports: airport name, location, airport manager, phone number, and e-mail address. This information was obtained from the Pennsylvania Bureau of Aviation, which is the regulatory agency responsible for the collection of such data.

To encourage a response and to provide an introduction to the study, I began with a telephone call that lasted no more than 10 minutes to each of the general aviation airport managers. The airport managers were provided with an introduction to me, an overview of the nature of the study, and how it was to be accomplished. The airport managers were advised of the informed consent form that was e-mailed to them along with the survey. The airport managers were asked to complete the informed consent form and e-mail it back to me and to review the airport survey. During this first phone interview, I scheduled a second phone interview with the airport manager so that the survey could be conducted. As an incentive, the airport manager was offered a copy of the results of the study.

I made the second phone call to the airport managers at the prearranged time during their regular working hours. Based on the duties of general aviation airport managers to support general aviation security, I believed that airport managers would come to the conclusion that it was ethical to take part in the survey during work hours. During this phone interview, which lasted no more than 20 minutes, I asked the airport managers the questions in the survey and while on the phone documented the response in writing on a paper copy of the survey. The airport managers were assured that their response would be kept confidential. The information collected during the second phone interview was evaluated as part of the research.

Research Questions and Hypotheses

The research examined and answered the questions detailed next.

Research Question 1

Is there a difference in the number of crimes between general aviation airports that have adopted the Aircraft Owners and Pilots Association Airport Watch program and those that have not?

> H1. There is a difference in the number of crimes between general aviation airports that have adopted the Aircraft Owners and Pilots Association Airport Watch program and those that have not.
>
> Ho1. There is no difference in the number of crimes between general aviation airports that have adopted the Aircraft Owners and Pilots Association Airport Watch program and those that have not.

Results

The dependent variable in the study was whether or not there was a change in crime (against people, property and aircraft) at the general aviation airports based on the adoption of the Aircraft Owners and Pilots Association Airport Watch program. Tables 13.1, 13.2, and 13.3 show that between 2002 the year before the Aircraft Owners and Pilots Association introduced the Airport Watch program, and 2004, the year after the program began, and there was a reduction in crime at the airports that adopted the Airport Watch program and an increase in crime at the airports that did not adopt the program. According to Table 1, crime against people at adopter airports went down from 5 to 0 and the number of crimes went up at non-adopter airports from 3 to 6. With regard to crime against property at adopter airports the number of crimes went down from 80 to 3 and the number of crimes went up at non adopter airports from 45 to 88. Related to crime against aircraft at adopter airports the number of crimes went down from 29 to 2 and the number of crimes went up at non adopter airports from to 4 to 13.

Table 13.1 Chi Square Crime Against People, Property and Aircraft-Years

Years Crime Reported	AOPA Adopters 37	AOPA Non-Adopters 30	Total	x^2	p
Crimes Against People					
2002	62.5% (5)	37.5% (3)	8	0.50	0.480
2004	0% (0)	100% (6)	6	—	—
Crimes Against Property					
2002	64% (80)	36% (45)	125	9.80	0.002
2004	3% (3)	97% (88)	91	79.40	0.001
Crimes Against Aircraft					
2002	88% (29)	12% (4)	33	18.9	0.001
2004	13% (2)	87% (13)	15	8.07	0.005

Table 13.2 ANOVAs on People 2002, to 2004, Property 2002 to 2004 and Aircraft 2002 to 2004 by AOPA (Adopters vs. Non-Adopters)

Variables	F	Sig.	Eta	Power	Adopters		Non-Adopters	
					M	SD	M	SD
People								
2002	0.15 (0.14)	.702	.002	.067	0.14	0.42	0.10	0.31
2004	6.34 (0.11)	.014	.089	.698	0.00	0.00	0.20	0.48
Property								
2002	3.62 (2.01)	.062	.053	.466	2.16	1.66	1.50	1.04
2004	63.20 (2.13)	.001	.493	1.00	0.08	0.28	2.93	2.16
Aircraft								
2002	9.96 (0.70)	.002	.133	.875	0.78	1.08	0.13	0.35
2004	13.76 (0.17)	.001	.175	.955	0.05	0.23	0.43	0.57

Table 13.3 ANOVAs on Crimes Against People, Property and Aircrafts by Year (2002 vs. 2004)

Variables	F	Sig.	Eta	Power	2002		2004	
					M	SD	M	SD
People	0.33	.568	0.01	0.09	0.12	0.37	0.09	0.34
	(0.09)							
Property	2.94	.091	0.04	0.39	1.87	1.44	1.36	2.04
	(2.93)							
Aircraft	4.75	.033	0.07	0.56	0.49	0.89	0.22	0.45
	(0.51)							

Statement of the Problem

The impact of crime prevention efforts such as the Aircraft Owners and Pilots Association Airport Watch crime prevention program is not known because of the lack of research in this area of the aviation community. This lack of research has created a gap in the knowledge related to general aviation and such programs. This limited knowledge and research leaves the general aviation community without a baseline of knowledge and information on the impact of crime prevention programs at general aviation airports such as the Aircraft Owners and Pilots Association Airport Watch program that had been established and adopted.

The research did bridge the gap between traditional community crime watch studies and the research that has been directed to commercial aviation crime prevention programs. This was accomplished by providing new research regarding the impact of general aviation security and the Aircraft Owners and Pilots Association Airport Watch program on crime at general aviation airports in the Commonwealth of Pennsylvania. The Aircraft Owners and Pilots Association Airport Watch program was established in 2003. It is the first and only crime watch program developed for general aviation airports and is still in operation in the Commonwealth of Pennsylvania and in the United States. The research did provide a review and comprehensive evaluation of the issues related to the Aircraft Owners and Pilots Association Airport Watch program at general aviation airports in the Commonwealth of Pennsylvania. It also explained the relationship between the Aircraft Owners and Pilots Association Airport Watch program and the crime at the general aviation airports that were examined in the research.

The Aircraft Owners and Pilots Association Airport Watch program is based on the concepts of traditional crime watch programs. There has been no research conducted with regard to general aviation airports and the Aircraft Owners and Pilots Association Airport Watch program or any other general aviation crime watch program. The purpose of this study that was conducted was to evaluate the effects of the Aircraft Owners and Pilots Association Airport Watch program on crime at the airports that adopted this program during the period from 2002 to 2004. The Ex post facto design was utilized for this study.

Conclusions

The hypothesis as presented in the completed research was that the Aircraft Owners and Pilots Association Airport Watch program would have an impact on crime against people, property and aircraft at the general aviation airports in the Commonwealth of Pennsylvania. The completed research shows that the general aviation airports in the Commonwealth of Pennsylvania that adopted the Aircraft Owners and Pilots Association Airport Watch program experienced a reduction in crime against people, property, and aircraft. Crime increased against people, property, and aircraft at the general aviation airports that did not adopt the Aircraft Owners and Pilots Association Airport Watch program. The Airport Owners and Pilots Association Airport Watch program works and is an effect tool in the reduction of crime at general aviation airports.

This is important to the continued use of crime prevention programs in the criminal justice and aviation security profession and to the future of aviation security. The completed study reaffirms the success of crime prevention programs regardless of the environment that they are implemented, be it in community neighborhoods, on the campus of universities, or at general aviation airports, they do have an impact in the reduction of crime.

The completed research shows that crime prevention programs, specifically the Aircraft Owners and Pilots Association Airport Watch program, can be a useful tool in general aviation security in the Commonwealth of Pennsylvania and across the United States in the reduction of crime. In light of the fears and concerns after 9/11, and the evolving homeland security initiatives to counter new aviation security threats, the completed study establishes that the Aircraft Owners and Pilots Association Airport Watch program is an important asset in the aviation security protocol in the reduction of crime and homeland security of the aviation infrastructure. It also allowed the general aviation community to be proactive in aviation security by developing and implementing a volunteer security program. This proactive approach was a key factor in the avoidance of new security mandates from the Department of Homeland Security Transportation Security Administration that could have been costly to the general aviation airports in Pennsylvania and the United States.

Recommendations of the Study

This was the first research effort that examined crime at general aviation airports. It was also the first study to explore the relationship between crime at general aviation airports and the adoption of the Aircraft Owners and Pilots Association Airport Watch program. The results of this study indicates the Aircraft Owners and Pilots Association Airport Watch program did reduce crime against people, property and aircraft at the general aviation airports that adopted the program. These results could be projected nationwide to provide an indication of the success of the Aircraft Owners and Pilots Association Airport Watch program.

It is recommended that this research be used as a baseline to expand research nationwide to examine the Aircraft Owners and Pilots Association Airport Watch program and the possible impact it has on crime at general aviation airports across the United States. This first study of general aviation security could possibly direct future research efforts towards many different facets of general aviation security and commercial aviation security in the United States benefiting the security and aviation profession as well as the academic community. See Appendix C.

BIBLIOGRAPHY

Aircraft Owners and Pilots Association (2003). *AOPA Airport Watch*. Frederick, MD: AOPA.

Barkan, S. E. (2006). *Criminology: A social understanding* (3rd ed.). Upper Saddle River, NY: Pearson.

Bartol, C. R,. & Bartol, A. M. (2005). *Criminal behavior: A psychosocial approach* (7th ed.). Upper Saddle River, NJ: Pearson/Prentice Hall.

Beeler, K. J., Bellandes, S. D. & Wiggins, C. A. (1991). *Campus safety: A survey of administrative perceptions and strategies*. Washington, DC: National Association of Student Personal Administrators, Inc.

Bennett, T. (1989). An assessment of the design, implementation, and effectiveness of neighborhood watch in London. *Howard Journal of Criminal Justice*, 274(4), 241–256.

Bisignani, G. (2006). Airlines. [Electronic version]. *Foreign Policy*, 22–28.

Boetig, B. (2006.) The routine activity theory: A model for addressing specific crime issues. *FBI Law Enforcement Bulletin*. June, 2006, 32–46.

Bohm, R. M., Reynolds, K. M. & Holmes, S. T. (2000). Perceptions of neighborhood problems and their solutions: Implications for community policing. *Policing: An International Journal of Police Strategies and Management,* 23(4), 439–465.

Brevard, R. (1995). Crime prevention at tuffs university. Hartford, CT: International Association for Campus Law Enforcement Administrators.

Bullock, J. A., Haddow, G. D., Coppola, D., Ergin, E., Westerman, L. & Yeletaysi, S. (2006). *Introduction to homeland security* (2nd ed.). Burlington, MA: Elsevier Butterworth-Heinemann.

Burling, P. (2003). *Acquaintance rape on campus*. Washington, DC: National Association of College and University Attorneys.

Carter, D. (2002). *The Police and the Community*, Upper Saddle River, NJ: Prentice Hall.

Champion, D. J. (2006). *Research methods for criminal justice and criminology*, (3rd Ed.). Upper Saddle River, NY: Pearson/Prentice Hall.

Clarke, R. V. (1992). *Situational crime prevention: Successful case studies*. Albany, NY: Harrow and Heston.

Clarke, R. V., & Cornish, D. B. (1983). *Crime control in Britain: A review of policy and research*. Albany, NY: State University of New York Press.

Cohen, L. E. & Felson, M. (1979). Social change and crime rate trends: A routine activity approach. *American Sociological Review*. 44, 588–608.

Cohen, J. Quantitative methods in psychology: A power primer. *Psychological Bulletin*. 112, no. 1 (1992), 155–159.

Commonwealth of Pennsylvania Bureau of Aviation (2007). *Regulations for general aviation airport operation*. Harrisburg, PA; Commonwealth of Pennsylvania.

Cornish, D. B., & Clarke, R. V. (1986). *The reasoning criminal*. New York, NY: Springer-Verlag.

Cronk, B. C. (2006). *How to use SPSS*. Glendale, CA: Pyrczak Publishing.

Culp, R. F., & Bracco, E. (2005). Examining prison escapes and the routine activities theory. *Corrections Compendium*. (2005, May-June) 1–5, 25–27.

Currran, D. J., & Renzetti, C. M. (2001). *Theories of crime* (2nd ed.). Boston, MA: Allyn & Bacon.

Criswell, J. W. (2003). *Research design qualitative, quantitative and mixed method approaches*. (2nd ed.).Thousand Oaks, CA: Sage Publications.

Emerson, S. (2006). *Jihad incorporated*. Amherst, NY: Prometheus Books.

Farrington, D. P., & Welsh, B. C. (2007). *Saving children form a life of crime: Early risk factors and early intervention studies on crime and public policy*. New York, NY: Oxford Press

Fischer, R. J.& Green, G. (2008). *Introduction to security* (8th ed). Burlington, MA: Elsevier.

Groff, E. (2007). Simulation for theory testing and experimentation: An example using routine activity theory and street robbery. *Journal of Quantitative Criminology*, Volume 23, 75–103.

Hope, T. (2005). The anti-social bias and the Maryland method scientific methods scale. *European Journal on Criminal Police and Research*, 275–296.

International Association of Campus Law Enforcement Administrators (2004). *University Crime Prevention Survey*. Hartford, CT: International Association of Campus Law Enforcement Administrators.

Jackson, A., Gilliland, K., & Veneziano, L. (2006). Routine activity theory and sexual deviance among male college students. *Journal of Family Violence*, 449–640.

Lindsay, B., & McGillis, D. (1986). Citywide community crime prevention: An assessment of the Seattle program. In D. P. Rosenbaum (Ed.), *Community crime prevention: Does it work?* Beverly Hills, CA: Sage, pp. 46–67.

Meadows, R. J. (2007). *Understanding violence and victimization* (4th ed.). Upper Saddle River, NY: Pearson/Prentice Hall.

Martin, G. (2006). *Understanding terrorism: Challenges, perspectives and issues* (2nd ed.). Thousand Oaks, CA: Sage Publications.

Mac Kenzie, D. L., & Hickman, L. J. (1998) *An examination of the effectiveness of the type of rehabilitation programs offered by Washington State Department of Corrections*. College Park, MD, University of Maryland.

Moore, K. C. (2000). *Airport, aircraft & airline security*. Burlington, MA: Elsevier Butterworth-Heinemann.

Morgan, D. (2006). Femicide: *The impact of victim/offender relationships on crime*. New York, NY: University of New York Press.

Neuman, W. L. (2006). *Social research methods qualitative and quantitative approaches*. New York, NY: Pearson.

Nyatepe-Coo, A. A., & Zeisler-Vralsted (2004). *Understanding terrorism: Threats in an uncertain world*. Upper Saddle River, NJ: Pearson/Prentice Hall.

Pizarro, J., Corsaro, N., & Violet, S. (2007). Journey to crime and victimization: An application of routine activity theory and environmental criminology to homicide. *Victims & Offenders*, 374–394.

Pennsylvania Bureau of Aviation (2008). *Directory of Pennsylvania general aviation airports*. Harrisburg, PA: Commonwealth of Pennsylvania.

Savage, M. (2003). *The enemy within*. Nashville, TN: WND Books.

San Miguel, C. (2005). *An analysis of neighborhood watch programs in Texas*. Huntsviille, TX: Sam Houston State University.

Schmalleger, F. (2007). *Criminal justice today* (9th ed.). Upper Saddle River, NJ: Prentice Hall.

Sherman, L. W., Farrington, D. P., Gottfredson, D. C., & Welsh, B. C. (2002). *Evidence-based crime prevention*. New York, NY: Routledge.

Simonse, C. E., & Spindlove, J. R. (2007). *Terrorism today: The past the players the future* (3rd ed.). Upper Saddle River, NJ: Pearson/Prentice Hall.

Smith, B. W., Novack, K. H., & Hurley, D. C. (1997). Neighborhood crime prevention: The influence of community-based crime prevention and neighborhood watch. *Journal of Crime and Justice*, 20(20), 69–86.

Sperry, P. (2005). *Infiltration: How muslin spies and subversives have penetrated Washington*. Nashville, TN: Nelson Current.

Straw, J. (2010). The evolving terrorist threat. *Security Management*. 4–10, 46–49.

Swanson, C., Territo, L., & Taylor, R. (2005). *Police administration.* Upper Saddle River, NJ: Prentice Hall.

Sweet, K. M., (2009). *Aviation and airport security.* Upper Saddle River, NJ: Pearson/ Prentice Hall.

Sperry, P. (2005). *Infiltration,* Nashville, TN: Nelson Current.

Transportation Security Administration. (2011). Retrieved from http://www.tsa.gov/

Turney, A. M., Bishop, J. C., & Fitzgerald, P. C. (2004). Measuring the importance of recent airport security interventions. [Electronic version]. *Journal of Air Transportation, 9,* 3.

Turvey, B. (2001). *Criminal profiling an introduction to behavioral evidence analysis,* San Diego, CA: Elsevier Academic Press.

Vold, G. B., Bernard, T., & Snipes, J. B. (2002). *Theoretical criminology* (5th ed.). New York, NY: Oxford University Press.

Wiencek, D. (2005). Open skies? *Journal of Counterterrorism and Homeland Security International* 11, 12–24.

Zhao, J., H., & Lovrich, N. P. (2003). Community policing: Did it change the basic function of policing in the 1990s? A national follow-up study. *Justice Quarterly,* 20(3), 697–724.

14

Transportation Security Administration Security Requirements and Recommendations for General Aviation

DEPARTMENT OF HOMELAND NATIONAL TERRORISM ADVISORY SYSTEM

The Department of Homeland Security National Terrorism Advisory System, or NTAS, replaces the color-coded Homeland Security Advisory System (HSAS). This new terrorism alert system was designed to communicate information about terrorist threats effectively by providing timely, detailed information to the public, government agencies, first responders, airports and other transportation hubs, and the private sector, including general aviation.

The concept of the terrorism alert system is to recognize that Americans all share responsibility for the nation's security and should always be aware of the heightened risk of terrorist attack in the United States and what they should do.

National Terrorism Advisory System Alerts

Imminent Threat Alert: Warns of a credible, specific, and impending terrorist threat against the United States.

Elevated Threat Alert: Warns of a credible terrorist threat against the United States.

After reviewing the available information, the secretary of Homeland Security will decide, in coordination with other federal entities, whether an National Terrorism Advisory System alert should be issued.

The National Terrorism Advisory System alerts will only be issued when credible information is available according to the Department of Homeland Security. These alerts will include a clear statement that there is an imminent threat or elevated threat. Using available information, the National Terrorism Advisory System alerts are to provide a concise summary of the potential threat, information about actions being taken to ensure public safety, and recommended steps that individuals, communities, businesses, and governments can take to help prevent, mitigate, or respond to the threat.

The National Terrorism Advisory System alerts are to be based on the nature of the threat; in some cases, alerts will be sent directly to law enforcement or affected areas of the private sector, while in others, alerts will be issued more broadly to the American people through both official and media channels.

Sunset Provision

Once an individual threat alert is issued for a specific time period, it will automatically expire at the end of the given time. The National Terrorism Advisory System alert may be extended if new information becomes available or the threat evolves.

The National Terrorism Advisory System alerts contain a sunset provision indicating a specific date when the alert expires. The Department of Homeland Security states that there will not be a constant National Terrorism Advisory System alert or blanket warning that there is an overarching threat. If threat information changes for an alert, the secretary of Homeland Security may announce an updated National Terrorism Advisory System alert. All changes, including the announcement that cancels a National Terrorism Advisory System alert, will be distributed the same way as the original alert.

The Transportation Security Administration has issued a Notice of Proposed Rulemaking that would reinforce the security of general aviation by minimizing the vulnerability of aircraft being used as weapons or to transport dangerous people or materials involved in criminal activity or terrorism. The goal of the proposed regulation is to reduce the susceptibility of large-aircraft misuse by individuals wishing to harm the United States and its citizens.

TRANSPORTATION SECURITY ADMINISTRATION LARGE AIRCRAFT SECURITY PROGRAM

The Transportation Security Administration Large Aircraft Security Program (LASP) regulation would require all U.S. operators of aircraft exceeding 12,500 pounds maximum take-off weight to implement security programs that would be subject to compliance audits by Transportation Security Administration agents. The proposed regulation would also require operators to have a program in place to be able to verify that passengers are not on the No-Fly list or on the U.S. terrorist watch list.

The LASP would require currently unregulated general aviation operations over a specific weight threshold to adopt security measures established by the Transportation Security Administration that would support these general aviation aircraft. Aspects of the program may include ensuring that flight crews have undergone a fingerprint-based criminal history record and terrorist name check; designating security coordinators as is now done at commercial airports and commercial airlines; conducting watch list matching of passengers through the Transportation Security Administration approved watch list.

TRANSPORTATION SECURITY ADMINISTRATION GENERAL AVIATION SECURE PROGRAM

The Transportation Security Administration, working with the Aircraft Owners and Pilots Association, supports the Aircraft Owners and

Pilots Association Airport Watch Program. The Transportation Security Administration is working with the general aviation profession and industry to develop and implement reasonable and effective security measures. As part of these efforts, the Transportation Security Administration has launched the General Aviation Secure Program. This program is designed to build on the Aircraft Owners and Pilots Association Airport Watch Program. The Transportation Security Administration General Aviation Secure Program encourages everyone to be vigilant about general aviation security and report any unusual activities to the Transportation Security Administration and Aircraft Owners and Pilots Association Airport Watch Program via the 1-866-GA-SECURE phone number, which is monitored by the Transportation Security Administration.

The key aspects of the Transportation Security Administration General Aviation Secure Program include observation and notification of crime or suspicious activity. Security concerns may include the following at a general aviation airport: aircraft with unusual modifications or activity; pilots appearing to be under the control of others; unfamiliar persons loitering around the field; suspicious aircraft lease or rental requests; anyone making threats; unusual, suspicious activities or circumstances.

The Transportation Security Administration General Aviation Secure Program also addresses aircraft security. The aspects of general aviation aircraft security would include doing the following: Always lock your aircraft; control the keys and do not leave keys in an unattended aircraft; utilize secondary security locks or aircraft; and keep the aircraft in a locked hangar when unattended.

TRANSPORTATION SECURITY ADMINISTRATION SECURE FIXED-BASE OPERATOR PROGRAM

In 2007, the Transportation Security Administration established the Secure Fixed-Base Operator Program (SFBOP). The program is a public-private sector partnership program that will allow fixed-base operators (FBOs) to check passenger and crew identification against manifests or Electronic Advance Passenger Information System (EAPIS) filings for positive identification of passengers and crew onboard general aviation aircraft.

DCA ACCESS STANDARD SECURITY PROGRAM

In response to the terror attack on Washington, D.C., on September 11, 2011, the Transportation Security Administration developed, in coordination with other Department of Homeland Security agencies and the Department of Defense, special security requirements for aircraft traveling in or out of Washington, D.C., using Washington Reagan National Airport (DCA). Under the Transportation Security Administration security plan, 48 flights in and out of DCA will be allowed each day. All aircraft will be required to meet the security measures set forth in the DCA Access Standard Security Program (DASSP), which include Transportation Security Administration (TSA) inspection of crew and passengers; Transportation Security Administration inspection of property (accessible and checked) and aircraft; indication of the start and end dates of the flight on the Transportation Security Administration flight authorization; identification checks of passengers by Transportation Security Administration; submission of passenger and crew manifests 24 hours in advance of flight; enhanced background checks for all passengers and fingerprint-based criminal history records check (CHRC) for flight crew; armed security officer (ASO) on board each flight program; all operations subject to cancellation at any time; and more. All unscheduled operations to/from KDCA (Ronald Reagan Washington National Airport) require a federal Aviation Administration slot reservation.

For general aviation to take part in the program, application must be made to the Transportation Security Administration DASSP. The application can be downloaded from the Transportation Security Administration Web site.

The Transportation Security Administration DASSP approval process is as follows as stated by the Transportation Security Administration:

1. *Once TSA receives your FBO and Aircraft Operator Application and NDA, TSA headquarters will contact the appropriate TSA field office to establish a local point of contact. The local point of contact will liaison between the applicant and TSA headquarters to assist in the preparation for DASSP compliance.*
2. *Once fully prepared, local TSA will revisit the operator for final review, and if fully compliant with the requirements, will notify TSA headquarters.*

3. *Upon receiving notification from the local TSA field office that the oper-ator is compliant with the DASSP requirements, TSA will approve the operator in writing and provide additional operating instructions.*

THE TRANSPORTATION SECURITY ADMINISTRATION PRIVATE CHARTER STANDARD SECURITY PROGRAM

The Transportation Security Administration Private Charter Standard Security Program (PCSSP) is similar to the TFSSP but adds additional requirements for aircraft operators using aircraft with a maximum take-off weight of greater than 45,500 kg (100,309.3 pounds) or with a seating configuration of 61 or more. Operators were required to be in compliance with the program by April 1, 2003.

MARYLAND THREE PROGRAM

The Maryland Three Program was established in response to the September 11, 2001, terror attack in Washington, D.C., and allows properly vetted private pilots to fly to, from, or between the three general aviation airports closest to the national capital region. These airports are collec-tively known as the "Maryland Three" airports, and include

- College Park Airport (CGS)
- Potomac Airfield (VKX)
- Hyde Executive Field (W32)

These airports are all within the Washington, D.C., Special Flight Rules Area (SFRA) and the Washington, D.C., Flight Restricted Zone (FRZ).

An interim final rule, published in February 2005, opened the Maryland Three to transient pilots. Based aircraft had been permitted operations at these airports since 2002. Flights in the Washington, D.C., SFRA and FRZ are highly controlled. Complete familiarity with *all* perti-nent regulations and NOTAMs (notice to airmen) pertaining to flying in the Washington, D.C., area is the responsibility of each pilot who wishes to fly in the vicinity. Several penalties can result from infractions commit-ted in the Washington, D.C., flight area and when departing to and from the three general aviation airports known as the Maryland Three.

All pilots wishing to operate into or out of the Maryland Three must complete a registration procedure in which a personal identification number (PIN) is issued. To be issued a PIN for aircraft operations to or from any of the Maryland Three airports, a pilot must complete the following as stated by the Transportation Security Administration:

1. Download and complete the PIN issuance form.
   - Check the appropriate box for the type of operation.
   - Complete all relevant applicant information. Mark all areas that are not applicable as "N/A."
2. Visit the appropriate FAA Flight Standards District Office (FSDO) in order for the FAA to review/inspect your certificate(s).
3. Visit the fingerprinting office located at the Ronald Reagan Washington National Airport (DCA) to be fingerprinted. Be sure to take an acceptable form of government issued photo identification. The representative at this location will then complete the appropriate sections of the PIN issuance form.
   - Acceptable forms of government issued photo ID include, but are not limited to:
     1. A driver's license issued by a U.S. State
     2. A U.S. passport
     3. A U.S. military ID
4. After reviewing the security briefing material at the airport for which you are applying, complete the signature section of the PIN issuance form and return it to the Airport Security Coordinator (ASC). The ASC must also complete the ASC signature section.
5. The application will be processed once the form is completed and received by TSA. Please note that applications that are not complete or do not contain the correct authorizing signatures may be returned.

TRANSPORTATION SECURITY ADMINISTRATION FLIGHT SCHOOL TRAINING REQUIREMENTS

The Transportation Security Administration prohibits a flight school from providing flight training to aliens and other individuals (candidates) designated by the Transportation Security Administration unless the flight school or the candidate submits certain information to the Transportation Security Administration, the candidate remits the specified fee to the Transportation Security Administration, and the Transportation Security

Administration determines that the candidate is not a threat to aviation or national security. The Transportation Security Administration requires flight schools to provide security awareness training to personnel. The Transportation Security Administration training is available for free on the Transportation Security Administration Web site.

BIBLIOGRAPHY

Transportation Security Administration. (2011). Retrieved from http://www.tsa.gov/

15

General Aviation Security Resources

GOVERNMENTAL ORGANIZATIONS WITH AVIATION SECURITY RESOURCES

In the late 1930s, more than 150,000 civil air patrol volunteers with a love for aviation argued for an organization to put their planes and flying skills to use in defense of their country. After much pressure, the Civil Air Patrol was born one week prior to the Japanese attack on Pearl Harbor. Thousands of volunteer members answered America's call to national service and sacrifice by accepting and performing critical volunteer wartime missions. Assigned to the War Department under the jurisdiction of the Army Air Corps, the Civil Air Patrol logged more than 500,000 flying hours, sank two enemy submarines, and saved hundreds of crash victims during World War II.

On July 1, 1946, President Harry Truman signed Public Law 476 incorporating the Civil Air Patrol as a benevolent, nonprofit organization. On May 26, 1948, Congress passed Public Law 557 permanently establishing the Civil Air Patrol as the auxiliary of the new U.S. Air Force. Three primary mission areas were set forth and continue to this day: aerospace education, cadet programs, and emergency services.

105 South Hansell Street
Building 714
Maxwell AFB, AL 36112-6332
http://www.cap.gov

Department of Homeland Security:
Transportation Security Administration

The origin of the Transportation Security Administration was in response to the terrorism attacks of September 11, 2001, in New York City, Washington, D.C., and over the skies of Pennsylvania. In an attempt to secure the airports and airlines within the United States as well as other modes of transportation, including maritime, rail, and trucking, the Transportation Security Act of 2001 was passed and signed into law.

The foundation of the Transportation Security Administration's airport security program is the Federal Aviation Administration Security Division. The Federal Aviation Administration Security Division was established due to an increase in airline hijackings through the 1960s. In 1971, the Aviation Security Act set forth new guidelines related to aviation security under the direction of the Federal Aviation Administration Security Division. The new law required that airlines and airports begin screening passengers and baggage. It also required that the airlines and airports establish security procedures. The Federal Aviation Administration Security Division was tasked with assisting airports and airlines in this endeavor and auditing the security systems put in place. It also established the air marshall program in which armed Federal Aviation Administration Security Division agents would travel on selected aircraft and routes.

After the terrorist attacks in September 2011 and the creation of the Department of Homeland Security, the function of the Federal Aviation Administration Security Division was transferred to the new agency under the Department of Homeland Security. The new agency, which was named the Transportation Security Administration, is now responsible for aviation, maritime, rail, and trucking security in the United States.

400 Seventh Street Southwest
Washington, DC 20590
http://www.tsa.gov/index.shtm
TSA General Aviation Security Guidelines: http://www.tsa.gov/assets/pdf/security_guidelines_for_general_aviation_airports.pdf
TSA Flight School Security Notice: http://www.tsa.gov/assets/pdf/ga_advisory_9-11-2006.pdf

Federal Aviation Administration

On August 23, 1958, the Federal Aviation Act transferred the Civil Aeronautics Authority's functions to a new independent Federal Aviation Agency (FAA) responsible for civil aviation safety. In 1966, Congress authorized the creation of a cabinet department that would combine major federal transportation responsibilities. This new Department of Transportation (DOT) began full operations on April 1, 1967. On that day, the Federal Aviation Agency became one of several organizations within the DOT and received a new name, the Federal Aviation Administration. The Federal Aviation Administration is responsible for aviation safety.

800 Independence Avenue, SW
Washington, DC 20591
http://www.faa.gov

Federal Bureau of Investigation

The Federal Bureau of Investigation's (FBI's) national security mission is to lead and coordinate intelligence efforts that drive actions to protect the United States. The goal of the FBI is develop a comprehensive understanding of the threats and penetrate national and transnational networks that have a desire and capability to harm the United States. Such networks include terrorist organizations, foreign intelligence services, those that seek to proliferate weapons of mass destruction, and criminal enterprises.

10th Street and Pennsylvania Avenue
Washington, DC 20530
http://www.fbi.gov

U.S. Department of State

The U.S. Department of State provides travel warnings to those in the aviation community, including general aviation such as corporate flights with a destination outside the United Sates. They provide extensive downloads and reference material related to travel security on their Web page.

2121 Virginia Avenue NW
Washington, DC 20522
http://travel.state.gov./travel/travel_1744.html

PROFESSIONAL AVIATION AND SECURITY ORGANIZATIONS

American Society for Industrial Security International

The American Society for Industrial Security (ASIS) International is the preeminent organization for security professionals. Founded in 1955, ASIS is dedicated to increasing the effectiveness and productivity of security professionals by developing educational programs and materials that address broad security interests globally. This is accomplished through the ASIS annual seminar and exhibits, workshops, and *Security Management* magazine.

1625 Prince Street
Alexandra, VA 22313-2818
http://www.asisonline.org/

Airlines for America (Formerly Air Transport Association)

Airlines for America, formerly the Air Transport Association, is America's oldest and largest airline trade association. The organization's member airlines and affiliates transport more than 90% of U.S. airline passengers and cargo traffic. Founded in 1936, the association is based in Washington, D.C., and it is the U.S. airlines key voice before Congress.

1301 Pennsylvania Avenue NW
Suite 1100
Washington, DC 2004-1717
http://www.airlines.org/Pages/Home.aspx

Aircraft Owners and Pilots Association

The Aircraft Owners and Pilots Association, a not-for-profit organization dedicated to general aviation, was incorporated on May 15, 1939. The goal of the organization is to provide education and legislative support to general aviation pilots and aircraft owners.

421 Aviation Way
Frederick, MD 21701
http://www.aopa.org

American Association of Airport Executives

The American Association of Airport Executives (AAAE) was founded in September 1928 when 10 airport directors met for the first time. Today, the organization has nearly 5,000 individual members, including some 3,000 airport professionals representing nearly 850 different airports, from large hubs to general aviation facilities. They provide education through their annual seminar, workshops, training, and *Airport* magazine.

4112 King Street
Alexandria, VA 33159
http://www.airportnet.org

Aviation Crime Prevention Institute

Since 1986, the Aviation Crime Prevention Institute organization has provided education to the aviation industry worldwide in security awareness and theft prevention methods. The organization also provides information on suspicious activity and security products and procedures.

226 North Nova Road
Ormond Beach, FL 32174
http://www.acpi.org

International Association for Counterterrorism and Security Professionals

The International Association for Counterterrorism and Security Professionals provides current information on counterterrorism and security issue through educational workshops, their publication *Counter Terrorism and Security,* and their newsletter.

P.O. Box 10265
Arlington, VA 22210
http://www.iacsp.com

AVIATION SECURITY: HIGHER EDUCATION

Embry-Riddle Aeronautical University (Daytona, Prescott, Worldwide Campuses)

Embry-Riddle Aeronautical University, the premier aeronautical university, offers degrees and a certificate program related to aviation security, homeland security, and intelligence through its Dayton Beach, Florida, and Prescott, Arizona, campuses and online through the Worldwide Web campus.

600 South Clyde Morris Boulevard
Daytona Beach, FL 32114
http://www.erau.edu

AVIATION SECURITY EDUCATION AND TRAINING

The following professional organizations provide aviation security education and training through seminars, workshops, and online learning:

ASIS International
1625 Prince Street
Alexandra, VA 22313-2818
http://asisonline.org

American Association of Airport Executives
4112 King Street
Alexandria, VA 22302
http://www.airportnet.org

Aircraft Owners and Pilots Association
421 Aviation Way
Frederick, MD 21701
http://www.aopa.org

AVIATION SECURITY PUBLICATIONS

Aviation Security International Magazine

The number one aviation security magazine globally, *Aviation Security International* provides up-to-date information on aviation security and news in the Air Watch segment of the publication.

Green Light Limited
375 Upper Richmond Road West
East Sheen
London, SW14 7NX United Kingdom
http://www.asi-mag.com

General Aviation Security Magazine

General Aviation Security, a free online publication, discusses the protection of general aviation aircraft and airports. The Web site also provides links to general aviation security videos that can be viewed at Planehook's YouTube® channel.

6010 Windhaven Drive
San Antonio, TX 78239
http://www.planehook.com

Jane's Airport Reviews is one of the industry's leading sources for global aviation security.

Jane's Airport Review
321 Inverness Drive South
Englewood, CO 80112
htp://www.janes.com/products/janes/transport/airport

APPENDIX A: GLOBAL TERRORIST GROUPS*

AFGHANISTAN

NAME: al Qaeda

DATE STARTED/FIRST ACTIVE: Established by Osama bin Laden in the late 1980s.

GOALS: Establish a pan-Islamic Caliphate throughout the world by working with allied Islamic extremist groups to overthrow regimes it deems "non-Islamic," and expelling Westerners and non-Muslims from Muslim countries.

MAIN ANTI-U.S. ACTIVITIES TO DATE: Is suspected of involvement in the October 2000 bombing of the *USS Cole* in Aden, Yemen. Conducted the bombings in August 1998 of the U.S. embassies in Nairobi, Kenya, and Dar es Salaam, Tanzania, that killed at least 301 persons and injured more than 5,000 others. Claims to have shot down U.S. helicopters and killed U.S. servicemen in Somalia in 1993, and to have conducted three bombings that targeted U.S. troops in Aden, Yemen, in December 1992.

STRENGTH: May have several hundred to several thousand members.

OPERATIONAL LOCATIONS: Al Qaeda has a worldwide reach with cells in a number of countries, and benefits from its ties to Sunni extremist networks. Bin Laden and his top associates resided in Afghanistan, and the group maintains terrorist training camps there.

AFFILIATIONS: Serves as the umbrella organization for a worldwide network that includes many Sunni Islamic extremist groups, such as Egyptian Islamic Jihad, some members of al-Gama'at al-Islamiyya, the Islamic Movement of Uzbekistan, and the Harakat ul-Mujahidin.

---

* From Mark Burgess, Center for Defense Information, The World Security Institute, www.cdi.org. With permission.

COMMENTS: Bin Laden was the son of a wealthy Saudi family, and uses his inheritance to finance the group. Al Qaeda also operates moneymaking front organizations, solicits donations, and illicitly siphons funds from donations to Muslim charitable organizations.

ALGERIA

NAME: Armed Islamic Group (GIA)

DATE STARTED/FIRST ACTIVE: 1992.

GOALS: GIA aims to overthrow the secular Algerian regime and replace it with an Islamic state.

MAIN ANTI-U.S. ACTIVITIES TO DATE: None.

STRENGTH: Unknown, probably several hundred to several thousand.

OPERATIONAL LOCATIONS: Algeria.

AFFILIATIONS: Algerian expatriates and members of the Salafi Group for Call and Combat (GSPC) splinter group abroad, many of whom reside in Western Europe, provide financial and logistic support. In addition, the Algerian government has accused Iran and Sudan of supporting Algerian extremists.

COMMENTS: The GSPC splinter faction appears to have eclipsed the GIA since approximately 1998 and is currently assessed to be the most effective remaining armed group inside Algeria. A U.S. Designated Foreign Terrorist Organization (FTO) listed as "active" during 2000.

NAME: The Salafist Group for Call and Combat (GSPC)

DATE STARTED/FIRST ACTIVE: 1996.

GOALS: Overthrow the Algerian government and impose fundamentalist Islamic theocracy.

MAIN ANTI-U.S. ACTIVITIES TO DATE: Unknown.

STRENGTH: Unknown; suspected to be several hundred to several thousand.

OPERATIONAL LOCATIONS: Algeria.

AFFILIATIONS: Algerian expatriates and GSPC members living abroad. The Algerian government has accused Iran and Sudan of supporting Algerian extremists. The GSPC may also receive support from the Armed Islamic Group (GIA) network in Europe, Africa and the Middle East. Some GSPC members in Europe are suspected of having ties with other North African extremists sympathetic to al Qaeda.

COMMENTS: GSPC is a splinter group of the GIA, and has gained popular support through its pledge not to attack civilians inside Algeria (although it has not kept the pledge). It was designated a Foreign Terrorist Organization (FTO) on March 27, 2002.

CAMBODIA

NAME: Khmer Rouge/The Party of Democratic Kampuchea

DATE STARTED/FIRST ACTIVE: 1970s.

GOALS: Overthrow the Cambodian government.

MAIN ANTI-U.S. ACTIVITIES TO DATE: None.

STRENGTH: Fewer than 500, possibly no more than 100.

OPERATIONAL LOCATIONS: Outlying provinces in Cambodia, particularly in the northwest along the border with Thailand.

AFFILIATIONS: None.

COMMENTS: The group was a Communist insurgency that conducted a campaign of genocide, killing more than 1 million in the late 1970s. Disintegrated due to defections in the late 1990s.

CHILE

NAME: Manuel Rodriguez Patriotic Front (FPMR)

DATE STARTED/FIRST ACTIVE: 1983.

GOALS: Carry out missions of the Chilean Communist Party as its armed wing.

MAIN ANTI-U.S. ACTIVITIES TO DATE: Attacks civilians and international targets, including U.S. businesses and Mormon churches. Bombed two restaurants in the United States in 1993.

STRENGTH: 50 to 100.

OPERATIONAL LOCATIONS: Chile, United States.

AFFILIATIONS: None.

COLOMBIA

NAME: National Liberation Army (ELN)—Colombia

DATE STARTED/FIRST ACTIVE: 1965.

GOALS: Replacing the current government with a Marxist regime.

MAIN ANTI-U.S. ACTIVITIES TO DATE: Conducted a campaign of mass kidnappings during the late 1990s, each of which involved at least one U.S. citizen.

STRENGTH: Approximately 3,000 to 6,000 armed combatants and an unknown number of active supporters.

OPERATIONAL LOCATIONS: Rural and mountainous areas of north, northeast, and southwest Colombia and Venezuela border regions.

AFFILIATIONS: Cuba provides some medical care and political consultation.

COMMENTS: Marxist insurgent group formed by urban intellectuals inspired by Fidel Castro and Che Guevara. A Designated Foreign Terrorist Organization (FTO) listed as "active" during 2000.

NAME: Revolutionary Armed Forces of Colombia (FARC)

DATE STARTED/FIRST ACTIVE: 1964.

GOALS: Replacing the current government with a Marxist regime.

MAIN ANTI-U.S. ACTIVITIES TO DATE: In March 1999, the FARC executed three U.S. Indian rights activists in Venezuela after it kidnapped them in Colombia.

STRENGTH: Approximately 9,000 to 12,000 armed combatants and an unknown number of supporters, mostly in rural areas.

OPERATIONAL LOCATIONS: Colombia with some activities—extortion, kidnapping, logistics—in Venezuela, Panama, and Ecuador.

AFFILIATIONS: Cuba provides some medical care and political consultation.

COMMENTS: Established as the military wing of the Colombian Communist Party. FARC continues peace negotiations with the Pastrana administration, which has granted the group several concessions, including a demilitarized zone used as a venue for negotiations. A Designated Foreign Terrorist Organization (FTO) listed as "active" during 2000.

NAME: United Self-Defense Forces/Group of Colombia (AUC-Autodefensas Unidas de Colombia)

DATE STARTED/FIRST ACTIVE: 1997.

GOALS: Claims its primary objective is to protect its sponsors from insurgents.

MAIN ANTI-U.S. ACTIVITIES TO DATE: The paramilitaries have not taken action against U.S. personnel.

STRENGTH: In early 2001, the government estimated there were 8,000 paramilitary fighters, including former military and insurgent personnel.

OPERATIONAL LOCATIONS: AUC forces are strongest in the north and northwest: Antioquia, Cordoba, Sucre, Bolivar, Atlantico, and Magdalena Departments of Colombia.

AFFILIATIONS: None outside Colombia. The AUC is supported by economic elites, drug traffickers, and local communities lacking effective government security.

COMMENTS: The AUC—commonly referred to as autodefensas or paramilitaries—is an umbrella organization formed in April 1997 to consolidate most local and regional paramilitary groups each with the mission to protect economic interests and combat insurgents locally. Listed as "active" during 2000, it was designated a Foreign Terrorist Organization (FTO) on October 5, 2001.

EGYPT

NAME: Al-Jihad a.k.a. Egyptian Islamic Jihad, Jihad Group, Islamic Jihad

DATE STARTED/FIRST ACTIVE: Late 1970s.

GOALS: Overthrow the Egyptian government and replace it with an Islamic state; attack U.S. and Israeli interests in Egypt and abroad.

MAIN ANTI-U.S. ACTIVITIES TO DATE: Car-bombing against official U.S. facilities.

STRENGTH: Unknown, suspected to be several hundred.

OPERATIONAL LOCATIONS: Mainly Cairo, but has a network outside Egypt, including Yemen, Afghanistan, Pakistan, Sudan, Lebanon, and the United Kingdom.

AFFILIATIONS: Close partner of Osama Bin Laden's al Qaeda; Iran. May get some funds via various Islamic non-governmental organizations, cover businesses, and criminal acts.

COMMENTS: The original Jihad was responsible for the 1981 assassination of Egyptian President Anwar Sadat.

NAME: Al-Gama'a al-Islamiyya (Islamic Group, IG)

DATE STARTED/FIRST ACTIVE: Late 1970s.

GOALS: The IG's primary goal is to overthrow the Egyptian government and replace it with an Islamic state, but certain group leaders also may be interested in attacking U.S. and Israeli interests.

MAIN ANTI-U.S. ACTIVITIES TO DATE: The IG has never specifically attacked a U.S. citizen or facility but has threatened U.S. interests.

STRENGTH: Unknown. At its peak, the IG probably commanded several thousand hard-core members and a like number of sympathizers. The 1998 cease-fire and security crackdowns following the attack on tourists in Luxor in 1997 probably have resulted in a substantial decrease in the group's numbers.

OPERATIONAL LOCATIONS: Operates mainly in the Al-Minya, Asyu't, Qina, and Sohaj Governorates of southern Egypt. Also appears to have support in Cairo, Alexandria, and other urban locations, particularly among unemployed graduates and students. Has a worldwide presence, including Sudan, the United Kingdom, Afghanistan, Austria, and Yemen.

AFFILIATIONS: Unknown. The Egyptian government believes that Iran, bin Laden, and Afghan militant groups support the organization. Also may obtain some funding through various Islamic non-governmental organizations.

COMMENTS: Al-Gama'a claims responsibility for the attempt in June 1995 to assassinate Egyptian President Hosni Mubarak in Addis Ababa, Ethiopia. The group's spiritual leader, Shaykh Umar Abd al-Rahman, is incarcerated in the United States. A Designated Foreign Terrorist Organization (FTO) listed as "active" during 2000.

GEORGIA

NAME: Zviadists

DATE STARTED/FIRST ACTIVE: 1991.

GOALS: Extremist supporters of deceased former Georgian President Zviad Gamsakhurdia. Overthrow Gamsakhurdia's successor Eduard Shevardnadze's rule.

MAIN ANTI-U.S. ACTIVITIES TO DATE: None.

STRENGTH: Unknown.

OPERATIONAL LOCATIONS: Georgia, especially Mingrelia and Russia.

AFFILIATIONS: Unknown.

COMMENTS: Some now operate anti-Shevardnadze activities from Russia.

GREECE

NAME: Revolutionary Nuclei (RN) a.k.a. Revolutionary Cells

DATE STARTED/FIRST ACTIVE: 1995.

GOALS: Believed to be the successor group to the Revolutionary People's Struggle (ELA), RN is a leftist group with an anti-establishment, anti-U.S., anti-NATO and anti-EU agenda. The ELA, which sought to oppose "imperialist domination, exploitation, and oppression," has not been active since 1995.

MAIN ANTI-U.S. ACTIVITIES TO DATE: In November 2000, RN bombed the Citigroup offices in Athens and the studio of a Greek/American sculptor. In December 1999, the group detonated explosives outside the Athens offices of Texaco.

STRENGTH: Unknown.

OPERATIONAL LOCATIONS: Mainly the Athens metropolitan area in Greece.

AFFILIATIONS: Unknown.

COMMENTS: RN was designated a Foreign Terrorist Organization (FTO) on March 27, 2002.

NAME: Revolutionary Organization 17 November (17 November)

DATE STARTED/FIRST ACTIVE: 1975.

GOALS: A radical leftist group, 17 November is described as anti-Greek establishment, anti-United States, anti-Turkey, anti-NATO, and committed to the ouster of U.S. bases, removal of Turkish military presence from Cyprus, and severing of Greece's ties to NATO and the European Union (EU).

MAIN ANTI-U.S. ACTIVITIES TO DATE: Initial attacks were assassinations of senior U.S. officials and Greek public figures.

STRENGTH: Unknown, but presumed to be small.

OPERATIONAL LOCATIONS: Athens, Greece.

AFFILIATIONS: Unknown.

COMMENTS: Added bombings in 1980s. Since 1990, has expanded targets to include EU facilities and foreign firms investing in Greece, and has added improvised rocket attacks to its methods. Most recent attack claimed was the murder in June 2000 of British Defense Attaché Stephen Saunders. A Designated Foreign Terrorist Organization (FTO) listed as "active" during 2000.

NAME: Revolutionary People's Struggle (ELA)

DATE STARTED/FIRST ACTIVE: 1971.

GOALS: To oppose "imperialist domination, exploitation, and oppression."

MAIN ANTI-U.S. ACTIVITIES TO DATE: Since 1974, has conducted bombings against Greek government and economic targets, as well as U.S. military and business facilities.

STRENGTH: Unknown.

OPERATIONAL LOCATIONS: Greece.

AFFILIATIONS: Received weapons and other assistance from international terrorist Carlos during 1980s. Currently no known foreign sponsors. Greek police believe they have established links between ELA and Revolutionary Organization 17 November.

COMMENTS: An extreme leftist group, the ELA is self-described as revolutionary, anti-capitalist, and anti-imperialist. Strongly anti-U.S., and seeks the removal of U.S. military forces from Greece. A Designated Foreign Terrorist Organization (FTO) listed as "active" during 2000.

HONDURAS

NAME: Morzanist Patriotic Front (FPM)

DATE STARTED/FIRST ACTIVE: Late 1980s.

GOALS: Protest U.S. intervention in Honduran economic and political affairs.

MAIN ANTI-U.S. ACTIVITIES TO DATE: Mainly operates attacks on U.S. military personnel in Honduras. Bus bombing in 1990 wounded seven U.S. servicemen, and one in 1989 wounded three servicemen. Attacked U.S. convoy in 1989. Grenade attack in La Ceiba in 1989 wounded seven U.S. soldiers. Claimed bombing of Peace Corps office in 1988.

STRENGTH: Unknown, probably relatively small.

OPERATIONAL LOCATIONS: Honduras.

AFFILIATIONS: Had ties to former government of Nicaragua and possibly Cuba.

INDIA

NAME: Al-Ummah

DATE STARTED/FIRST ACTIVE: 1992.

GOALS: Unknown.

MAIN ANTI-U.S. ACTIVITIES TO DATE: None.

STRENGTH: Unknown.

OPERATIONAL LOCATIONS: Southern India.

AFFILIATIONS: Unknown.

COMMENTS: Radical Indian Muslim group believed responsible for the Coimbatore bombings in Southern India in 1998.

IRAQ

NAME: Abu Nidal organization (ANO) a.k.a. Fatah Revolutionary Council, Arab Revolutionary Brigades, Black September, and Revolutionary Organization of Socialist Muslims.

DATE STARTED/FIRST ACTIVE: Split from the PLO in 1974.

GOALS: Establishment of a Palestinian State.

MAIN ANTI-U.S. ACTIVITIES TO DATE: Targets include the United States, the United Kingdom, France, Israel, moderate Palestinians, the PLO, and various Arab countries. Has not attacked Western targets since the late 1980s.

STRENGTH: A few hundred plus limited overseas support structure.

OPERATIONAL LOCATIONS: Its leader, Sabri Al-Banna, relocated to Iraq in December 1998, where the group maintains a presence. Has an operational presence in Lebanon, including in several Palestinian refugee camps. Authorities shut down the ANO's operations in Libya and Egypt in 1999. Has demonstrated ability to operate over wide area, including the Middle East, Asia, and Europe. Has carried out terrorist attacks in 20 countries, killing or injuring almost 900 persons.

AFFILIATIONS: Has received considerable support, including safe haven, training, logistic assistance, and financial aid from Iraq, Libya, and Syria (until 1987), in addition to close support for selected operations.

COMMENTS: Financial problems and internal disorganization have reduced the group's activities and capabilities. A Designated Foreign Terrorist Organization (FTO) listed as "active" during 2000.

NAME: Mujahedin-e Khalq Organization (MEK or MKO) a.k.a. The National Liberation Army of Iran (NLA, the militant wing of the MEK), the People's Mujahidin of Iran (PMOI), National Council of Resistance (NCR), Muslim Iranian Student's Society (front organization used to garner financial support).

DATE STARTED/FIRST ACTIVE: 1960s.

GOALS: The MEK continues to conduct a worldwide campaign against the Iranian government, which stresses propaganda and occasionally uses terrorist violence.

MAIN ANTI-U.S. ACTIVITIES TO DATE: During the 1970s, the MEK staged terrorist attacks inside Iran and killed several U.S. military personnel and civilians working on defense projects in Tehran. Supported the takeover in 1979 of the U.S. Embassy in Tehran.

STRENGTH: Several thousand fighters based in Iraq with an extensive overseas support structure. Most of the fighters are organized in the MEK's National Liberation Army (NLA).

OPERATIONAL LOCATIONS: In the 1980s, the MEK's leaders were forced by Iranian security forces to flee to France. Most resettled in Iraq by 1987. In the mid-1980s, the group did not mount terrorist operations in Iran at a level similar to its activities in the 1970s. In the 1990s, however, the MEK claimed credit for an increasing number of operations in Iran.

AFFILIATIONS: Beyond support from Iraq, the MEK uses front organizations to solicit contributions from expatriate Iranian communities.

COMMENTS: Formed by the college-educated children of Iranian merchants, the MEK sought to counter what it perceived as excessive Western influence in the Shah's regime. Following a philosophy that mixes Marxism and Islam, the MEK has developed into the largest and most active armed

Iranian dissident group. Its history is studded with anti-Western activity, and, most recently, attacks on the interests of the clerical regime in Iran and abroad. A Designated Foreign Terrorist Organization (FTO) listed as "active" during 2000.

NAME: Palestine Liberation Front (PLF)

DATE STARTED/FIRST ACTIVE: Broke away from the PFLP-GC in mid-1970s.

GOALS: Creation of a Palestinian state.

MAIN ANTI-U.S. ACTIVITIES TO DATE: The Abu Abbas-led faction was responsible for the attack in 1985 on the cruise ship *Achille Lauro* and the murder of U.S. citizen Leon Klinghoffer.

STRENGTH: Unknown.

OPERATIONAL LOCATIONS: Based in Tunisia until the *Achille Lauro* attack, it is now based in Iraq.

AFFILIATIONS: Receives support mainly from Iraq. Has received support from Libya in the past.

COMMENTS: After its initial break with the PFLP-GC, split again into pro-PLO, pro-Syrian, and pro-Libyan factions. Pro-PLO faction is led by Muhammad Abbas (Abu Abbas), who became member of PLO Executive Committee in 1984 but left it in 1991. A warrant for Abu Abbas's arrest is outstanding in Italy. A Designated Foreign Terrorist Organization (FTO) listed as "active" during 2000.

ISRAEL

NAME: Kach and Kahane Chai

DATE STARTED/FIRST ACTIVE: Both organizations were declared to be terrorist organizations in March 1994 by the Israeli Cabinet under the 1948 Terrorism Law.

GOALS: Stated goal is to restore the biblical state of Israel.

MAIN ANTI-U.S. ACTIVITIES TO DATE: None.

STRENGTH: Unknown.

OPERATIONAL LOCATIONS: Israel and West Bank settlements, particularly Qiryat Arba' in Hebron.

AFFILIATIONS: Receives support from sympathizers in the United States and Europe.

COMMENTS: Kach was founded by radical Israeli-American rabbi Meir Kahane, while its offshoot Kahane Chai (which means "Kahane Lives") was founded by Meir Kahane's son Binyamin following his father's assassination in the United States. They have threatened to attack Arabs, Palestinians, and Israeli government officials. A Designated Foreign Terrorist Organization (FTO) listed as "active" during 2000.

JAPAN

NAME: Aum Supreme Truth (Aum) a.k.a. Aum Shinrikyo, Aleph

DATE STARTED/FIRST ACTIVE: 1987.

GOALS: To take over Japan and then the world.

MAIN ANTI-U.S. ACTIVITIES TO DATE: None.

STRENGTH: The Aum's current membership is estimated at 1,500 to 2,000 persons. At the time of the 1995 Tokyo subway attack, the group claimed to have 9,000 members in Japan and up to 40,000 worldwide.

OPERATIONAL LOCATIONS: The Aum's principal membership is located only in Japan, but a residual branch comprising an unknown number of followers has surfaced in Russia.

AFFILIATIONS: None.

COMMENTS: A cult established by Shoko Asahara, the Aum is responsible for the March 20, 1995, sarin nerve gas attacks on several Tokyo subway trains that killed 12 persons and injured up to 6,000. In 2000, Fumihiro Joyu took control of the Aum following his three-year jail sentence for perjury. Joyu was previously the group's spokesman and Russia Branch leader. Under Joyu's leadership the Aum changed its name to Aleph and claims to have rejected the violent and apocalyptic teachings of its founder. A Designated Foreign Terrorist Organization (FTO) listed as "active" during 2000.

NAME: Chukaku-Ha (Nucleus or Middle Core Faction)

DATE STARTED/FIRST ACTIVE: 1957.

GOALS: Protest Japan's imperial system, Western imperialism, and events such as the Gulf War and the expansion of Tokyo's Narita Airport.

MAIN ANTI-U.S. ACTIVITIES TO DATE: None.

STRENGTH: 3,500.

OPERATIONAL LOCATIONS: Japan.

AFFILIATIONS: None.

COMMENTS: Largest domestic militant group; has small covert action wing called Kansai Revolutionary Army.

NAME: Japanese Red Army (JRA) a.k.a. Anti-Imperialist International Brigade (AIIB)

DATE STARTED/FIRST ACTIVE: Around 1970.

GOALS: To overthrow the Japanese government and monarchy and to help foment world revolution.

MAIN ANTI-U.S. ACTIVITIES TO DATE: In 1972 the JRA attempted a takeover of the U.S. Embassy in Kuala Lumpur. In April 1988, JRA operative Yu Kikumura was arrested with explosives on the New Jersey Turnpike, apparently planning an attack to coincide with the bombing of a USO club in Naples, a suspected JRA operation that killed five, including a U.S. servicewoman.

STRENGTH: About six hard-core members; undetermined number of sympathizers.

OPERATIONAL LOCATIONS: The JRA has carried out a series of attacks around the world. Location unknown, but possibly traveling in Asia or Syrian-controlled areas of Lebanon.

AFFILIATIONS: Unknown. Has history of close relations with Palestinian terrorist groups based and operating outside Japan. May control or at least have ties to Anti-Imperialist International Brigade (AIIB); also may have links to Antiwar Democratic Front—an overt leftist political organization—inside Japan.

COMMENTS: The JRA is a break away from the Japanese Communist League-Red Army Faction. A Designated Foreign Terrorist Organization (FTO) in 2000, it was removed from the FTO list on October 5, 2001.

LEBANON

NAME: 'Asbat al-Ansar (The Partisans' League)

DATE STARTED/FIRST ACTIVE: Early 1990s.

GOALS: Overthrow the Lebanese government and thwart anti-Islamic influences in Lebanon.

MAIN ANTI-U.S. ACTIVITIES TO DATE: None.

STRENGTH: About 300 fighters.

OPERATIONAL LOCATIONS: Primary base of operations is the 'Ayn al-Hilwah Palestinian refugee camp in southern Lebanon.

AFFILIATIONS: Overseas Sunni extremist networks and Osama bin Laden's al Qaeda.

COMMENTS: A Lebanon-based group composed mainly of Palestinians, Asbat al-Ansar adheres to an extremist interpretation of Islam and justifies the use of violence against civilian targets. The group raised its profile in 2000 with a rocket-propelled grenade attack on the Russian Embassy in Beirut. It was designated a Foreign Terrorist Organization (FTO) on March 27, 2002.

NAME: Hezbollah (Party of God) a.k.a. Islamic Jihad, Revolutionary Justice Organization, Organization of the Oppressed on Earth, and Islamic Jihad for the Liberation of Palestine

DATE STARTED/FIRST ACTIVE: Unknown.

GOALS: Increasing its political power in Lebanon, and opposing Israel and the Middle East peace negotiations.

MAIN ANTI-U.S. ACTIVITIES TO DATE: Known or suspected to have been involved in numerous anti-U.S. terrorist attacks, including the suicide truck bombing of the U.S. embassy and U.S. Marine barracks in Beirut in October 1983, and the U.S. embassy annex in Beirut in September 1984.

STRENGTH: Several thousand supporters and a few hundred terrorist operatives.

OPERATIONAL LOCATIONS: Operates in the Bekaa Valley, the southern suburbs of Beirut, and southern Lebanon. Has established cells in Europe, Africa, South America, North America, and Asia.

AFFILIATIONS: Receives substantial amounts of financial, training, weapons, explosives, political, diplomatic, and organizational aid from Iran and Syria.

COMMENTS: A radical Shia organization founded in Lebanon. A Designated Foreign Terrorist Organization (FTO) listed as "active" during 2000.

NORTHERN IRELAND

NAME: Continuity Irish Republican Army (CIRA) a.k.a. Continuity Army Council

DATE STARTED/FIRST ACTIVE: 1994.

GOALS: The reunification of Ireland and to forcing British troops from Northern Ireland.

MAIN ANTI-U.S. ACTIVITIES TO DATE: None.

STRENGTH: Fewer than 50 hard-core activists.

OPERATIONAL LOCATIONS: Northern Ireland, Irish Republic.

AFFILIATIONS: Suspected of receiving funds and arms from sympathizers in the United States. May have acquired arms and materiel from the Balkans in cooperation with the Real IRA.

COMMENTS: A radical terrorist splinter group formed as the clandestine armed wing of the political organization Republican Sinn Fein (RSF). RSF formed after the Irish Republican Army announced a cease-fire in September 1994. Targets include British military and Northern Ireland security targets and Northern Ireland Loyalist paramilitary groups. Also has launched bomb attacks against civilian targets in Northern Ireland. Does not have an established presence or capability to launch attacks on the U.K. mainland. NOT a Designated Foreign Terrorist Organization (FTO), but listed as "active" during 2000.

NAME: Irish Republican Army (IRA) a.k.a. Provisional Irish Republican Army (PIRA), the Provos

DATE STARTED/FIRST ACTIVE: 1969.

GOALS: Removing British forces from Northern Ireland and unifying Ireland.

MAIN ANTI-U.S. ACTIVITIES TO DATE: None.

STRENGTH: Several hundred members, plus several thousand sympathizers.

OPERATIONAL LOCATIONS: Northern Ireland, Irish Republic, Great Britain, Europe.

AFFILIATIONS: Has, in the past, received aid from a variety of groups and countries and considerable training and arms from Libya and the PLO. Is suspected of receiving funds, arms, and other terrorist-related materiel from sympathizers in the United States. Similarities in operations suggest links to the ETA.

COMMENTS: Terrorist group formed as the clandestine armed wing of Sinn Fein, a legal political movement. Has a Marxist orientation. Organized into small, tightly knit cells under the leadership of the Army Council. Despite of some members to the dissident splinter groups, its numbers have remained steady. The IRA has been observing a cease-fire since July 1997 and previously observed a cease-fire from September 1994 to February 1996. NOT a Designated Foreign Terrorist Organization (FTO), but listed as "active" during 2000.

NAME: Loyalist Volunteer Force (LVF)

DATE STARTED/FIRST ACTIVE: 1996.

GOALS: Prevent a political settlement with Irish nationalists in Northern Ireland by attacking Catholic politicians, civilians, and Protestant politicians who endorse the Northern Ireland peace process.

MAIN ANTI-U.S. ACTIVITIES TO DATE: None.

STRENGTH: Approximately 150.

OPERATIONAL LOCATIONS: Ireland, Northern Ireland.

AFFILIATIONS: None.

COMMENTS: Terrorist group formed as a faction of the mainstream loyalist Ulster Volunteer Force (UVF), the LVF did not emerge publicly until February 1997. Composed largely of UVF hardliners. Has been observing a cease-fire since May 1998. The LVF decommissioned a small but significant amount of weapons in December 1998, but it has not repeated this gesture, and in fact threatened in 2000 to resume killing Catholics. In 2000, the LVF also engaged in a brief but violent feud with other loyalists in which several individuals were killed. NOT a Designated Foreign Terrorist Organization (FTO) but listed as "active" during 2000.

NAME: Orange Volunteers (OV)

DATE STARTED/FIRST ACTIVE: Late 1990s.

GOALS: Prevent a political settlement with Irish nationalists.

MAIN ANTI-U.S. ACTIVITIES TO DATE: None.

STRENGTH: Up to 20 hard-core members, some of whom are experienced in terrorist tactics and bomb making.

OPERATIONAL LOCATIONS: Northern Ireland.

AFFILIATIONS: None.

COMMENTS: Comprised largely of disgruntled loyalist hardliners who split from groups observing the cease-fire. The OV declared a cease-fire in September 2000, but the group maintains the ability to conduct bombings, arson, beatings, and possibly robberies. NOT a Designated Foreign Terrorist Organization (FTO) but listed as "active" during 2000.

NAME: Real IRA (RIRA) a.k.a. True IRA

DATE STARTED/FIRST ACTIVE: February-March 1998.

GOALS: Removing British forces from Northern Ireland and unifying Ireland.

MAIN ANTI-U.S. ACTIVITIES TO DATE: None.

STRENGTH: 150 to 200.

OPERATIONAL LOCATIONS: Northern Ireland, Irish Republic, Great Britain.

AFFILIATIONS: Possible limited support from IRA hardliners dissatis-fied with the IRA cease-fire and other republican sympathizers. Suspected of receiving funds from sympathizers in the United States. RIRA also is thought to have purchased sophisticated weapons from the Balkans, according to press reports.

COMMENTS: The clandestine armed wing of the 32-County Sovereignty Movement, a "political pressure group" opposed to Sinn Fein's adoption of the Mitchell principles of democracy and nonviolence 1999 additions to the Irish Constitution, which lay claim to Northern Ireland. Listed as "active" during 2000, it was designated a Foreign Terrorist Organization (FTO) on October 5, 2001.

NAME: Red Hand Defenders (RHD)

DATE STARTED/FIRST ACTIVE: Late 1990s.

GOALS: Prevent a political settlement with Irish nationalists by attacking Catholic civilian interests in Northern Ireland.

MAIN ANTI-U.S. ACTIVITIES TO DATE: None.

STRENGTH: Up to 20 members.

OPERATIONAL LOCATIONS: Northern Ireland.

AFFILIATIONS: None.

COMMENTS: Extremist terrorist group composed largely of Protestant hardliners from other loyalist groups observing a cease-fire. RHD was quiet in 2000, following a damaging crackdown by security forces in late 1999. In prior years, the group has carried out numerous pipe bombings and arson attacks against "soft" civilian targets, such as homes, churches, and private businesses, to cause outrage in the republican community and to provoke IRA retaliation. NOT a Designated Foreign Terrorist Organization (FTO) but listed as "active" during 2000.

OCCUPIED TERRITORIES

NAME: Al-Aqsa Martyrs Brigade

DATE STARTED/FIRST ACTIVE: 2000.

GOALS: Drive the Israeli military and people from the West Bank, Gaza Strip, and Jerusalem and establish a Palestinian state.

MAIN ANTI-U.S. ACTIVITIES TO DATE: At least five U.S. citizens have been killed in attacks, but probably not because of their citizenship. The group mainly targets Israeli military personnel and civilians.

STRENGTH: Unknown.

OPERATIONAL LOCATIONS: Mainly in the West Bank, but has also claimed responsibility for attacks inside Israel and the Gaza Strip.

AFFILIATIONS: Unknown.

COMMENTS: Al-Aqsa Martyrs Brigade is composed of cells of Fatah-affiliated activists that emerged with the onset of the intifadah in 2000. In January 2002, an al-Aqsa member became the first female suicide bomber in the intifadah. The group was designated a Foreign Terrorist Organization (FTO) on March 27, 2002.

NAME: Democratic Front for the Liberation of Palestine (DFLP)

DATE STARTED/FIRST ACTIVE: 1969.

GOALS: Achieve Palestinian national goals through revolution of the masses.

MAIN ANTI-U.S. ACTIVITIES TO DATE: None.

STRENGTH: 500.

OPERATIONAL LOCATIONS: Syria, Lebanon, and the Israeli-occupied territories.

AFFILIATIONS: One of the two factions joined with other rejectionist groups to form the Alliances of Palestinian Forces (APF), but broke it off. Has made limited moves toward merging with the Popular Front for the Liberation of Palestine (PFLP) since the mid-1990s. Receives limited financial and military aid from Syria.

COMMENTS: Marxist-Leninist organization founded when it split from the PFLP. Opposed the Israel-PLO peace agreement.

NAME: HAMAS (Islamic Resistance Movement)

DATE STARTED/FIRST ACTIVE: 1987.

GOALS: Establishing an Islamic Palestinian state in place of Israel.

MAIN ANTI-U.S. ACTIVITIES TO DATE: Unknown.

STRENGTH: Unknown number of hard-core members; tens of thousands of supporters and sympathizers.

OPERATIONAL LOCATIONS: Primarily the occupied territories, Israel. In August 1999, Jordanian authorities closed the group's Political Bureau offices in Amman, arrested its leaders, and prohibited the group from operating on Jordanian territory.

AFFILIATIONS: Receives funding from Palestinian expatriates, Iran, and private benefactors in Saudi Arabia and other moderate Arab states. Some fundraising and propaganda activities take place in Western Europe and North America.

COMMENTS: Formed as an outgrowth of the Palestinian branch of the Muslim Brotherhood. Various HAMAS elements have used both political and violent means, including terrorism. Loosely structured, with some elements working clandestinely and others working openly through mosques and social service institutions to recruit members, raise money, organize activities, and distribute propaganda. Also has engaged in peaceful political activity, such as running candidates in West Bank Chamber of Commerce elections. A Designated Foreign Terrorist Organization (FTO) listed as "active" during 2000.

NAME: The Palestine Islamic Jihad (PIJ)

DATE STARTED/FIRST ACTIVE: 1970s.

GOALS: The creation of an Islamic Palestinian state and the destruction of Israel through holy war.

MAIN ANTI-U.S. ACTIVITIES TO DATE: Because of its strong support for Israel, the United States has been identified as an enemy of the PIJ, but the group has not specifically conducted attacks against U.S. interests in the past. In July 2000, however, publicly threatened to attack U.S. interests if the U.S. Embassy is moved from Tel Aviv to Jerusalem.

STRENGTH: Unknown.

OPERATIONAL LOCATIONS: Primarily Israel and the occupied territories and other parts of the Middle East, including Jordan and Lebanon. Headquartered in Syria.

AFFILIATIONS: Receives financial assistance from Iran and limited logistic assistance from Syria.

COMMENTS: Originated among militant Palestinians in the Gaza Strip during the 1970s. Also opposes moderate Arab governments that it believes have been tainted by Western secularism. A Designated Foreign Terrorist Organization (FTO) listed as "active" during 2000.

PAKISTAN

NAME: Harakat ul-Ansar (HUA)

DATE STARTED/FIRST ACTIVE: October 1993.

GOALS: Oppose Indian troops in Kashmir.

MAIN ANTI-U.S. ACTIVITIES TO DATE: U.S. nationals were kidnapped in New Delhi in 1994 in effort to secure the release of imprisoned HUA leader Maulana Masood Azhar.

STRENGTH: Several thousand armed supporters.

OPERATIONAL LOCATIONS: Based in Pakistan, but operates mainly in Kashmir.

AFFILIATIONS: Collects funds from supporters in Saudi Arabia and other Gulf and Islamic states, and from Pakistanis and Kashmiris. Has been linked to the Kashmiri militant group Al-Faran. See "Army of Muhammad (JEM)."

NAME: Harakat ul-Mujahidin (HUM)

DATE STARTED/FIRST ACTIVE: Early 1990s.

GOALS: Unite Kashmir with Pakistan.

MAIN ANTI-U.S. ACTIVITIES TO DATE: None, although new leader Farooq Kashmiri. Khalil, who took control of HUM in February 2000, has been linked to Bin Laden and signed his *fatwah* in February 1998 calling for attacks on U.S. and Western interests.

STRENGTH: Several thousand armed supporters.

OPERATIONAL LOCATIONS: Based in Muzaffarabad, Rawalpindi, and several other towns in Pakistan and Afghanistan, but members conduct insurgent and terrorist activities primarily in Kashmir. The HUM trains its militants in Afghanistan and Pakistan.

AFFILIATIONS: Collects donations from Saudi Arabia and other Gulf and Islamic states, and from Pakistanis and Kashmiris. The sources and amount of HUM's military funding are unknown. Leadership has been linked to Osama Bin Laden.

COMMENTS: Formerly known as the Harakat al-Ansar, the HUM is an Islamic militant group based in Pakistan that operates primarily in Kashmir. Supporters are mostly Pakistanis and Kashmiris, and also include Afghans and Arab veterans of the Afghan war. Uses light and heavy machineguns, assault rifles, mortars, explosives, and rockets. HUM lost some of its membership in defections to the Jaish-e-Mohammed (JEM). Continues to operate terrorist training camps in eastern Afghanistan. A Designated Foreign Terrorist Organization (FTO) listed as "active" during 2000.

NAME: Jaish-e-Mohammed (JEM) (Army of Mohammed)

DATE STARTED/FIRST ACTIVE: February 2000.

GOALS: Unite Kashmir with Pakistan.

MAIN ANTI-U.S. ACTIVITIES TO DATE: None. JEM's leader, Maulana Masood Azhar, is a former leader of Harakat ul-Ansar (HUA), and was imprisoned until 1999 when he was released in a hostage exchange. U.S. nationals were kidnapped in New Delhi in 1994 in an earlier HUA effort to secure his release.

STRENGTH: Several hundred armed supporters.

OPERATIONAL LOCATIONS: Based in Peshawar and Muzaffarabad, but members conduct terrorist activities primarily in Kashmir. The JEM maintains training camps in Afghanistan.

AFFILIATIONS: Most of the JEM's cadre and material resources have been drawn from the militant groups Harakat ul-Jihad al-Islami (HUJI) and the Harakat ul-Mujahidin (HUM). The JEM has close ties to Afghan Arabs and the Taliban. Osama Bin Laden was suspected of giving funding to the JEM.

COMMENTS: The JEM is an Islamist group based in Pakistan that has rapidly expanded in size and capability. Supporters are mostly Pakistanis and Kashmiris, and also include Afghans and Arab veterans of the Afghan war. Uses light and heavy machineguns, assault rifles, mortars, improvised explosive devices, and rocket grenades. NOT a Designated Foreign Terrorist Organization (FTO), but listed as "active" during 2000.

NAME: Lashkar-e-Tayyiba (LT) (Army of the Righteous)

DATE STARTED/FIRST ACTIVE: 1989.

GOALS: Unite Kashmir with Pakistan.

MAIN ANTI-U.S. ACTIVITIES TO DATE: None.

STRENGTH: Several hundred members.

OPERATIONAL LOCATIONS: Based in Muridke (near Lahore) and Muzaffarabad. The LT trains its militants in mobile training camps across Pakistan-administered Kashmir and Afghanistan.

AFFILIATIONS: Collects donations from the Pakistani community in the Persian Gulf and United Kingdom, Islamic NGOs, and Pakistani and Kashmiri businessmen. The amount of LT funding is unknown. The LT maintains ties to religious/military groups around the world, ranging from the Philippines to the Middle East and Chechnya through the MDI fraternal network.

COMMENTS: The LT is the armed wing of the Pakistan-based religious organization, Markaz-ud-Dawa-wal-Irshad (MDI)—a Sunni anti-U.S. missionary organization. One of the three largest and best-trained groups fighting in Kashmir against India, it is not connected to a political party. The group has conducted a number of operations against Indian troops and civilian targets in Kashmir since 1993. Almost all LT cadres are foreigners— mostly Pakistanis from seminaries across the country and Afghan veterans of the Afghan wars. Uses assault rifles, light and heavy machineguns, mortars, explosives, and rocket propelled grenades. NOT a Designated Foreign Terrorist Organization (FTO) but listed as "active" during 2000.

PERU

NAME: Sendero Luminoso (Shining Path)

DATE STARTED/FIRST ACTIVE: Late 1960s.

GOALS: Destroy existing Peruvian institutions and replace them with a Communist peasant revolutionary regime. Oppose any influence by foreign governments, as well as by other Latin American guerrilla groups, especially the Tupac Amaru Revolutionary Movement (MRTA).

MAIN ANTI-U.S. ACTIVITIES TO DATE: Attempted to car-bomb the U.S. embassy in Peru in 1990.

STRENGTH: 100–200 armed militants.

OPERATIONAL LOCATIONS: Peru, with most activity in rural areas.

AFFILIATIONS: None.

COMMENTS: In the 1980s, SL became one of the most ruthless terrorist groups in the Western Hemisphere—approximately 30,000 persons have died since SL took up arms in 1980. A Designated Foreign Terrorist Organization (FTO) listed as "active" during 2000.

NAME: Tupac Amaru Revolutionary Movement (MRTA)

DATE STARTED/FIRST ACTIVE: 1983.

GOALS: Establish a Marxist regime and rid Peru of all imperialist elements (primarily U.S. and Japanese influence).

MAIN ANTI-U.S. ACTIVITIES TO DATE: None.

STRENGTH: No more than 100.

OPERATIONAL LOCATIONS: Peru with supporters throughout Latin America and Western Europe. Controls no territory.

AFFILIATIONS: None.

COMMENTS: Previously conducted bombings, kidnappings, ambushes, and assassinations, but recent activity has fallen drastically. Peru's counter-terrorist program has diminished the group's ability to carry out terrorist attacks. A Designated Foreign Terrorist Organization (FTO) in 2000, it was removed from the FTO list on October 5, 2001.

PHILIPPINES

NAME: Abu Sayyaf Group (ASG)

DATE STARTED/FIRST ACTIVE: 1991.

GOALS: Promote an independent Islamic state in western Mindanao and the Sulu Archipelago, areas in the southern Philippines heavily populated by Muslims.

MAIN ANTI-U.S. ACTIVITIES TO DATE: Kidnapped more than 30 foreigners, including a U.S. citizen, in 2000.

STRENGTH: 200 core fighters and more than 2,000 supporters.

OPERATIONAL LOCATIONS: Mainly southern Philippines with members occasionally traveling to Manila. Operated in Malaysia in 2000.

AFFILIATIONS: Probably receives support from Islamic extremists in the Middle East and South Asia. Some have ties to *Mujahidin* in Afghanistan.

COMMENTS: Smallest and most radical of the Islamic separatist groups operating in the southern Philippines. The group split from the Moro National Liberation Front in 1991. A Designated Foreign Terrorist Organization (FTO) listed as "active" during 2000.

NAME: Alex Boncayao Brigade (ABB)

DATE STARTED/FIRST ACTIVE: Mid-1980s.

GOALS: [A breakaway urban hit squad of the Communist Party of the Philippines New People's Army.]

MAIN ANTI-U.S. ACTIVITIES TO DATE: Suspected involved in the murder in 1989 of U.S. Army Col. James Rowe in the Philippines.

STRENGTH: 500.

OPERATIONAL LOCATIONS: Manila and central Philippines.

AFFILIATIONS: Formed an alliance with the Revolutionary Proletarian Army in 1997.

COMMENTS: Breakaway urban hit squad of the Communist Party of the Philippines New People's Army. NOT a Designated Foreign Terrorist Organization (FTO), but listed as "active" during 2000.

NAME: New People's Army (NPA)

DATE STARTED/FIRST ACTIVE: 1969.

GOALS: Overthrow the government of the Philippines through protracted guerrilla warfare.

MAIN ANTI-U.S. ACTIVITIES TO DATE: Opposes any U.S. military presence in the Philippines and attacked U.S. military interests before the U.S. base closures in 1992. Press reports in 1999 indicated that the NPA would target U.S. troops participating in joint military exercises under the Visiting Forces Agreement and U.S. embassy personnel.

STRENGTH: 6,000–8,000.

OPERATIONAL LOCATIONS: Rural Luzon, Visayas, and parts of Mindanao. Has cells in Manila and other metropolitan centers.

AFFILIATIONS: Derives most of its funding from contributions of supporters and so-called revolutionary taxes extorted from local businesses.

COMMENTS: The military wing of the Communist Party of the Philippines (CPP). Although primarily a rural-based guerrilla group, the NPA has an active urban infrastructure to conduct terrorism and uses city-based assassination squads called sparrow units. NOT a Designated Foreign Terrorist Organization (FTO), but listed as "active" during 2000.

RWANDA

NAME: Army for the Liberation of Rwanda (ALIR), a.k.a. Interahamwe, Former Armed Forces (ex-FAR)

DATE STARTED/FIRST ACTIVE: 1994.

GOALS: Topple Rwanda's Tutsi-dominated government, reinstitute Hutu control, and, possibly, complete the genocide begun in 1994.

MAIN ANTI-U.S. ACTIVITIES TO DATE: In 1996, a message—allegedly from the ALIR—threatened to kill the U.S. Ambassador to Rwanda and other U.S. citizens. In 1999, ALIR guerrillas critical of alleged U.S.-U.K. support for the Rwandan regime kidnapped and killed eight foreign tourists, including two U.S. citizens, at the Congo-Uganda border.

STRENGTH: Several thousand.

OPERATIONAL LOCATIONS: Mostly Democratic Republic of the Congo and Rwanda, but a few may operate in Burundi.

AFFILIATIONS: In the Congolese war, the ALIR is allied with Kinshasa against the Rwandan invaders. From the Rwandan invasion of 1998 until his death in early 2001, the Laurent Kabila regime in the Democratic Republic of the Congo provided the ALIR with training, arms, and supplies.

COMMENTS: The FAR was the army of the Rwandan Hutu regime that carried out the genocide of 500,000 or more Tutsis and regime opponents in 1994. The Interahamwe was the civilian militia force that carried out much of the killing. The groups merged after they were forced from Rwanda into the Democratic Republic of the Congo (then-Zaire) in 1994. They are now often known as the Army for the Liberation of Rwanda (ALIR), which is the armed branch of the PALIR or Party for the Liberation of Rwanda. NOT a Designated Foreign Terrorist Organization (FTO), but listed as "active" during 2000.

SIERRA LEONE

NAME: Revolutionary United Front (RUF)

DATE STARTED/FIRST ACTIVE: Unknown.

GOALS: Topple the current government of Sierra Leone and retain control of the lucrative diamond-producing regions of the country.

MAIN ANTI-U.S. ACTIVITIES TO DATE: None directly, but held hundreds of UN peacekeepers hostage in 2000.

STRENGTH: Several thousand fighters and possibly a similar number of supporters and sympathizers.

OPERATIONA LOCATIONS: Sierra Leone, Liberia, Guinea.

AFFILIATIONS: President Charles Taylor of Liberia reportedly provides support and leadership to the RUF. The United Nations has identified Libya, Gambia, and Burkina Faso as conduits for weapons and other materiel for the RUF.

COMMENTS: NOT a Designated Foreign Terrorist Organization (FTO), but listed as "active" during 2000.

SOUTH AFRICA

NAME: Qibla and People Against Gangsterism and Drugs (PAGAD)

DATE STARTED/FIRST ACTIVE: Qibla: 1980s; PAGAD: 1996.

GOALS: Qibla: Establish an Islamic state in South Africa; PAGAD: Fight drug lords in Cape Town. The two groups share anti-Western stance as well as some members and leadership, and promote greater political voice for South African Muslims.

MAIN ANTI-U.S. ACTIVITIES TO DATE: Qibla protests U.S. policies toward the Muslim world through its radio station 786. PAGAD is suspected of conducting hundreds of bombings and other violent actions.

STRENGTH: Qibla: 250; PAGAD: at least 50 gunmen, and larger than Qibla.

OPERATIONAL LOCATIONS: Cape Town, South Africa.

AFFILIATIONS: Probably have ties to Islamic extremists in the Middle East.

COMMENTS: Often uses names such as Muslims Against Global Oppression (MAGO) and Muslims Against Illegitimate Leaders (MAIL) when launching anti-Western campaigns. NOT a Designated Foreign Terrorist Organization (FTO), but listed as "active" during 2000.

SPAIN

NAME: Basque Fatherland and Liberty (ETA), a.k.a. Euzkadi Ta Askatasuna

DATE STARTED/FIRST ACTIVE: 1959.

GOALS: Establish an independent homeland based on Marxist principles in the northern Spanish provinces of Vizcaya, Guipuzcoa, Alava, and Navarra and the southwestern French departments of Labourd, Basse-Navarra, and Soule.

MAIN ANTI-U.S. ACTIVITIES TO DATE: None.

STRENGTH: Unknown; may have hundreds of members, plus supporters.

OPERATIONAL LOCATIONS: Operates primarily in the Basque autonomous regions of northern Spain and southwestern France, but also has bombed Spanish and French interests elsewhere.

AFFILIATIONS: Has received training at various times in the past in Libya, Lebanon, and Nicaragua. Some ETA members allegedly have received sanctuary in Cuba while others reside in South America. Also appears to have ties to the Irish Republican Army through the two groups' legal political wings.

COMMENTS: Primarily bombings and assassinations of Spanish government officials, especially security and military forces, politicians, and judicial figures. ETA finances its activities through kidnappings, robberies, and extortion. The group has killed more than 800 persons since it began lethal attacks in the early 1960s. A Designated Foreign Terrorist Organization (FTO) listed as "active" during 2000.

NAME: First of October Antifascist Resistance Group (GRAPO), Grupo de Resistencia Anti-Fascista Premero de Octubre.

DATE STARTED/FIRST ACTIVE: 1975.

GOALS: Overthrow of the Spanish government and replace it with a Marxist-Leninist regime.

MAIN ANTI-U.S. ACTIVITIES TO DATE: GRAPO is vehemently anti-U.S., calls for the removal of all U.S. military forces from Spanish territory, and has conducted and attempted several attacks against U.S. targets since 1977.

STRENGTH: Unknown but likely fewer than a dozen hard-core activists. Numerous GRAPO members also currently are in Spanish prisons.

OPERATIONAL LOCATIONS: Spain.

AFFILIATIONS: None.

COMMENTS: Armed wing of the illegal Communist Party of Spain of the Franco era. Advocating the NOT a Designated Foreign Terrorist Organization (FTO), but listed as "active" during 2000.

SRI LANKA

NAME: Liberation Tigers of Tamil Eelam (LTTE) Other known front organizations: World Tamil Association (WTA), World Tamil Movement (WTM), the Federation of Associations of Canadian Tamils (FACT), the Ellalan Force, the Sangilian Force.

DATE STARTED/FIRST ACTIVE: 1976.

GOALS: Establish an independent Tamil state.

MAIN ANTI-U.S. ACTIVITIES TO DATE: None.

STRENGTH: 8,000 to 10,000 armed combatants in Sri Lanka, with a core of trained fighters of approximately 3,000 to 6,000. Has significant overseas support structure for fundraising, weapons procurement, and propaganda activities.

OPERATIONAL LOCATIONS: Sri Lanka.

AFFILIATIONS: Lobbies foreign governments and the UN. Uses its international contacts to procure weapons, communications, and any other equipment and supplies it needs. Exploits large Tamil communities in North America, Europe, and Asia to obtain funds and supplies for its fighters in Sri Lanka.

COMMENTS: A Designated Foreign Terrorist Organization (FTO) listed as "active" during 2000.

SYRIA

NAME: Popular Front for the Liberation of Palestine (PFLP)

DATE STARTED/FIRST ACTIVE: 1967.

GOALS: Oppose current negotiations with Israel. Promote national unity and the reinvigoration of the PLO.

MAIN ANTI-U.S. ACTIVITIES TO DATE: None.

STRENGTH: 800.

OPERATIONAL LOCATIONS: Syria, Lebanon, Israel, and the occupied territories.

AFFILIATIONS: Receives safe haven and some logistic assistance from Syria.

COMMENTS: Joined the Alliance of Palestinian Forces (APF) to and suspended participation in the PLO. Broke away from the APF, along with the DFLP, in 1996 over ideological differences. A Designated Foreign Terrorist Organization (FTO) listed as "active" during 2000.

NAME: Popular Front for the Liberation of Palestine-General Command (PFLP-GC)

GOALS: Oppose Arafat's PLO.

MAIN ANTI-U.S. ACTIVITIES TO DATE: None.

STRENGTH: Several hundred.

OPERATIONAL LOCATIONS: Europe, Middle East, southern Lebanon, Israel, West Bank, and Gaza Strip. Headquartered in Damascus with bases in Lebanon.

AFFILIATIONS: Receives logistic and military support from Syria and financial support from Iran.

COMMENTS: Known for cross-border terrorist attacks into Israel using unusual means. A Designated Foreign Terrorist Organization (FTO) listed as "active" during 2000.

TURKEY

NAME: Kurdistan Workers' Party (PKK)

DATE STARTED/FIRST ACTIVE: 1974.

GOALS: Establish an independent Kurdish state in southeastern Turkey, where the population is predominantly Kurdish. Improve rights for Kurds in Turkey.

MAIN ANTI-U.S. ACTIVITIES TO DATE: None.

STRENGTH: 4,000 to 5,000, with thousands of sympathizers in Turkey and Europe.

OPERATIONAL LOCATIONS: Turkey, Europe, and the Middle East.

AFFILIATIONS: Has received safe haven and modest aid from Syria, Iraq, and Iran. The Syrian government expelled PKK leader Abdullah Ocalan and known elements of the group from its territory in October 1998.

COMMENTS: In the early 1990s, the PKK moved beyond rural-based insurgent activities to include urban terrorism. The group now claims it would use only political means to achieve its goals. A Designated Foreign Terrorist Organization (FTO) listed as "active" during 2000.

NAME: Revolutionary People's Liberation Party/Front (DHKP/C) a.k.a. Devrimci Sol (Revolutionary Left), Dev Sol

DATE STARTED/FIRST ACTIVE: 1978.

GOALS: Uphold Marxist ideology and demonstrate its anti-U.S. and anti-NATO stance.

MAIN ANTI-U.S. ACTIVITIES TO DATE: Assassinated two U.S. military contractors and wounded a U.S. Air Force officer to protest the Gulf war. Launched rockets at U.S. Consulate in Istanbul in 1992. Turkish authorities thwarted DHKP/C attempt in June 1999 to fire light antitank weapon at U.S. Consulate in Istanbul.

STRENGTH: Unknown.

OPERATIONAL LOCATIONS: Turkey, primarily in Istanbul, Ankara, Izmir, and Adana. Raises funds in Western Europe.

AFFILIATIONS: Unknown.

COMMENTS: A Designated Foreign Terrorist Organization (FTO) listed as "active" during 2000.

UNITED STATES

NAME: Jamaat ul-Fuqra

DATE STARTED/FIRST ACTIVE: Early 1980s.

GOALS: Purify Islam through violence.

MAIN ANTI-U.S. ACTIVITIES TO DATE: Assassinations and fire-bombings across the United States in the 1980s. Members in the United States have been convicted of criminal violations, including murder and fraud.

STRENGTH: Unknown.

OPERATIONAL LOCATIONS: North America, Pakistan.

AFFILIATIONS: None.

COMMENTS: Members have purchased isolated rural compounds in North America to live communally, practice their faith, and insulate themselves from Western culture.

UZBEKISTAN

NAME: Islamic Movement of Uzbekistan (IMU)

DATE STARTED/FIRST ACTIVE: Unknown.

GOALS: Oppose Uzbekistani President Islom Karimov's secular regime and establish an Islamic state in Uzbekistan.

MAIN ANTI-U.S. ACTIVITIES TO DATE: Took hostages on several occasions in 1999 and 2000, including four U.S. citizens. The group's propaganda includes anti-Western and anti-Israeli rhetoric.

STRENGTH: Militants probably number in the thousands.

OPERATIONAL LOCATIONS: Militants based in Afghanistan and Tajikistan. Area of operation includes Uzbekistan, Tajikistan, Kyrgyzstan, and Afghanistan.

AFFILIATIONS: Other Islamic extremist groups in Central and South Asia.

COMMENTS: A U.S. Designated Foreign Terrorist Organization (FTO) listed as "active" during 2000.

APPENDIX B: SAMPLE GENERAL AVIATION AIRPORT SECURITY PLAN

SAMPLE

General Aviation Airport Security Plan

Airport Name
Airport Designator
Town and State

CONTENTS

PART I: INTRODUCTION

A. Purpose

The goal of this general aviation airport security plan is to provide an overview of the security measures that have been established for the _____ airport to ensure the security and safety of the pilots, aircraft owners, tenants, and staff of the airport. The security plan will provide the procedures to use in an emergency security or safety situation and the protocol to report suspicious behavior.

B. Airport Security Coordinator and Committee

An airport security coordinator has been named, and an airport security committee has been established consisting of the airport manager, a fixed-base operator (FBO), and the flight school director, chief of police, fire chief, and a pilot/aircraft owner. The committee will meet annually to review security at the airport and establish and update security procedures as needed.

C. Points of Contact

The airport manager/security coordinator point of contact is _____, who can be contacted at _____ during working hours and at _____ after hours.

The secondary point of contact is the fixed-base operator, _____, who can be contacted at _____ during working hours and at _____ after hours.

PART II: COMMUNICATION

A. Contact Information

The contact information is posted in the fixed-base operator office and in the pilot lounge.

Airport Emergency Contact Information

Agency	Contact	Telephone	Alternate #
Airport manager/ security			
Fixed-base operator			
Fire department			
Police department			
Emergency medical service			
Federal Aviation Administration Flight Standards District Office			
National Transportation Safety Board			
Aircraft Owners and Pilots Association (AOPA) Watch	AOPA HQ Frederick, MD	1-866-GA-SECURE	

B. Pilots/Tenants

Airport Tenants

Fixed-Base Operator: _____

Address: _____

Telephone: _____

Aircraft Owner Name	Telephone	Aircraft	N Number	Hangar #

PART III: AIRPORT PHYSICAL SECURITY

A. General Information

_____ Airport is a general aviation airport with a primary runway length of _____ feet and width of _____ feet.

Secondary runways are RW _____; Length _____; Width _____.
RW _____; Length _____; Width _____.

There are _____ single engine aircraft, _____ multiengine aircraft, and _____ jet aircraft based at the airport.

Approximately _____ total operations (take-offs and landings) take place at the airport in 1 year.

Twin turbo-prop and jet operations: _____.

Activities at the Airport

Flight instruction: Agriculture Operations:
Aircraft rental: Air ambulance:
Charter service: Aircraft repair:
Law enforcement: Aircraft sales:

Military bases within 30 nm (nautical miles)? _____ .

Power plants within 30 nm? _____ .

Highly populated areas (50,000+) within 30 nm? _____ .

Fixed-base operator flight school

B. Landscaping and Grounds

Building entrances should be accentuated through landscaping and/or paving features.

All public entrances should be clearly defined by walkways and signage.

Landscape should be maintained to provide good visibility around buildings.

Vegetation should be trimmed to eliminate potential hiding places on the airport property.

Ensure that trees or other landscape features do not provide access to the roof or other upper levels of hangars and buildings or over any security fencing on the airport property.

Trees and vegetation should be kept trimmed to prevent from interfering with lighting.

Ensure that trash dumpsters and trash enclosures do not create blind spots or hiding areas.

Ensure that the airport perimeter is clearly defined by landscaping or fencing.

C. Access Control

The airport should have chain-link perimeter security fencing.

The perimeter of the airport should be completely fenced.

Vehicle access to the air-side area must be controlled or restricted by fencing, gates, use of security signs, access control, and security cameras.

Maintenance roads that provide access to the air-side area must be controlled at all times.

Law enforcement and emergency personnel should be provided a key or access code to all locked gates at the airport.

Security camera surveillance should be installed at the airport and monitored.

Pedestrian access must be controlled to air-side areas.

A photo-badge ID system should be in use for all staff, pilots, and aircraft owners based at the airport.

Sign-in/sign-out procedures should be in place for all transients (vendors, contractors, pilots) entering the air side.

D. Intrusion Detections System

An instruction detection system should be utilized to protect buildings and hangars.

The intrusion detection system should be certified by the Underwriters Laboratory.

The intrusion detection system should be tested daily.

The intrusion detection system should report to a contract central station or proprietary central station.

Automatic backup power supply that activates during power failures should be installed.

The intrusion detection system should employ antitamper technology.

E. Hangars

The airport has _____ conventional hangar buildings and _____
T-hangar buildings with a total capacity of _____ aircraft.
Each hangar should be equipped with padlocks on pedestrian doors
and a locking system for the main hangar doors.
It should be the policy of this airport to keep hangar doors shut and
locked when tenants are not present and aircraft are in the hangar.
Control vehicle and pedestrian traffic to hangars.

F. Aircraft

All aircraft owners should be encouraged to practice good security
with regard to their aircraft.
Pilots of all tie-down aircraft should be advised to lock or otherwise
secure aircraft with prop locks or throttle locks.
Logbooks and other valuables should be removed from aircraft.
Cockpit windows should be covered to prevent thieves from observ-
ing avionics and other contents.
Throttle and propeller locks and/or wheel locks should be installed.

G. Lighting

Hangar, fueling, flight school, and all key access areas must be well
lit from dusk to dawn.
Proper lighting levels should be maintained at all door and window
openings during hours of darkness.
Develop a schedule for maintenance inspections to ensure that lights
are in good working order at all times.

H. Signage

Restrictive signs should be posted at vehicular and pedestrian access
points to control access.
Clear signage related to perimeter, building entry, and visitor parking needs to be displayed.
No trespassing and restricted area signs should be posted along the
perimeter fencing and at restricted areas.

I. Fueling

100LL AvGas tank(s): Number _____ Capacity _____.
  Below/above ground? _____.
Jet A fuel tank(s): Number _____ Capacity _____.
  Below/above ground? _____.
MoGas tank(s): Number _____ Capacity _____.
  Below/above ground? _____.

Fueling pumps must be locked when the airport is unattended.

If 24-hour self-fueling is allowed at this airport, then access control cards or keys should be issued to the authorized individuals.

The fuel storage should not be accessible from exterior perimeter public roads.

The fueling area should be secured by fencing, security cameras, and locked when not in use or after operating hours of the airport.

Vehicle parking areas must separated from the fueling areas for security and safety.

Fuel trucks on the airport should be locked and parked in a secure fenced area of the airport.

J. Airport Layout

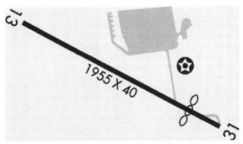

Figure C.1   Reigle Airport, 58 N.

K. Flight School Operations

- All flight school staff should be trained annually in accordance with Transportation Security Administration requirements.
- The identity of individuals renting aircraft or joining a flying club must be validated by checking a government-issued photo ID.

- There must be controls on a student pilot's access to aircraft keys until the student pilot has reached a specific point in the training curriculum that would include successful completion of the presolo written test.
- Before their solo, keep student pilots under the supervision of a flight instructor at all times.
- Have all student pilots check in with a specific flight instructor or management official before being allowed access to aircraft.
- Establish positive identification of any student pilot before every flight lesson.
- Be sure that if the student pilot is not yet a legal adult at the time of enrollment, do have the enrollment application, if applicable, cosigned by a parent or legal guardian.
- With rental and instruction aircraft, ensure that the aircraft ignition key differs from the door lock key.
- Ensure that only authorized personnel are issued keys to rental/flying club aircraft.
- Awareness training for all instructors, pilots, ramp personnel, and other flight school staff should be provided to advise them to be aware of suspicious activity on or near the airport to include the next four items:
- Aircraft with unusual or unauthorized modifications.
- Persons loitering for extended periods in the vicinity of parked aircraft or in air operations areas.
- Pilots who appear to be under the control of other persons.
- Persons wishing to obtain aircraft without presenting proper credentials or persons who present apparently valid credentials but do not have a corresponding level of aviation knowledge.

L. Restricted Areas

- Barriers such as fences and locked gates should be utilized to prevent unauthorized vehicles and pedestrians entry to restricted areas such as hangars, aircraft tie-downs, and fueling and fuel storage areas.
- Ramp personnel and regular airport users should be instructed to challenge and report unauthorized individuals in restricted areas.

- Ramp personnel and regular airport users should be instructed to report suspicious persons and activities to the airport management, the AOPA GA-SECURE number, or law enforcement authorities.
- Restricted areas must be properly posted to keep out unauthorized individuals.
- Signage should be prominently displayed near areas of public access warning against tampering with aircraft or unauthorized use of aircraft.
- The restricted areas should be fully secured with fencing.
- The fence and gates must always be in good repair.
- The security fence should be at least 7 feet high with a 1-foot top guard facing outward at a 45° angle.
- Adequate security lighting needs to be utilized during the hours of darkness.
- All gates should be secured with high-security padlocks.
- A security seal should be used on all locked gates in the restricted area.

M. Doors, Windows, and Utility Ports on Building and Hangars

Doors
- All exterior doors should be made of metal or solid core wood design.
- Sliding glass doors need to be equipped with supplemental pin locks and antilift devices.
- Exposed hinges need to have nonremovable pins.
- High-security dead-bolt locks should be used.
- The lock needs to be designed, or the doorframe constructed, so that the door cannot be forced open by spreading the frame.
- Key control of the doors is vital to the security of the structure.
- Doors with panic hardware must be properly secured to prevent opening and activation from the exterior.

Windows
- Unused windows should be permanently sealed. Are accessible windows protected by burglary-resistant glazing, security film, heavy screen, or bars wherever possible?

- Window locks need to be designed so they cannot be defeated by merely breaking the glass.
- Horizontal sliding windows need to be equipped with secondary locks and antilift devices.

Utility Ports
- Skylights should be protected by bars or polycarbonate glazing or an intrusion detection system.
- Roof hatches must be securely locked.
- Ports for ventilators or air conditioning ducts and fan openings must be adequately protected with bars or wire mesh.
- Roof ladders and other roof access points must be removed or secured against unauthorized use.
- Roll-up and sliding doors should be properly mounted and secured with high-quality locks.
- Utility rooms both inside and outside the building or hangar need to be properly secured.

N. Office and Cash-Handling Security

Office
- Restrict office keys to those who actually need them.
- Keep strict key control of the office keys issued and up-to-date records of the disposition of all office keys.
- Prohibit duplication of office keys except for those that are specifically ordered in writing.
- Mark "Do not duplicate" on all keys to prevent legitimate locksmiths from making copies without your knowledge.
- Procedures need to be in place for the collection of keys from terminated employees.
- All keys need to be stored in a secure wall cabinet.
- Secure all office equipment, such as computers and calculators, with some locking device.
- Keep a record showing issuance and return of every key, including name of person, date, and time.
- Use telephone locks to prevent unauthorized phone usage when offices are unattended.

- Provide secure areas for employees to store their personal property.
- Record all equipment serial numbers and file them in a safe place.
- Have a paper shredder and shred sensitive documents before discarding them.
- Lock briefcases and bags containing important material in a safe place when not in use.
- Insist on proper identification from all vendors and repair persons who come into the airport facility.
- Keep desk clear of important papers when the office is closed.
- Frequently change the combination to your safe.
- Emergency phone numbers should be posted near all phones.

Cash Handling
- Cash registers and cash drawers need to be located beyond the reach of customers.
- Make regular bank deposits or utilize an armored transport service to avoid keeping large sums of money in the office when closed.
- Train employees in proper cash-handling procedures.
- Employees need to be trained in proper procedures to follow during and after a robbery.
- Install panic/robbery alarm stations that may be used by employees during robberies or emergency situations.
- Leave cash registers and cash drawers empty and open after hours.

The Transportation Security Administration Airport Characteristics Measurement Tool is provided. It can be used to give guidance in the type of voluntary security measures that are recommended based on the airport and potential risk and threat to that airport.

TRANSPORTATION SECURITY ADMINISTRATION AIRPORT CHARACTERISTICS MEASUREMENT TOOL

Use this tool developed by the Transportation Security Administration to assess which security enhancements might be most appropriate for your airport. Each airport characteristic is assigned a point. Add points for every characteristic that applies to your facility.

TSA Assessment Scale

	Assessment Scale	
Security Characteristics	Public Use Facility	Private Use Facility
Location		
Within 30 nm of mass population area	5	3
Within 30 nm of a sensitive site	4	2
Falls within outer perimeter of Class B Airspace	3	1
Falls within the boundaries of restricted airspace	3	1
Based Aircraft		
Greater than 101 based aircraft	3	1
26–100 based aircraft	2	0
11–25 based aircraft	1	0
10 or fewer based aircraft	0	0
Based aircraft over 12,500 lbs	3	1
Runways		
Runway length greater than 5001 ft	5	3
Runway length less than 5000 ft, but greater than 2001 ft	4	2
Runway length 2000 ft or less	2	0
Asphalt or concrete runway	1	0
Operations		
Over 50,000 annual aircraft operations	4	2
Part 135 Operations	3	1
Part 137 Operations	3	1
Part 125 Operations	3	1
Flight Training	3	1
Flight Training in aircraft over 12,500 lbs	4	2
Rental Aircraft	4	2
Maintenance, Repair, and Overhaul facilities conducting long term storage of aircraft over 12,500 lbs	4	2
Total points		

SUGGESTED AIRPORT SECURITY ENHANCEMENTS

Use the accumulated score from the TSA Assessment Scale to determine the suggested security enhancements for your facility. Refer to the "TSA Guidelines for General Aviation Airports" for section reference.

Points/Suggested Guidelines

>45 Points

Fencing (Section 3.3.3)
Hangars (Section 3.3.1)
CCTV (Section 3.4.5)
Intrusion Detection System (Section 3.4.6)
Access Controls (Section 3.3.3)
Lighting System (Section 3.3.4)
Personal ID System (Section 3.3.6)
Vehicle ID System (Section 3.3.6)
Challenge Procedures (Section 3.4.1)
LEO (Law Enforcement Officer) Support (Section 3.4.4)
Security Committee (Section 3.4.3)
Transient Pilot Sign-In/Out Procedures (Section 3.1.4)
Signs (Section 3.3.5)
Documented Security Procedures (Section 3.5.1)
Positive Passenger/Cargo/Baggage ID (Section 3.1.1)
All Aircraft Secured (Section 3.2)
Community Watch Program (Section 3.4.1)
Contact List (Section 3.5.3)

25–44 Points

Access Controls (Section 3.3.3)
Lighting System (Section 3.3.4)
Personal ID System (Section 3.3.6)
Vehicle ID System (Section 3.3.6)
Challenge Procedures (Section 3.4.1)
LEO Support (Section 3.4.4)
Security Committee (Section 3.4.3)
Transient Pilot Sign-In/Out Procedures (Section 3.1.4)

continued

Points/Suggested Guidelines (continued)

Signs (Section 3.3.5)
Documented Security Procedures (Section 3.5.1)
Positive Passenger/Cargo/Baggage ID (Section 3.1.1)
All Aircraft Secured (Section 3.2)
Community Watch Program (Section 3.4.1)
Contact List (Section 3.5.3)

Suggested Airport Security Enhancements

Use the accumulated score from the TSA Assessment Scale to determine the suggested security enhancements for your facility. Refer to the "TSA Guidelines for General Aviation Airports" for section reference.

Points/Suggested Guidelines

15–24 Points

LEO Support (Section 3.4.4)
Security Committee (Section 3.4.3)
Transient Pilot Sign-In/Out Procedures (Section 3.1.4)
Signs (Section 3.3.5)
Documented Security Procedures (Section 3.5.1)
Positive Passenger/Cargo/Baggage ID (Section 3.1.1)
All Aircraft Secured (Section 3.2)
Community Watch Program (Section 3.4.1)
Contact List (Section 3.5.3)

0–14 Points

Signs (Section 3.3.5)
Documented Security Procedures (Section 3.5.1)
Positive Passenger/Cargo/Baggage ID (Section 3.1.1)
All Aircraft Secured (Section 3.2)
Community Watch Program (Section 3.4.1)
Contact List (Section 3.5.3)

PART IV: SECURITY AND LAW ENFORCEMENT SUPPORT

A. Airport Watch Program

- The airport should use the AOPA Watch Program.
- AOPA Watch signs should be posted at strategic locations.
- Local police need to be aware of the Airport Watch Program.

B. Routine Patrols

- A law enforcement agency should provide for routine patrols.
- Law enforcement personnel should be trained on building, hangar, locations, runways, and airport operation procedures.
- Law enforcement personnel should be trained on airport/aircraft communication procedures.
- Proprietary or contract security patrols should be considered to provide security for the airport.

PART V: INCIDENT REPORTING/EMERGENCY RESPONSE

A. Suspicious Activity

- Notify the following:
- Airport manager
- Fixed-base operator
- AOPA Airport Watch

B. Criminal Activity, Bomb Threats, Terrorism, or other Emergency

- Call 911 and initiate emergency response plan.
- Restrict site access until it is secured by public safety staff.
- Notify airport manager/airport security coordinator, fixed-base operator, tenants, key airport staff.
- Contact Flight Standards District Office (FSDO).
- Call 24/7 FAA Operations Center.

SIGNATURE PAGE

Signed this _____ day of _____, 2012

_____

Airport Manager

_____

Mailing Address

_____

City/State/Zip

_____

Telephone

APPENDIX C: THE IMPACT OF THE AIRCRAFT OWNERS AND PILOTS ASSOCIATION AIRPORT WATCH PROGRAM ON CRIME AT PENNSYLVANIA GENERAL AVIATION AIRPORTS

THE IMPACT OF THE AIRCRAFT OWNERS AND PILOTS ASSOCIATION AIRPORT WATCH PROGRAM ON CRIME AT PENNSYLVANIA GENERAL AVIATION AIRPORTS

by

Daniel J. Benny, Ph.D.

© Daniel J. Benny, 2010

Capella University

ABSTRACT

The study examined the Aircraft Owners and Pilots Association (AOPA) Airport Watch program that has been implemented at general aviation airports throughout the Commonwealth of Pennsylvania in an endeavor to prevent and reduce crime at general aviation airports. The study's sample included 122 general aviation airports located in the Commonwealth of Pennsylvania. Data were collected using an e-mailed questionnaire. The purpose of this study was to examine the descriptive differences between the characteristics of the general aviation airports and determine the effects of the AOPA Airport Watch program on crime at the airports that adopted this program during the period from 2002 to 2004 using an ex post facto design. In addition, the Routine Activity theory was used to conceptualize the research questions. The study with the focus on the AOPA Airport Watch program and the impact it had on crime at general aviation airports in the Commonwealth of Pennsylvania could suggest the impact of the Airport Watch program across the United States.

DEDICATION

This is dedicated to all security and aviation professionals in the United States and my loyal dog Magnum.

ACKNOWLEDGMENTS

Jennifer Rounds-Bryant, Ph.D., Faculty Mentor and Chair
Craig J. Spencer, Vice President Aviation Security AOPA
Kathleen R. Martian, FASSTA Team Program Manager FAA
General Aviation Airports in the Commonwealth of Pennsylvania
Embry-Riddle Aeronautical University

TABLE OF CONTENTS

LIST OF TABLES

Chapter 1

Introduction

INTRODUCTION TO THE PROBLEM

In March 2003, the Aircraft Owners and Pilots Association developed the Airport Watch program. The goals of the Airport Watch program were to enhance security at general aviation airports, to aid in the prevention and reduction of crime in the general aviation community, and to prevent mandated security regulations from the Transportation Security Administration (AOPA, 2003). This was the focus of the completed research along with the application of the Routine Activity theory.

The Routine Activity theory has been utilized in the analysis of crime watch programs and the programs' impact on the crime (Cohen & Felson, 1979). The Routine Activity theory is based on the assumption that a perpetrator seeking to commit a criminal act will examine the routine or day-to-day activity of the target. Since people are creatures of habit and establish routines, individuals and business operations have established routines. Based on the Routine Activity theory, an individual seeking to take part in criminal activity will use this routine or predictable behavior of the individuals at the target site to their advantage in taking part in criminal activity. It will allow the perpetrator to commit the crime at a time best suited to allow access to their target in a situation in which the offender is most likely to accomplish the criminal act and not be identified or apprehended for taking part in such criminal activity (Vold, Bernard, & Snipes, 2002).

To counter such threats, the target individual or business must take steps to counter such criminal acts by changing the routine and introducing capable guardians that can discourage and prevent criminal activity from occurring. Capable guardians according to the theory would include the use of security officers, lighting, security awareness training, access control in the form of fencing, CCTV, use of card access and locks (Cohen & Felson, 1979).

The Routine Activity theory was tested by evaluating the Aircraft Owners and Pilots Association Airport Watch program. The evaluation of the Aircraft Owners and Pilots Association Airport watch program tested the Routine Activity theory by exploring if the use of capable guardians at general aviation airports as recommend by the Aircraft Owners and Pilots Association Airport watch program had an impact on crime. The capable guardians are the central component of the Routine Activity theory and the airport watch program because the premise for committing a criminal act at a location can be dependent on the effective use of guardians that establish barriers and changes in the environment that may impact the decision of a perpetrator to commit a criminal act at a location (Cohen & Felson, 1979).

BACKGROUND OF THE STUDY

The Aircraft Owners and Pilots Association Airport Watch program is not a new concept as it is based on existing crime watch programs. The modern concepts of the community crime watch programs were conceived and implemented in the United States during the 1970s. These neighborhood crime prevention programs were based on two crime prevention models: (1) social control and (2) opportunity diminution. In 1975, research was conducted in the state of Washington encompassing the cities of Seattle and Portland. The research that was conducted in the two cities in the state of Washington concluded that the crime watch programs that were implemented that included the posting of crime watch signs, increased lighting, police patrols, and community involvement resulted in a significant reduction in the crime rate in the two cities that were studied (Lindsay & McGillis, 1986). Another significant study was one that evaluated the crime watch programs in London, England, in 1987. In that research, it was concluded that such crime watch and prevention programs did not result in a reduction in crime, but it did make the residences of the area feel much safer as it relates to crime and the incidents that took place in their community (Bennett, 1989).

Some research related to crime prevention and commercial aviation has been accomplished. In 2005, a qualitative study was conducted within the United States airline industry. The goal was to evaluate the fears of pilots, aircrew, and passengers related to the implementation of the new Department of Homeland Security commercial airport and airline crime prevention procedures. The research did indicate that all target areas of the study, pilots, aircrew, and passengers had reduced fears from terrorism and aviation crime with the implementation of the new Department of Homeland Security crime prevention and security programs. The elements of the new program include use of Department of Homeland Security screeners at commercial airports, improved security detection equipment, secure doors on airline cockpits, the carrying of weapons by airline pilots, and increased security awareness training of employees working in the airline profession. While the study did cover commercial aviation airports and airline carriers, it did not examine crime prevention and crime at general aviation airports, which is the nature of this research (Wiencek, 2005). Since the events of September 11, 2001, the revelations of the use of the general aviation community by the terrorists and the establishment of the Aircraft Owners and Pilots Association Airport Watch program, there has been no research on the impact of the Aircraft Owners and Pilots Association Airport Watch crime prevention program and crime at general aviation airports.

The AOPA Airport Watch program encompasses two concepts related to security. The two concepts are physical security and security awareness. As it relates to physical security, the program recommends and encourages general aviation airport managers, aircraft owners, and pilots to utilize physical security practices to prevent and reduce crime (AOPA, 2003).

The security awareness aspect of the program focuses on making general aviation airport owners and employees, as well as aircraft owners and pilots, aware of their surroundings. This includes being aware as to what is considered normal activity at the general aviation airports and what is not (AOPA, 2003). General aviation aircraft are non-commercial aircraft that may be owned and operated by a private individual, corporation or public safety organization such as police or emergency service organization (Sweet, 2009).

The crimes that may occur at a general aviation airport would be crimes against persons, the airport property, or the fixed-base operation (FBO), and aircraft located at the airport in hangars or at the aircraft tie-down area. Crimes against a person would include any crime that has an impact on the person or victim of the crime who is at the airport. This would include the crimes of murder, rape, robbery, assault, stalking, kidnapping, and harassment (Sweet, 2009).

Crimes against airport property or the FBO only affect the physical structures at the airport. Such crimes would include burglary, theft, arson, and vandalism. The crimes that could be perpetrated against the aircraft situated in a hangar or tie-down area at the airports would include theft of the aircraft, theft of aircraft avionics, sabotage of the aircraft, hijacking, and vandalism (Sweet, 2009). There has been no research conducted on commercial aviation security and crime prevention programs since the terrorist attack in September 2001. There is a solid foundation of research on what is known as traditional community crime prevention programs that operate in the United States and in the United Kingdom. While there has been research related to traditional crime prevention programs, there has been no research conducted related to general aviation and the Aircraft Owners and Pilots Association Airport Watch program or general aviation security and crime prevention programs at airports (Sweet, 2004).

STATEMENT OF THE PROBLEM

The impact of crime prevention efforts such as the Aircraft Owners and Pilots Association Airport Watch crime prevention program is not known because of the lack of research in this area of the aviation community. This lack of research has created a gap in the knowledge related to general aviation and such programs. This limited knowledge and research leaves the general aviation community without a baseline of knowledge and information on the impact of crime prevention programs at general aviation airports such as the Aircraft Owners and Pilots Association Airport Watch program that had been established and adopted (Bisignani, 2006).

PURPOSE OF THE STUDY

The completed research bridged the gap between community crime watch research and commercial aviation crime prevention research. This was accomplished by providing new knowledge with regard to the impact of general aviation security and the Aircraft Owners and Pilots Association Airport Watch program. The completed research provided a comprehensive and a complete review of the Aircraft Owners and Pilots Association Airport Watch program at general aviation airports in the Commonwealth of Pennsylvania. The relationship between the Aircraft Owners and Pilots Association Airport Watch program and the crime at the general aviation airports was examined. The purpose of the study was to determine effects of the AOPA Airport Watch program on crime at the airports that adopted this program during the period from 2002 to 2004 using an ex post facto design.

One of the tenets of the Routine Activity theory is that the offender will make a decision to take part in criminal activity based on the situation and opportunities at the target location. The offender will use the routine activity of the target to their advantage. The Aircraft Owners and Pilots Association Airport Watch program proposes security measures that can manipulate the opportunities of the offender (Clarke & Cornish, 1983).

RATIONALE AND SIGNIFICANCE OF THE STUDY

The rationale and significance of the completed research provided general aviation administrators, aircraft owners, and security practitioners with a new and relevant knowledge base that will be useful to practitioners at the general aviation airports in the Commonwealth of Pennsylvania. This is an area in which no research has been conducted, resulting in a failure to bridge the gap in the professional research related to general aviation security and crime prevention. This new knowledge will contribute to the Routine Activity theory and the prevention of crime in an environment that has not been researched before. The results of the study did bridge the gap and provided the general aviation community and security practitioners with useful knowledge on which future research can be built.

This new information that was developed in the study will also be of value to scholars. This would include scholars who conduct research and teach general aviation security and criminal justice crime prevention theories and procedures. They may be working at colleges and universities, as well as for governmental and private research institutions. Many professional organizations related to security, criminal justice, and aviation also utilize scholars who could benefit from the research conducted in this study.

RESEARCH QUESTIONS AND HYPOTHESES

The research examined and answered the following questions:

Research Question 1

Is there a difference in the number of crimes between general aviation airports that have adopted the Aircraft Owners and Pilots Association Airport Watch program and those that have not?

> H1. There is a difference in the number of crimes between general aviation airports that have adopted the Aircraft Owners and Pilots Association Airport Watch program and those that have not.
>
> Ho1. There is no difference in the number of crimes between general aviation airports that have adopted the Aircraft Owners and Pilots Association Airport Watch program and those that have not.

Research Question 2

Is there a difference in the routine activity between general aviation airports that have adopted the program and those that have not?

> H2. There is a difference in the routine activity between general aviation airports that have adopted the program and those that have not.
>
> Ho2. There is no difference in the routine activity between general aviation airports that have adopted the program and those that have not.

NATURE OF THE STUDY

The ex post facto design was developed that utilized an intervention group and one control group to study the impact on crime by the Aircraft Owners and Pilots Association Airport Watch program the year before implementation of the program in 2002, in 2003, and the year after the implementation of the program in 2004. These two groups were general aviation airports in the Commonwealth of Pennsylvania that have adopted the Aircraft Owners and Pilots Association Airport Watch program, the intervention group, and all general aviation airports in Pennsylvania that have not adopted the Aircraft Owners and Pilots Association Airport Watch program, the control group. A questionnaire titled, "Aircraft Owners and Pilots Association Airport Watch Program Questionnaire," was utilized to conduct a survey by telephone and mail of the general aviation airports in the Commonwealth of Pennsylvania.

DEFINITION OF TERMS

Card Access. Card access is an electronic card reader that controls the access to structures by unlocking doors and also records who has entered or left the facility (Fischer & Green, 2004).

Capable Guardians. Capable guardians are protective measures such as intrusion detection systems, CCTV, fencing, access control, and use of security officers that have been established and put in place at general aviation airports in the Commonwealth of Pennsylvania to provide protection and prevent crime under the Routine Activity theory (Boetig, 2006).

CCTV. CCTV or closed circuit television is a monitoring system that is utilized in security and crime prevention programs to monitor areas of risk (Fischer & Green, 2004).

General Aviation Aircraft. General aviation aircraft are non-commercial aircraft that may be owned and operated by a private individual, corporation, or public safety organization such as police or emergency service organization (Sweet, 2004).

General Aviation Airports. General aviation airports are airport that are used for non-commercial, private aircraft (Sweet, 2004).

Crime. Actions committed by a perpetrator that are violations of the Crimes Code of Pennsylvania and would include murder, rape, robbery, assault, stalking, kidnapping, and harassment (Sweet, 2004).

Commercial Aircraft. Commercial aircraft are aircraft that carry passengers or cargo for a fee (Sweet, 2004).

Fixed-Base Operation. A fixed-base operation is the administrative or managerial area of a general aviation airport (Sweet, 2004).

Intrusion Detection Systems. Intrusion detection systems (IDSs) are alarm systems that activate when an intrusion onto the protected property is identified and are used at general aviation airports. This allows for a response by security or law enforcement officers (Fischer & Green, 2004).

Local Police. Local police are law enforcement officers that are authorized by a city, town, or township to enforce the laws of the state and the community in which they were hired (Fischer & Green, 2004).

Physical Security. This includes intrusion detection systems, card access/locks, fencing, CCTV, lighting, and use of security officers.

Routine Activity. This is activity at a general aviation airport that is common practice each day that follows the same schedule and is predictable.

Routine Activity Theory. A theory developed by Cohen and Felson for analyzing crime trends based on activity at the target location.

Security Awareness Training. Security training is education covering the protection of general aviation airports that is provided to airport staff and flight instructors (Fischer & Green, 2004).

Security Lighting. Lighting used for security applications in general aviation airports to deter crime (Fischer & Green, 2004).

Security Patrol. A security patrol is the utilization of a private security officer at a general aviation airport to deter or respond to crime and other emergency situations that may occur at a general aviation airport (Fischer & Green, 2004).

State Police. State police are law enforcement officers who are authorized to enforce the laws of the state, with the authority coming from the state legislature of said state (Fischer & Green, 2004).

ASSUMPTIONS AND LIMITATIONS

The researcher assumed that all of the 122 general aviation airports in the Commonwealth of Pennsylvania have been exposed to the Aircraft Owners and Pilots Association Airport Watch program because notification of the program was sent to all of the general aviation airports in the United States, including Pennsylvania. The researcher states that not all of the airports in Pennsylvania have adopted the Aircraft Owners and Pilots Association Airport Watch program.

Regarding the methodological assumption, the researcher purports that the ex post facto design was the best method to conduct the research to examine the intervention and the control groups without the need for manipulation of the target groups since the manipulation has already occurred after the implementation of the Aircraft Owners and Pilots Association Airport Watch program. The researcher states that the Routine Activity theory was applied to the research because the adoption of the Airport Watch program, which includes the awareness and the use of physical security measures, will modify the routine activity at the airport and take away the sense of privacy and predictability with the introduction of the guardians (Criswell, 2003).

The limitations of the research can be attributed to the use of the ex post facto design. The utilization of this design does not allow for any current manipulation of the intervention and control groups during the research by the researcher since the manipulation has already occurred with the adoption of the Aircraft Owners and Pilots Association Airport Watch program in 2003 compared to a true experimental design that is subject to random treatment of the study group. The final results of the research were based on what occurred prior to the start of this research and the impact of crime on general aviation airports in Pennsylvania that adopted the Aircraft Owners and Pilots Association Airport Watch program (Criswell, 2003).

Because of the fact that the only source of crime data for the research was from the general aviation airports, the accuracy of the crime data was dependent on the proper recording of crime data information by the researcher in the survey provided to the general aviation airports during a phone interview. Additional limitations could have occurred due to lack of control related to factors in the research. This lack of control could have resulted in the inability to establish a cause-and-effect relationship. There are those who view the ex post facto design as not being flexible and not a reliable method of research (Vold et al., 2002). This is because during the research the outcome could have arrived from a different cause. This is due to the fact that it has a limited casual validity because there is no control of the experiment since it already occurred. The design could not measure cause and effect because the study, in this research related to crime at general aviation airports, is being completed after the fact. The Aircraft Owners and Pilots Association Airport Watch program was developed in 2003. This study did explore the crime at general aviation airports in the Commonwealth of Pennsylvania between 2002 and 2004. Based on the fact that the time has passed, the researcher used the ex post facto design (Champion, 2006).

There was the possibility of some differences between the interventions and the comparison groups as it relates to variables that might have had an impact on dependent variables such as location of the airport, police presence, the size of the police force, frequency of police patrols, police crime prevention efforts, changes in population, the impact of funding such as grants, changes in public safety rules or guidelines, airport security patrols, airport security training, and the utilization of physical security measures.

The Static Group Comparison was explored during the study of the two research groups. The two research groups, the airports that received experimental treatment by adopting the Aircraft Owners and Pilots Association Watch Program and those that have not adopted the Aircraft Owners and Pilots Association Watch Program, were examined to determine if there was a difference (Vold et al., 2002).

Chapter 2
Literature Review

INTRODUCTION

The research did bridge the gap between traditional community crime watch studies and the research that has been directed on commercial aviation crime prevention programs. This was accomplished by providing new research regarding the impact of general aviation security and the Aircraft Owners and Pilots Association Airport Watch program on crime at general aviation airports in the Commonwealth of Pennsylvania. The Aircraft Owners and Pilots Association Airport Watch program was established in 2003. It is the first and only crime watch program developed for general aviation airports and is still in operation in the Commonwealth of Pennsylvania and in the United States. The research did provide a review and comprehensive evaluation of the issues related to the Aircraft Owners and Pilots Association Airport Watch program at general aviation airports in the Commonwealth of Pennsylvania. It also explained the relationship between the Aircraft Owners and Pilots Association Airport Watch program and the crime at the general aviation airports that were examined in the research (AOPA, 2003).

The Aircraft Owners and Pilots Association Airport Watch program is based on the concepts of traditional crime watch programs. There has been no research conducted with regard to general aviation airports and the Aircraft Owners and Pilots Association Airport Watch program or any other general aviation crime watch program. The purpose of this study that was conducted was to evaluate the effects of the Aircraft Owners and Pilots Association Airport Watch program on crime at the airports that adopted this program during the period from 2002 to 2004. The ex post facto design was utilized for this study (AOPA, 2003).

The concepts of the Routine Activity theory were also examined in the research to determine if the offender made a decision to take part in criminal activity based on the situations and opportunities at the target airport location. As described in the theory, the offender will use the routine activity of the target to their advantage. The Aircraft Owners and Pilots Association Airport Watch program includes security measures such as the use of security officers, lighting, fencing, card access, locks, intrusion detection systems, and CCTV, which can create an impact on the opportunities of the offender by altering the routine activity at the airport to the disadvantage of the perpetrator (Clarke & Cornish, 1983).

The themes of the review of the literature included an examination of the writings and research that has been conducted as it relates to the Aircraft Owners and Pilots Association Airport Watch program to determine if any critical research has been explored and documented. This study did build on that existing research and expand the professional database of information on the topic. There was no significant research related to the Aircraft Owners and Pilots Association Airport Watch program; this study did break new ground in that area of research and built a foundation for further studies related to this general aviation security topic.

Due to the lack of research related to general aviation and commercial aviation crime prevention, a review of literature related to traditional crime prevention programs supports the concepts of crime prevention and the application of the Routine Activity theory and its relation to crime activity and crime prevention in various cities in the United States. Several traditional crime prevention programs will be evaluated because of their significant contribution to the professional literature related to crime prevention programs.

An examination of the literature related to commercial aviation crime watch programs was also explored since it is closely related to the general aviation security and crime prevention concerns. This relationship is based on the type of industry, even if the operations of the two types of aviation, general aviation and commercial aviation, are different in that general aviation is for private and public safety aircraft use and commercial is for paying clients who utilize aircraft for transportation of individuals or cargo (AOPA, 2003).

The next area of review was the traditional crime watch programs that have been established in neighborhoods across the United States. They are based on police crime prevention programs that have been in use since Sir Robert Peel established the Metropolitan Police of London, England, in 1829 (Bennett, 1989). These crime prevention programs are relevant to general aviation security concerns and the Aircraft Owners and Pilots Association Airport Watch program because they both deal with private, non-governmental crime prevention programs that have an impact on individuals, private business, non-commercial neighborhoods, or private general airport operations (AOPA, 2003).

THEORETICAL FRAMEWORK

The Routine Activity theory was selected to be tested as part of the research of the Aircraft Owners and Pilots Association Airport Watch program and the impact of that program on crime at general aviation airports in the Commonwealth of Pennsylvania. The rationale for the selection of the Routine Activity theory is because the implantation of the Aircraft Owners and Pilots Association Airport Watch program embraces the two important concepts of the Routine Activity theory.

The Routine Activity theory was developed by Lawrence Cohen and Marcus Felson in 1979. The theory was utilized to study the crime rate in the United States between the period of 1947 and 1974 (Cohen & Felson, 1979).

One of the concepts of the Routine Activity theory includes the premise that perpetrators seeking to take part in criminal activity will examine the routine events and activities of a neighborhood or target location where they intend to commit a crime. If the target is an individual, the perpetrator will study the routine activity of the individual who is targeted. By exploring this routine activity of a location or an individual and identifying flaws and vulnerabilities in security procedures, it allows the perpetrator to plan their criminal activity during a period of time that will be most successful to the perpetrator. Utilizing that method of operation falls within the concepts of the Routine Activity theory (Cohen & Felson, 1979).

Another concept of the Routine Activity theory includes the examination of the use of capable guardians that can change the routine activity at the target location or of an individual who may be targeted. The use of the capable guardians, such as schedule changes and security measures that include the use of security officers, CCTV, fencing, lighting, intrusion detection, and access control systems, can change the routine schedule and activities. This change in routine activity through the introduction of capable guardians may prevent a perpetrator from carrying out their criminal activity and have a positive impact on crime against the location or targeted individual (Cohen & Felson, 1979).

There have been studies in the past that examined the Routine Activity theory. Perhaps the most comprehensive study dealing with the Routine Activity theory was the research conducted by Lawrence Cohen and Marcus Fleson, which was published in 1979. The research examined social changes and trends in crime rates through the lens of the Routine Activity theory. In the published study, the researchers considered paradoxical trends in the rate of crime and the relationship to a change in the routine activity of the potential targets or victims of the perpetrators. It was the belief of the researchers that any structural change in everyday patterns, or what they identified as routine activity, can have an impact on criminal activity and the crime rate by disturbing the space and time considered to be key factors in direct-contact predatory criminal activity. The key factors as described by the researchers include a motivated offender who will take advantage of the lack of security to act in a criminal manner. There must be a suitable target and, according to the researchers, a lack of security or capable guardians that can be utilized and put in place as a prevention to crime (Cohen & Felson, 1979).

Cohen and Felson concluded in their research that there was a statistically positive significant relationship between the activity in the homes and the rate of crime in the neighborhood in which the homes were located. Based on the results of the research, they argued that the Routine Activity theory is valid, and that a change in the capable guardians and the routine activity around a home can have a significant impact on the crime rate. Cohen and Felson provided a new outlook on crime prevention. Their focus on the criminal act rather than on the criminal as well as how capable guardians and changes in activity impacted the criminal activity was a new and significant approach to the research of crime prevention (Cohen & Felson, 1979).

Parsi Boetig in 2006 conducted research exploring the Routine Activity theory as a model for addressing a very specific crime issue. The research explores the use of the Routine Activity theory at a specific setting, that being the campus environment. Rather than looking at a more open and public environment such as a neighborhood in a city or town, a campus environment was selected for the research (Boetig, 2006).

The study concluded that the Routine Activity theory presents an alternative approach to the examination of the impact of a crime prevention program. The study further stated that with the Routine Activity theory, the researcher can determine the impact on crime based on the actions of the target individual or location. This is accomplished through the examination of the use of capable guardians and the changes in the routine of daily activity on the part of the potential individual or institutional victim of crime. The Routine Activity theory provided an alternative lens through which to view and examine the impact of a crime prevention program on the reduction of crime at a given location. Other conceptual models support the study, such as the research by Richard Culp and Elizabeth Bracco that explored prison escapes. The study concluded that prison escapes occur when the inmates, after a study of the prison security activities, identify a weakness and low threat to apprehension if they try and escape (Culp and Bracco, 2005).

When examining the professional literature with regard to research on crime prevention at other airports, only one significant study emerges that examined commercial airports. That research is the 2004 study of the impact of recent airport security interventions on commercial aviation carriers and airports since the terrorist attack of September 11, 2001. That qualitative study, conducted by Turney, Bishop, and Fitzgerald and published in the *Journal of Air Transportation*, examined the impact of new aviation security measures on how safe airline pilots, crew, and passengers felt since the implementation of the new security procedures (Turney, Bishop, & Fitzgerald, 2004).

The new security procedures addressed in the 2004 study include the establishment the United States Department of Homeland Security Transportation Security Administration and its new role in providing security screening to passengers and cargo bound for commercial aircraft at commercial aviation airports. This includes the quality of the individuals hired by the Transportation Security Administration and the screening equipment utilized such as x-ray, metal detectors, and explosives detectors. The study also addressed the operational effectiveness of such security measures and the new restrictions regarding what was permitted to be carried onto a commercial aircraft and the items that are now prohibited (Turney et al., 2004).

The study also explored additional new security measures implemented since the terrorist attack of September 11, 2001. This included such security measures as the hardening of aircraft cockpit doors with reinforcement of the doors and locking devices. The carrying of firearms by the pilot and copilot of commercial aircraft was also a new security measure that was implemented. The research also examined other new security measures, including increased security training for all flight crew members in the identification of possible threat situations and how to react to such incidents. New operational procedures by the pilot and copilot as well as the United States military air response in the event of a hijacking of a commercial aircraft were also considered in the research (Turney et al., 2004).

The qualitative study concluded that airline pilots, crew, and passengers felt safer with the introduction of the new security procedures in the commercial airports and on the commercial airlines. The research was focused on how safe the pilots, crew, and passengers felt and did not examine the number or impact of such crimes related to the introduction of the new security measures. While not part of the 2004 study, since an aircraft has not been hijacked since the establishment of the new security procedures at the airports and on the commercial airlines, one could come to the conclusion from a quantitative approach that there was a reduction in crime related to the hijacking of a commercial aircraft based on the new security measures (Turney et al., 2004).

The research on commercial aviation also focused on the Rational Choice theory; based on the increased security at the commercial airports, any attempt to hijack an aircraft would result in detection and the inability to carry out the criminal act. The application of the Routine Activity theory to the study that was completed on commercial aviation can be accomplished when examining some of the new security measures that were implemented (Turney et al., 2004). With the changes in the security screening procedures and airline security enhancements, the routine activity of the airport and airlines security programs changed. This change in routine activity as seen in the commercial aviation study can prevent and reduce crime.

This research conducted by Turney, Bishop, and Fitzgerald is unique in that it is the only study that addressed the security of commercial airports and commercial airlines (Turney et al., 2004). It is also significant in that the results were viewed through the lens of a qualitative study that concluded the new security measures did have a positive impact on how the airline pilots, crew, and passengers felt with regard to safety and security. After examining the research, one can make the inference from the quantitative lens that since there has been no hijacking of United States commercial aircraft since the integration of the new security procedure into the overall security program, that in addition to individuals feeling positive, secure, and safe when flying and traveling on commercial aircraft, the new security procedures in the airports and on the airlines did in fact reduce crime.

The traditional neighborhood crime watch programs now used in the United States began in the 1970s with funding from the Law Enforcement Assistance Administration along with the National Institute of Justice in the form of grants that were provided to police agencies through-out the United States (Schmalleger, 2007). The concept of self-protection by the citizens is not new to security and law enforcement in the United States. While the crime prevention program format that is now in place in the United States began in the 1970s, the use of citizens to protect the neighborhoods began while the colonies were under British rule in the 1700s (Schmalleger, 2007). During that period of time, law enforcement consisted of sheriffs and constables to keep the peace. Their primary goal was to support the crown, and they did not provide security for the shops and homes of the towns in the colonies. Town watches were established to provide protection for the communities. The town watch consisted of private citizens who patrolled the community at night to prevent and reduce crime. These town watch programs began in the cities of Philadelphia, Boston, and New York City. These private town watches became the foundation of the paid public police departments in the larger cities of the United States (Schmalleger, 2007).

One of the first crime prevention programs to be studied was the Seattle, Washington, Neighborhood Watch program, which was funded by grants from the Law Enforcement Assistance Administration. The watch program included home security surveys, the engraving of property, meet-ings, the use of lighting around the homes, the posting of neighborhood watch signs, and members of the community being observant to possible suspicious and criminal activity. The components of the research included the comparison of crime data from residential burglaries before the incep-tion of the crime watch program and a year after the inception of the pro-gram. The second component of the study was to examine if there was a difference not only in the number of residential burglaries but also in the frequency of reporting residential burglaries (Lindsay & McGillis, 1986).

Based on the results of the research, it was determined that the fre-quency of reported residential burglaries did not increase during the study period. Based on the findings of the research, it was sufficient for the researchers to make the determination that the Seattle, Washington, Crime Watch program was a success (Lindsay & McGillis, 1986). With the increase of security awareness, the perpetrators would be placed in a situ-ation in which it was more likely that they would be caught and made the rational choice for their own survival not to take part in burglaries in the neighborhood that had established a crime watch program (Lindsay & McGillis, 1986).

A more recent study of a community crime watch program was conducted in the city of Cincinnati, Ohio, in 1997 (Smith, Novack, &

Hurley, 1997). The goal of the research was to evaluate if there was a relationship between crime and the number of crime watch programs that had been implemented in Cincinnati. The Strain theory was the focus of the ex post facto design, and the conclusion of the research supported this theory. It was determined that the number of crime watch programs that were established in all areas of Cincinnati, Ohio, did not have an impact on the crime. The research established that there were other variables, including poverty, population increase, mobility, and racial heterogeneity, that contributed to the finding of the study (Smith et al., 1997).

Upon review of the research and the findings, it would appear that there would be no means to associate the Routine Activity theory to the reduction of crime. The utilization of the concept of the Routine Activity theory would not be suitable in that situation and research project. The Strain theory would be the appropriate theory based on the research that was conducted.

A 2005 study of neighborhood watch programs in Texas was conducted by Claudia San Miguel in which the operational characteristics of the watch programs were researched to determine the relationship between residential burglaries and the characteristics of the Texas watch programs. The research concluded that there was a variation in the programs across the state of Texas, but that there was no significant difference in the residential burglary rate between the various watch programs in Texas (San Miguel, 2005).

The research of the Texas watch programs did not focus on a criminology theory but was rather a quantitative look at the crime rates across the state and an examination of the impact of the crime watch programs. As with all crime watch programs, various criminology theories can be argued as being the most suitable based on the situation and type of crime watch program. The Routine Activity theory could be applicable to these crime watch programs just as the Routine Activity theory has been identified with other crime watch programs across the United States (San Miguel, 2005).

CRUCIAL CONCEPTUAL DEBATES

When researching crime watch programs, there can be a debate as to the effectiveness of the programs being studied based on the location, components of the watch program, and the method of research that was used during the study. The more interesting debate with regard to crime watch programs is that of the criminology theory that can be used to explain why a crime watch program may have failed to reduce crime or why it was successful in reducing crime in the neighborhoods where the research took place. The two theories often cited, the Routine Activity theory developed by Lawrence Cohen and Marcus Felson and the Rational Choice theory inspired by Cesare Beccaria and elaborated by Jeremy Bentham, can be debated as to which is the actual reason for the reduction in crime where a crime watch program has been established (Boetig, 2006).

The Routine Activity theory is the criminology theory that was presented for the Aircraft Owners and Pilots Association Airport Watch program; it is based on the assumption that an individual seeking to take part in criminal acts will look at the routine activity of the target. Individuals are creatures of habit and establish routines; individuals and business operations such as general aviation airports have established routines. Based on the Routine Activity theory, a perpetrator will use this routine or predictable behavior of the individuals at the general aviation airports to their advantage in taking part in criminal activity. It will allow the perpetrator to commit the crime at a time best suited to the offender with access to their target in a situation in which the offender is most likely to accomplish the criminal act and not be identified or apprehended for taking part in such criminal activity. To counter such threats, the target individual or business, and in the case of this study a general aviation airport, must takes steps to counter such criminal acts. This is done by changing the routine at the airport and introducing capable guardians that can discourage and prevent criminal activity from occurring, such as the use of security patrols, CCTV, fencing, lighting, and access control devices (Fischer & Green, 2004).

Another criminology theory that could be rationalized as the reason for the reduction in crime when crime watch programs are utilized is the Rational Choice theory. In this theory, it is supposed that all individuals, including those with criminal intent, have the ability to make a rational choice between committing the crime or not taking part in the criminal act. Often, this is based on the evaluation of whether the perpetrator can take part in the criminal act and not be identified or apprehended. In the debate with regard to crime watch programs, the perpetrator could make a decision not to take part in the crime based on the Rational Choice theory because of countermeasures that have been put in place, or the capable guardians that have been established, created an atmosphere in which the perpetrator felt it was not safe to take part in the crime as they may be apprehended and prosecuted. This is because the offender evaluated the risk and made a rational choice not to commit the crime because of the fear of being exposed (Boetig, 2006).

When conducting research on a crime watch program such as the Aircraft Owners and Pilots Association Airport Watch, one can make the argument that the Rational Choice theory should be employed. The rationale for that decision would be that the countermeasures put in place, including the change in the routine activity at the general aviation airports, created an atmosphere in which the perpetrator believed there was too much risk to take part in the criminal activity. The offender made a conscious decision using rational choice in the thinking process regarding the decision to commit a crime.

When using the Rational Choice theory, the emphasis is on the offender and not the crime watch program. In most situations in which a crime is or is not committed, the offender will examine the risk and make the rational choice to take part in the criminal act or not. The more important aspect of a crime watch program such as the Aircraft Owners and Pilots Association Airport Watch program was to determine if the capable guardians or security countermeasures and the change in the routine activity of the general aviation airport contributed to the prevention and reduction in criminal activity. While the Rational Choice theory was useful to the study of the Aircraft Owners and Pilots Association Airport Watch program, the focus is the capable guardians, a key factor of the Routine Activity theory, and the impact on crime better supports the hypothesis of the research.

By using the Routine Activity theory over the Rational Choice theory, the research focused on the airport crime watch program and the acts of the general aviation airports rather than that of the offender. The Routine Activity theory also provides for a realization of the impact of the Aircraft Owners and Pilots Association Airport Watch program on the reduction of crime at general aviation airports in the Commonwealth of Pennsylvania by examining the impact of the change in routine activity and the use of the capable guardians.

BRIDGING THE GAPS

Past research has focused on traditional crime prevention programs that are found in neighborhoods across the United States. However, there has been no previous research conducted related to the Aircraft Owners and

Pilots Association Airport Watch program or general aviation security crime prevention programs. The research was the first research related to the study of the Aircraft Owners and Pilots Association Airport Watch program and the first study of general aviation security and crime prevention programs. Because it was the first research in this area of aviation security, it established a baseline of knowledge related to this area of aviation security and crime prevention. The research through the establishment of this new baseline of general aviation security and crime prevention knowledge did bridge the gap in the research from general aviation security to commercial aviation security and crime prevention programs as well as bridge the gap to traditional crime prevention programs.

The research did resolve the issue with regard to the effectiveness of a crime prevention program established at a general aviation airport. The research did resolve the issue of the effectiveness of the Aircraft Owners and Pilots Association Airport Watch program and if it contributed to the reduction in crimes and is an effective aviation crime prevention program for general aviation airports. The findings of the study answered these questions about the effectiveness of the Aircraft Owners and Pilots Association Airport watch program and crime prevention for us at general aviation airports.

REVIEW OF THE CRITICAL LITERATURE

When examining the critical literature related to the study on the Aircraft Owners and Pilots Association Airport Watch program and security and crime prevention at general aviation airports in the Commonwealth of Pennsylvania, there are several relevant themes that emerge in the literature. These themes relating to crime prevention build upon each other as well as the new research at general aviation airports in the Commonwealth of Pennsylvania.

The first theme is the literature related to traditional crime prevention programs that have been established in the Commonwealth of Pennsylvania and across the United States. The second theme is the literature as it relates to the crime prevention and security programs that have been established and implemented in a specialized environment such as a campus community. The third theme explored the literature related to crime prevention programs at commercial aviation airports and commercial air carriers in the Commonwealth of Pennsylvania and across the United States. The final theme of the study is the Routine Activity theory as it relates to traditional crime prevention programs, commercial aviation crime prevention, and the new research that was examined and did analyze the Aircraft Owners and Pilots Association Airport Watch program and security and crime prevention at general aviation airports in the Commonwealth of Pennsylvania and the programs' impact on crime at general aviation airports.

Traditional Crime Prevention Programs

Traditional crime prevention programs have been utilized to reduce crime and provide protection in neighborhoods across the United States and in the Commonwealth of Pennsylvania. The Seattle, Washington, Neighborhood Watch program, which was studied, provided an opportunity to examine the impact of a neighborhood crime watch program and the effect it had on the specific crime of home burglaries. During the study, a comparison of crime reports of residential burglaries before and after the establishment of a neighborhood crime watch program was conducted based on the Rational Choice theory (Lindsay & McGillis, 1986).

The components of the crime watch program included crime prevention methods to reduce all types of crime, such as patrols, the posting of signs, and security lighting. The crime watch program also utilized methods designed to prevent burglaries. This included the conducting of home security surveys and engraving of valuable property. The study also examined the frequency of the reporting of residential burglaries in the neighborhoods before and after the implementation of the crime watch program. Upon conclusion of the study, the results indicated that there was no increase in the frequency of reporting burglaries during the time frame of the research. The study also supported the fact that there was a decrease in residential burglaries during the time period of the research in the target neighborhoods resulting from the utilization of the crime watch programs (Lindsay & McGillis, 1986).

The research presented a solid argument that the introduction of crime prevention programs in the neighborhoods and the components of the crime watch program contributed to the reduction in residential burglaries. This conclusion based on the research does not address the impact of the crime watch program on the reduction of other property crimes or crime against persons in the neighborhood. It does not provide any evidence on the effectiveness of the crime watch program across a larger spectrum of criminal activity.

The 1977 Cincinnati, Ohio, ex post facto study of the community crime watch program was successful in determining the relationship between the level of crime and the number of crime watch programs that were implemented in Cincinnati, Ohio, utilizing the Strain theory (Smith et al., 1997). The conclusion of the research was that the crime watch program did not have a significant impact on the reduction of crime. The Cincinnati, Ohio, study established that not all crime watch programs are successful in the reduction of crime even when using traditional crime prevention methods. The utilization of a traditional crime watch program does not in itself imply that there will be a reduction in crime as many other variables may change the expected outcome (Smith et al., 1997).

A neighborhood watch program covering the state of Texas was conducted in 2005 to determine the relationship between residential burglaries and the Texas watch programs that had been established (San Miguel, 2005). The conclusion of the research was that there was a variation in the type of crime watch programs in Texas, and they did reduce crime. An interesting aspect of the study was that with the variety of the different crime watch programs across Texas, there was no significant difference in the residential burglary rate between the various watch programs in Texas (San Miguel, 2005).

The research that was conducted related to traditional crime watch programs as demonstrated in the cited studies often focuses on the use of a crime watch program in the reduction of a specific type of criminal activity. The research may explore some different aspects of the crime watch programs such as the consistence of the several different crime watch programs in a target research area and their impact on crime or the unique methods utilized for a specific crime watch program. Some of the research attempts to link the success or failure of a crime watch program with a criminology theory, while others do not examine the crime watch program through the lens of a criminology theory. The Cincinnati study does demonstrate how a criminology theory such as the Routine Activity theory that is to be used for the research of general aviation airports manifests itself in the later research to support new and future research.

Campus Crime Prevention Programs

In addition to research related to crime prevention programs in community neighborhoods, there has been research that has examined crime prevention programs in a different environment from the community neighborhood setting. In 1991, the campus community was explored through the Campus Safety Survey of Administrative Perceptions, in which research was conducted to examine the professional literature related to campus crime prevention programs. That research identified a need for more research related to crime prevention at college campuses (Beeler, Bellandes, & Wiggins, 1991).

A 1995 study that examined the Tufts University crime prevention program and the impact on rape concluded that such crime watch programs did reduce the crime of rape within the campus community (Brevard, 1995). A mixed methods research was also conducted in the campus environment by the Association of College and University Attorneys in 2003 (Brevard, 1995). This study focused on the topic of acquaintance rape in the campus community. The study concluded that, because of effective crime prevention methods that included crime prevention awareness training, the methods were successful in the reduction of the crime of acquaintance rape on campus. The study further stated that the acquaintance date rape crime prevention training that was provided to students on the campus community made the students more aware of the risk on campus, which resulted in the students feeling safer from acquaintance rape and other crimes on the grounds and property of the campus (Burling, 2003).

In 2004, a study by the International Association of Campus Law Enforcement Administrators, a professional organization comprised of campus law enforcement and security professionals, explored the impact of campus crime prevention programs on the crime rate at state residential universities (International Association of Campus Law Enforcement Administrators, 2004). The University Crime Prevention Survey conducted by the International Association of Campus Law Enforcement Administrators concluded that crime prevention programs on a state college or university campus did reduce the crime at the state universities where the crime watch programs were implemented (International Association of Campus Law Enforcement Administrators, 2004).

The campus research related to crime prevention programs within the campus programs, such as a neighborhood watch program for a unique environment, the college and university campus. The research in this area focused on the impact of crime prevention programs in a unique environment. The research will expand the professional literature related to crime prevention to another unique environment, the general aviation airport.

Commercial Aviation Crime Prevention Programs

There has been negligible research related to commercial aviation crime and crime prevention programs. One significant qualitative study conducted in 2005 did examine new security regulations and practices that were mandated for the commercial aviation industry after the terrorist attacks of September 11, 2001 (Wiencek, 2005). The qualitative research examined the impact of the new security requirements and the impact of the new security measures on the fears of the pilots, aircrew, and passengers (Wiencek, 2005).

The research concluded that the mandating of the new security procedures by the United States Department of Homeland Security Transportation Security Administration did reduce the fears from terrorism and aviation-related crime of the target individuals who were studied. The target group included pilots, aircrew, and passengers of commercial aviation carriers. The elements of the new program included the use of Department of Homeland Security screeners and improved security explosive and weapons detection equipment at commercial airports. The new security countermeasures also included secure doors on airline cockpits, the carrying of weapons by airline pilots, and increased security awareness training for the airline profession. There was also a mandated increase in the number of armed Transportation Security Administration sky marshals who fly on domestic and international commercial air carriers as part of the new aviation crime prevention program (Wiencek, 2005).

The qualitative research did not explore the impact of the new security procedures on terrorism or traditional crimes committed against persons, property, or aircraft at commercial aviation airports. One can come to an unscientific conclusion that, since there have been no successful terrorist attacks directed against the commercial aviation community, the new procedures have been effective in the reduction of terrorism. Had a mixed method of research been conducted, the study could have also explored the quantitative impact of the new security procedure on the number and type of traditional crimes committed at the commercial aviation airports against persons, property, and aircraft. Such an examination would have been a valuable contribution to the professional literature in determining if the new security countermeasures designed to prevent terrorism had an impact on traditional crime in the commercial aviation community. The completed research on the Aircraft Owners and Pilot Association Airport Watch program did add knowledge to the general aviation community and the professional literature that the Wiencek study did not contribute to the commercial aviation community and the professional literature.

General Aviation Crime Prevention Program

The research on the Aircraft Owners and Pilots Association Airport Watch program at general aviation airports in the Commonwealth of Pennsylvania did navigate and explore a different path than the traditional crime watch programs. The study examined the impact of the Aircraft Owners and Pilots Association Airport Watch program on all crime against persons and property rather than focusing on one type of criminal activity. Another different aspect of the Aircraft Owners and Pilots Association Airport Watch program study is that it will be examining a nationally established crime prevention program with benchmark guidelines to be followed at general aviation airports across the United States.

The Aircraft Owners and Pilots Association Airport Watch program research permitted a determination to be made as to the impact of the Airport Watch program on different types of crime against persons, airport property, and general aviation aircraft at general aviation airports in the Commonwealth of Pennsylvania. The research also explored an area in which other crime prevention programs have not: the effectiveness of having a standardized crime prevention program such as the one developed by the Aircraft Owners and Pilots Association. The Aircraft Owners and Pilots Association Airport Watch program was the first to establish a national standard for crime prevention in that the airports are able to apply benchmark guidelines at their airport.

The AOPA Airport Watch program encompasses two concepts related to security. The two concepts are physical security and security awareness. As it relates to physical security, the program recommends and encourages general aviation airport managers, aircraft owners, and pilots to utilize physical security practices to prevent and reduce crime. This would include adopting the program, as would be evident in the posting of the Aircraft Owners and Pilots Association Airport Watch program signs, use of intrusion detection systems, CCTV, access control in the form of fencing, card readers, and locks (AOPA, 2003).

The security awareness aspect of the program focuses on making general aviation airport owners and employees, as well as aircraft owners and pilots, aware of their surroundings. This includes being aware as to what is considered normal activity at the general aviation airports and what is not. This awareness will allow these individuals to notice what may be criminal or suspicious behavior at the general aviation airport and then to report it to the proper authorities, be it airport management or members of the law enforcement community or the homeland security profession. If the activity that is witnessed is an obvious criminal act in nature and creates an immediate threat to people, property, or aircraft, then the police are to be notified by calling 911 on a telephone. If the activity is suspicious in nature, the Aircraft Owners and Pilots Association Airport Watch phone number, 1-800-GA-SECURE, that is provided, is to be utilized to report the suspicious activity (AOPA, 2003). This phone number is a direct line to the Transportation Security Administration. The Transportation Security Administration, when notified, will document the information provided by a caller. They will then take the appropriate action based on the situation and information provided to investigate the circumstances of the report of suspicious activity (AOPA, 2003).

The research examined the impact on crime at the airports that made a deviation from the recommended components or benchmark guidelines of the Aircraft Owners and Pilots Association Airport Watch program and only implemented a portion of the established crime prevention guidelines. These results were utilized to compare and evaluate the crime levels at the general aviation airports in the Commonwealth of Pennsylvania that did not implement the Aircraft Owners and Pilots Association Airport Watch program.

Evaluation of Viable Research Designs

Upon examination of the professional literature and research that has been conducted related to traditional crime prevention programs, specialized campus and university crime prevention programs, and commercial aviation crime watch programs, it is evident that different research designs have been utilized for the various studies. The research has primarily been quantitative in nature, and some have used mixed methods utilizing quantitative and qualitative evaluation. Qualitative research was also utilized in determining how safe individuals felt with the use of a crime watch program. All of these research methods are valid in the evaluation of crime prevention programs and have resulted in meaningful research and a significant contribution to the professional literature in the area of criminal justice and crime prevention.

One of the instruments that have been used in the research of crime prevention programs is the Maryland Scale of Scientific Methods that was developed in 1997 at the University of Maryland. In 1998, the Maryland Scale of Scientific Methods was used by the University of Maryland Criminal Justice Department as an instrument in the study of the effect of rehabilitation programs and security measures in the Washington State Department of Corrections to determine the impact of such programs and the reduction of crime in prisons. The study concludes that the use of effective physical security measures contributed to a reduction of crime in the prison system (MacKenzie & Hickman, 1998).

In a 2002 research project titled "Evidence-Based Crime Prevention," the Maryland Scale of Scientific Methods was utilized to examine the effects of criminological interventions in the reduction of crime and the use of the Maryland Scale of Scientific Methods. The study concluded that the Maryland Scale of Scientific Methods was a simple and effective method of communicating the results of research to scholars, practitioners, and policy makers in criminal justice (Sherman et al., 2002).

The research did seek to examine the impact on the number of crimes committed at general aviation airports in the Commonwealth of Pennsylvania in relation to the implementation of the Aircraft Owners and Pilots Association Airport Watch program and not how individuals feel about the watch program. In order to make this determination through the research, the quantitative method was selected. The quantitative method is the most appropriate method to be utilized in the collection, examination, and reporting of the findings of the study because the research is dealing with numbers and facts rather then emotions and opinions about a general aviation crime prevention watch program (Criswell, 2003).

The research that has been conducted as identified in the review of literature has utilized the time-line design in the study of crime prevention programs. This design allows the researcher to conduct a study of a crime prevention program as it is occurring by establishing a time line to begin the research and to end the research. This allows the research team to obtain a current evaluation of the effectiveness of the crime prevention program. It also allows the researchers to manipulate the research to evaluate different variables since the research is being conducted in real time. This is an excellent method when conducting real-time evaluations and can provide the researcher with viability in the research (Criswell, 2003).

Since the research examined the impact of the Aircraft Owners and Pilots Association Airport Watch program after the fact, the time-line design would, of course, not be appropriate. The ex post facto design was selected in view of the fact that such a design is intended to be utilized in the study of events that previously occurred (Criswell, 2003). Since one of the goals of the research was to study and evaluate the impact of the Aircraft Owners and Pilots Association Airport Watch program on crime before its implementation at general aviation airports in the Commonwealth of Pennsylvania and the effect it had on crime after its introduction to the general aviation community in Pennsylvania, the ex post facto design is the appropriate method to be utilized in this type of research.

All of the research questions in the survey that were asked of the target group were questions regarding what had occurred in the past rather than in the present. This further justifies the use of the ex post facto design as the most appropriate and effective for the research.

CHAPTER CONCLUSIONS

The topic that was used for the research is of vital interest to the aviation community and the security profession with regard to its historical context and the issue of terrorism and aviation security. The study is timely in that it was the first study to address not only the Aircraft Owners and Pilots Association Airport Watch program but also general aviation security crime prevention. As the aviation community and security profession continue to explore methods of providing protection for general aviation, the research will provide a new foundation on which to build for future research in this critical area of general aviation security.

As revealed in the review of the literature, there have been similar studies related to the research that have covered traditional crime prevention, specialized crime prevention programs for college and universities, and some research related to commercial aviation. None of these previous research projects addressed general aviation security or the Aircraft Owners and Pilots Association Airport Watch program. Because of this lack of research related to general aviation security, the research did bridge the gap from the traditional crime prevention research and commercial aviation studies to the general aviation environment. Based on the research history related to crime prevention and aviation security, the selection of this topic for the research is justified and is a study that should be done in order to provide research in all areas of the aviation community and aviation security.

The research design and methodological procedures were appropriate for the research. Due to the nature of the research, it was able determine if there was an impact on the number of crimes at general aviation airports in the Commonwealth of Pennsylvania due to the implementation of the Aircraft Owners and Pilots Association Airport Watch program, so the quantitative research method is justified. Because the study examined the crime rate at general aviation airports for a period of time that has already passed, the ex post facto methodology is the logical and most suitable design to employ in this study (Criswell, 2003).

The one area of research that is lacking in the professional literature as it is related to crime prevention and aviation security is the effectiveness of a crime prevention program adapted to the general aviation security surroundings. The other unique aspect of the research is not only the examination of the impact of a crime prevention program at general aviation airports in the Commonwealth of Pennsylvania but also the impact of a nationally standardized crime watch program within the aviation community as developed by the Aircraft Owners and Pilots Association in the Airport Watch program.

The research was able to answer the questions about the effectiveness of a crime prevention program in the general aviation community as well as the viability and effectiveness of a standardized crime watch program while incorporating the concepts of the Routine Activity theory. It will further enhance the professional literature related to the Routine Activity theory by providing additional data for future research. The study of the Aircraft Owners and Pilots Association in the Airport Watch program did not support the impact of the Routine Activity theory on crime prevention programs at general aviation airports. It did show that the use of capable guardians had no impact on the outcome of criminal activity at general aviation airports by altering the routine activity at the airports and interrupting the plans of the perpetrator.

Based on this information, the research provided research and bridged the gap in the professional and scholarly literature. It also offered original and valuable research data to the aviation, security, and criminal justice professions. Considering these facts, the research was appropriate.

Chapter 3

Methodology

INTRODUCTION

The aim of the research was to provide a comprehensive and complete review of the Aircraft Owners and Pilots Association Airport Watch program at general aviation airports in the Commonwealth of Pennsylvania. The relationship between the Aircraft Owners and Pilots Association Airport Watch program and the crime at the general aviation airports was examined. The study was conducted using an ex post facto design to determine effects of the Aircraft Owners and Pilots Association Airport Watch program on crime at the airports that adopted this program during the period from 2002 to 2004. The Routine Activity theory was applied to the Aircraft Owners and Pilots Association Airport Watch program. One of the tenets of the Routine Activity theory is that the offender will make a decision to take part in criminal activity based on the situation and opportunities at the target location. The offender will use the routine activity of the target to their advantage. The Aircraft Owners and Pilots Association Airport Watch program proposes security measures that can manipulate the opportunities of the offender (Clarke & Cornish, 1983).

PHILOSOPHY FRAMEWORK

The quantitative research method was selected for this study because it is the most effective research method that can be utilized for the collection and evaluation of factual data relating to crime statistics and the use of capable guardians at general aviation airports. The philosophical foundation for quantitative research has been found to originate from the logical positivist, post-positivist, post-modernism, or the pragmatism traditions (Champion, 2006).

279

The philosophy is derived from the logical positivist view. The logical positivist view is that all knowledge can be based on logical inference that can be obtained by the study of observable facts (Champion, 2006). This research approach supports my philosophy based on my ontological assumptions, epistemological assumptions, and methodological assumptions. The view on the nature of reality or ontological assumptions is that one must collect observable facts such as the number of crimes that were committed at the general aviation airports in order to make a determination as to the impact of a crime watch program at such aviation facilities.

The epistemological assumptions or the philosophical view on how knowledge is acquired and transmitted is based on the foundation that the knowledge one collects must be factual, obtained and transmitted from the source. As in the case of the research of the impact of the Aircraft Owners and Pilots Association Airport Watch program, the data was obtained and transmitted directly from the source, the general aviation airports.

The method of research that was utilized in this study is compatible with my methodological assumptions as it relates to the research questions in the study. To make a determination of the impact of the Aircraft Owners and Pilots Association Airport Watch on crime at general aviation airports, the collection of data based on observable facts conforms to my logical positivist approach to the completed research.

RESEARCH DESIGN

A quantitative statistical methodology was utilized to examine the intervention and the control groups. The intervention group consisted of those airports that have adopted the watch program, and the control group was the airports that did not adopt the study. The completed research examined two existing groups that have not been manipulated during the study. This is because the manipulation has already occurred at the general aviation airports in the Commonwealth of Pennsylvania who have adopted the Aircraft Owners and Pilots Association Airport Watch program and general aviation airports in the Commonwealth of Pennsylvania who have not adopted the Aircraft Owners and Pilots Association Airport Watch program (Criswell, 2003). The source of the data was derived from a survey of the general aviation airports located in the Commonwealth of Pennsylvania. This ex post facto design was selected because of the fact that the research explored the impact of the Aircraft Owners and Pilots

Association Airport Watch program on the crime at the general aviation airports after the fact. What was researched has already occurred, and there is no treatment applied. The ex post facto design can be utilized to examine the possible independent variables that may be apparent in the research and where experimentation is impossible because the events have already taken place. Ex post facto design can also be utilized as a possible causal model that may be tested via experimentation in additional research (Champion, 2006).

Method

The study's sample based on the data from the research was collected by the use of a survey that was e-mailed to the 122 general aviation airports in the Commonwealth of Pennsylvania along with the consent form and a letter of introduction and instructions. Of the 122 general aviation airports that were sent the survey, it was determined that four had closed, leaving a total of 118 general aviation airports. Of the 118 general aviation airports, 67 responded to the survey. Of the 67, 37 adopted the AOPA Airport Watch Program, and 30 did not. This equates to 55% that adopted and 45% that did not. To establish the sample size necessary for the statistical analysis, one should consider the power, effect size, and level of significance. These components exploit the relationships among the variables to include sample size (N), significance criterion (ft), population effect size (ES), and the statistical power (Cohen, 1992). Considering this large effect size of 0.50, a generally accepted power of 0.80, and a 0.05 level of significance, the necessary sample size to achieve empirical validity for this study is 26 per group. For this study, 52 observations (26 adopters and 26 non-adopters) is the desired sample size. This would be a response rate of 42.5% in each group (Cohen, 1992).

The sample plan examined the criteria for the airports to be studied. The airports were located in the Commonwealth of Pennsylvania and were general aviation airports. The airports studied were obtained from a list of the licensed general aviation airports in the Commonwealth of Pennsylvania that is compiled by the Pennsylvania Department of Transportation Bureau of Aviation (Pennsylvania Bureau of Aviation, 2008).

Instruments

The Maryland Scale of Scientific Methods instrument that was developed in 1998 at the University of Maryland has been used in the research of

281

crime prevention programs in prisons and various communities in the United States (Sherman et al., 2002). It measures the impact of a crime prevention program on crime in the target area studied. It has been described as an effective instrument to provide simple findings that can be of value to policy makers and scholars in the criminal justice profession (Farrington et al., 2007).

The Maryland Scale of Scientific Methods includes core criteria to develop a correlation between a crime prevention program and how much crime occurred or did not occur during the time and location of the study. There are five scoring methods. Level 1 Correlation. Level 2 Temporal sequence, Level 3 Comparison between comparable units one adopting the program and one not adopting the program, Level 4 Comparison between multiple units and Level 5 Random assignment and the analysis of comparable units (Sherman et al., 2002). An example of how the scale was used can been seen in a 2007 study by Farrington and Welsh when they conducted research on saving children from a life of crime based on risks factors and interventions. They examined the correlation between the risk factors of where a child lives and their involvement in crime. The research also explored the difference between comparable units, those children who were exposed to intervention techniques and those who were not. The results concluded that with intervention, there was less of a chance that the child would become involved in crime (Farrington and Welsh, 2007).

A 2005 report by Tom Hope explored the Maryland Scale of Scientific Methods and the anti-social bias in crime prevention intervention programs. The study examined numerous crime prevention programs and the correlation in the reduction of crime and sequence of criminal activity. The report also examined the crime prevention policy that was utilized by looking at random comparable units and comparing the results of the effectiveness of the crime prevention program that was implemented. The conclusion was that application of methodological approaches on crime prevention policy can have an impact on the outcome of the crime prevention intervention (Hope, 2005).

The survey for this study was a modification of the Maryland Scale of Scientific Methods in that it explored two of the five areas listed in the Maryland scale. Level 3 is a comparison between comparable units one adopting the program and one not adopting the program. There was an examination between the several comparable units of analysis, the general aviation airports located in the suburbs with local police protection and the general aviation airports located in rural areas with no local police protection. Level 4 is a comparison between multiple units. There was also a comparison between units with and without the program, general aviation airports that have adopted the crime watch program and those that have not (Sherman et al., 2002).

Procedures

The data for the research was collected by the use of a survey. The survey was reviewed by the Aircraft Owners and Pilots Association located in Frederick, Maryland and the Federal Aviation Administration in Harrisburg, Pennsylvania, being the premier professional organizations related to general aviation and comprised of general aviation experts. These organizations were utilized as the resources by having general aviation professionals who are associated with the Aircraft Owners and Pilots Association and the Federal Aviation Administration review the survey questions and provide a professional opinion as to the validity of the survey related to the study of crime and the impact of the Aircraft Owners and Pilots Association Airport Watch program at general aviation airports in the Commonwealth of Pennsylvania. The Aircraft Owners and Pilots Association provided a letter. The Federal Aviation Administration provided a letter.

The first step in the process was to obtain current information on the general aviation airports in the Commonwealth of Pennsylvania. This included the name of the airport, location of the airport, airport manager, the phone number, and e-mail address. This information will be obtained from the Pennsylvania Bureau of Aviation that is the regulatory agency responsible for the collection of such data (Pennsylvania Bureau of Aviation, 2008).

To encourage a response and to provide an introduction to the study, the researcher began with a telephone call to each of the general aviation airport managers that lasted no more than ten minutes. The airport managers were provided with an introduction to the researcher and an overview of the nature of the study and how it was to be accomplished. The airport manger was advised of the informed consent form that was e-mailed to them along with the survey. The airport managers were asked to complete the informed consent form and e-mail it back to the researcher and to review the airport survey. During this first phone interview, the researcher scheduled a second phone interview with the airport manager so that the survey could be conducted. As an incentive, the airport manager was offered a copy of the results of the study.

The second phone call was made by the researcher to the airport manager at the prearranged time during their regular working hours. Based on the duties of general aviation airport managers to support general aviation security, the researcher believes that airport managers will come to the conclusion that it is ethical to take part in the survey during work hours. During this phone interview that lasted no more then twenty minutes, the researcher asked the airport manager the questions in the survey and documented the response in writing on a paper copy of the survey while on the phone with the airport manager. The airport manager was assured that their response will be kept confidential. The information collected during the second phone interview was evaluated as part of the research.

Variable Definitions

The dependent variable is based on changes that have occurred due to the independent variable as it relates to general aviation airports and their adoption of the Aircraft Owners and Pilots Association Airport Watch program. The independent variable is the adoption of the Aircraft Owners and Pilots Association Airport Watch Program and the components of the program. The Maryland Scale of Scientific Methods Level 3 methods score, comparison between airports that did or did not adopt the Airport Watch program, was used for this area of the research. The control variables were based on the descriptive difference of the airports, such as location of the airports, are they suburban or rural, and the type of police support they receive. Local police or state police coverage at the airport locations was considered. The Maryland Scale of Scientific Methods Level 4 methods score, comparison between airports that did or did not adopt the Airport Watch program controlling for other factors, were used for this area of the research (Neuman, 2006).

DATA ANALYSIS PROCEDURES

Data was entered into SPSS 16.0 for Windows. Descriptive statistics were conducted on the demographic data. SPSS, Statistical Package for the Social Sciences, was developed in 1968 by Norman Nie, C. Hadlai Hull, and Dale H. Bent. The SPSS software system was based on the idea of using statistics to turn raw data into useful information or intelligence that could be used in business and the intelligence community for decision making (Cronk, 2006). It was used in this research to convert the raw data collected from the general aviation airports to useful information to determine the impact of the airport watch program on crime at general aviation airports.

To examine research question 1, Level 3 of the Maryland Scale of Scientific Methods was used to make a comparison between comparable units, one adopting the program and one not adopting the program. There was an examination between the several comparable units of analysis, the general aviation airports located in the suburbs with local police protection and the general aviation airports located in rural areas with no local police protection. With regard to research question 1, "Is there a difference in the number of crimes between general aviation airports that have adopted the Aircraft Owners and Pilots Association Airport Watch program and those that have not?" A one-way ANOVA (analysis of variance) on the number of crimes (i.e., people, property, and aircraft) by AOPA adoption (adopters vs. non-adopters) was conducted. The assumptions of ANOVA—normality and homogeneity of variance—were assessed. ANOVA is the appropriate analysis based on the dependent variable, and the independent variable is categorical (Cronk, 2006). The independent variable is the adoption of the Aircraft Owners and Pilots Association Airport Watch Program and the components of the program. To examine research question 2, Level 4 of the Maryland Scale was used, and to make a comparison between airports that did or did not adopt the Airport Watch program, controlling for other factors will be used for this area of the research. With regard to research question 2, "Is there a difference in the routine activity between general aviation airports that have adopted the program and those that have not?" A chi-square analysis was conducted between adoption of Airport Watch program (yes vs. no) and routine activities. The chi-square was used to test if the variables are independent of each other. The chi-square allows the research to compare the categorical response between two or more independent groups (Cronk, 2006).

LIMITATIONS OF METHODOLOGY

The methodology, being ex post facto in design, has a limitation in that it is examining events that have already taken place. Based on this fact, there is no ability to control the research. The issues of internal validity and external validity were also addressed.

Internal Validity

Internal validity can be described as the approximate truth with regard to cause-effect and a casual relationship associated with the research

(Champion, 2006). The primary concern was whether observed changes in the number of crimes at the general aviation airports in the Commonwealth of Pennsylvania can be attributed to the Aircraft Owners and Pilots Association Airport Watch program and the interventions of that program or capable guardians. Other causes or alternative explanations included a decrease in crime in the area of the airports due to changes in demographic situations in the community. Other explanations included possible variables, such as the type of the police force near the airports.

External Validity

External validity can be described as a generalization based on research and the study of a specialized area. The research of the general aviation airports in the Commonwealth of Pennsylvania and the results of the impact on crime with the adoption of the Aircraft Owners and Pilots Association Airport Watch program can be generalized to state that the results in Pennsylvania are relevant to other comparable general aviation airports in other states with reference to the impact or proximal similarity of the Aircraft Owners and Pilots Association Airport Watch program. The sampling model can improve the external validity and the proximal similarity theory. This was accomplished because the sample represents the general aviation community (Champion, 2006).

EXPECTED FINDINGS

The expected findings were different in each hypothesis.

H1. There is a difference in the number of crimes between general aviation airports that have adopted the Aircraft Owners and Pilots Association Airport Watch program and those that have not.

Ho1. There is no difference in the number of crimes between general aviation airports that have adopted the Aircraft Owners and Pilots Association Airport Watch program and those that have not.

H2. There is a difference in the routine activity between general aviation airports that have adopted the program and those that have not.

Ho2. There is no difference in the routine activity between general aviation airports that have adopted the program and those that have not.

As a result of the study, the researcher found that many of the general aviation airports in the Commonwealth of Pennsylvania have adopted the Aircraft Owners and Pilots Association Airport Watch program. As part of that adoption of the crime watch program, the research showed that some capable guardians were implemented at the general aviation airports.

Because of the adoption of the Aircraft Owners and Pilots Association Airport Watch program, the research illustrated that there was a reduction in crimes against people, property, and aircraft that can be contributed to the Aircraft Owners and Pilots Association Airport Watch program. Some of the possible variables, such as the size of the police force near the airports, police budgets, and precise accounting of changes in demographics and population were explored as to their impact on the crime rate at the airports.

ETHICAL ISSUES

In order to conduct the research on the general aviation airports that are operated independent of each other, no permission was required from any aggregate body. The research followed the highest ethical guidelines in areas of protection from harm, informed consent, assurance of volunteerism, right to privacy, anonymity, confidentiality, and honesty with professional colleagues. Based on the nature of the research, there was no risk or potential for harm to the airport managers who completed the surveys or to the general aviation airports. Regarding informed consent and the assurance of volunteerism, the completion of the surveys took place with the full knowledge and consent of the general aviation airport managers.

Regarding the issues of privacy, anonymity, and confidentiality, only the researcher knew the identity of the airports that responded. The report of the results of the amount of crime against persons, property, or aircraft or the level of security that has or has not been adopted by the general aviation airports did not identify any of the individual general aviation airports that responded.

The data that was collected during the research was not associated or identified with the general aviation airports who responded to the survey. The original copies of the survey are secured in a locked security container at the researcher's office, which is protected by an intrusion detection system. The researcher was honest with professional colleagues in the reporting of the results of the research.

CONCLUSION

To summarize, the completed research provided a comprehensive review of the Aircraft Owners and Pilots Association Airport Watch program at general aviation airports in the Commonwealth of Pennsylvania. The research examined the relationship between the Aircraft Owners and Pilots Association Airport Watch program and the crime at the general aviation airports. The research was quantitative, utilizing the ex post facto design because the data that was collected during the research was based on information and events from the past. The researcher's philosophy was derived from the logical positivist view. The logical positivist view is that knowledge can be based on logical inferences that can be obtained by the investigation of observable facts (Champion, 2006).

The sampling took into account the large effect size of 0.50, a generally accepted power of 0.80, and a 0.05 level of significance. The necessary sample size to achieve empirical validity for this study is 26 per group. For this research, 52 observations (26 adopters and 26 non-adopters) were considered the desired sample size.

The survey was the instrument that was used for the research. The research survey is the most common method of measurement in criminal justice research (Champion, 2006). This method of research encompasses a measurement procedure that involves asking questions of the general aviation airports in the Commonwealth of Pennsylvania, the target group, in written form.

The data analysis procedures entered the data into SPSS 16.0 for Windows so that descriptive statistics can be conducted on the demographic data. The methodology used to gather data to be analyzed, the ex post facto design, has a limitation in that it is examining events that have already taken place (Champion, 2006).

The final results of the study of the Aircraft Owners and Pilots Association Airport Watch program illustrated that there was a reduction in crimes against people, property, and aircraft that can be contributed to the Aircraft Owners and Pilots Association Airport Watch program.

Chapter 4

Results

This chapter presents the results of the study techniques used to analyze the data and answer the research questions.

Research Question 1

Is there a difference in the number of crimes between general aviation airports that have adopted the Aircraft Owners and Pilots Association Airport Watch program and those that have not?

Research Question 2

Is there a difference in the routine activity between general aviation airports that have adopted the program and those that have not?

DESCRIPTION OF SAMPLE

The data for the completed research was collected by the use of a survey that was e-mailed to the 122 general aviation airports in the Commonwealth of Pennsylvania. Of the 122 general aviation airports that received the survey, it was determined that 4 had closed, leaving a total of 118 general aviation airports. Of the 118 general aviation airports, 67 responded to the survey. Of the 67 airports, 37 adopted the AOPA Airport Watch Program, and 30 did not.

VARIABLES

The dependent variable in the study was whether or not there was a change in crime (against people, property, and aircraft) at the general aviation airports based on the adoption of the Aircraft Owners and Pilots Association Airport Watch program. Tables 1, 2, and 3 show that between 2002, the year before the Aircraft Owners and Pilots Association introduced the Airport Watch program, and 2004, the year after the program began, there was a reduction in crime at the airports that adopted the Airport Watch program and an increase in crime at the airports that did not adopt the program. According to Table 1, crime against people at adopter airports went down from 5 to 0, and the number of crimes went up at non-adopter airports from 3 to 6. With regard to crime against property at adopter airports, the number of crimes went down from 80 to 3, and the number of crimes went up at non-adopter airports from 45 to 88. Related to crime against aircraft at adopter airports, the number of crimes went down from 29 to 2, and the number of crimes went up at non-adopter airports from to 4 to 13.

The independent variables considered in the completed research, shown in Table 4, are related to the Routine Activity theory. The majority of the airports did not make any changes in their routine activity. Table 4 shows the percentage of airports by status (adopter and non-adopter) that made any change in their routine activity. As it relates to a change in routine activity in the use of security lights (14% adopters, 0% non-adopters) made a change. As it relates to a change in the routine activity in the locking of buildings (24% adopters, 7% non-adopters) made a change. As it

Table 1   Chi Square Crime Against People, Property, and Aircraft-Years

Years Crime Reported	AOPA Adopters 37	AOPA Non-Adopters 30	Total	x^2	p
Crimes Against People					
2002	62.5% (5)	37.5% (3)	8	0.50	0.480
2004	0% (0)	100% (6)	6	—	—
Crimes Against Property					
2002	64% (80)	36% (45)	125	9.80	0.002
2004	3% (3)	97% (88)	91	79.40	0.001
Crimes Against Aircraft					
2002	88% (29)	12% (4)	33	18.9	0.001
2004	13% (2)	87% (13)	15	8.07	0.005

290

Table 2 ANOVAs on People 2002, to 2004, Property 2002 to 2004 and Aircraft 2002 to 2004 by AOPA (Adopters vs. Non-Adopters)

Variables	F	Sig.	Eta	Power	Adopters		Non-Adopters	
					M	SD	M	SD
People								
2002	0.15	.702	.002	.067	0.14	0.42	0.10	0.31
	(0.14)							
2004	6.34	.014	.089	.698	0.00	0.00	0.20	0.48
	(0.11)							
Property								
2002	3.62	.062	.053	.466	2.16	1.66	1.50	1.04
	(2.01)							
2004	63.20	.001	.493	1.00	0.08	0.28	2.93	2.16
	(2.13)							
Aircraft								
2002	9.96	.002	.133	.875	0.78	1.08	0.13	0.35
	(0.70)							
2004	13.76	.001	.175	.955	0.05	0.23	0.43	0.57
	(0.17)							

Table 3 ANOVAs on Crimes Against People, Property, and Aircrafts by Year (2002 vs. 2004)

Variables	F	Sig.	Eta	Power	2002		2004	
					M	SD	M	SD
People	0.33	.568	0.01	0.09	0.12	0.37	0.09	0.34
	(0.09)							
Property	2.94	.091	0.04	0.39	1.87	1.44	1.36	2.04
	(2.93)							
Aircraft	4.75	.033	0.07	0.56	0.49	0.89	0.22	0.45
	(0.51)							

relates to a change in the routine activity and setting of security alarms, 8% of adopters and 7% of non-adopters made a change. As it relates to a change in the routine activity and the use of security patrols, 5% of adopters and 0% of non-adopters made a change. Other independent variables related to the Routine Activity theory include the location (rural/ suburban) of the airport. The study shows 89.9% of the rural airports were

Table 4   Chi Square AOPA (Adopters vs. Non-Adopters)

Independent Variables		AOPA		Total	x^2	p
		Adopters 37	Non-Adopters30			
Located in rural area	Yes	89% (33)	66.7% (20)	53	5.08	0.024
Local police presence in area	Yes	24.3% (9)	75.7% (28)	37	9.76	0.002
Observed population increase	Yes	40.5% (15)	59.5% (22)	37	1.32	0.250
Change when security lights on	Yes	14% (5)	0% (0)	5	4.38	0.036
Change when buildings locked	Yes	24% (9)	7% (2)	11	3.76	0.052
Change when alarm systems on	Yes	8% (3)	7% (2)	5	0.05	0.838
Change when security patrol schedule	Yes	5% (2)	0% (0)	2	1.67	0.196

adopters, and 67.7% of the rural airports were non-adopters; for local police presence, 24.3% of adopter airports had local police presence, and 75.7% of non-adopter airports had local police presence; and for any observed change in population near the airport, 40.5% of adopter airports observed a population change near the airport, and 59.5% of non-adopter airports observed a population change near the airport. Based on the completed research, the results were not significant, and the Routine Activity theory had no impact.

DATA ANALYSIS

Research Question 1

To examine research question 1, analyses of variance (ANOVAs) were conducted to assess if there is a difference in the number of crimes between general aviation airports that have adopted the Aircraft Owners and Pilots Association Airport Watch program and those that have not. As exhibited in Tables 1, 2, and 3, based on the results of the survey and the completed research, there was a significant reduction in the number of crimes against people, property, and aircraft at general aviation airports that adopted the Aircraft Owners and Pilots Association Airport Watch program. Tables 1, 2, and 3 clearly show the reduction in crime at the adopter airports. The results of the research also establish that the airports that adopted the Aircraft Owners and Pilots Association Airport Watch program not only utilized the capable guardians, or physical security measures, but also utilized awareness and training initiatives. This total commitment to the Airport Watch program resulted in the reduction of crime at adopter airports. Based on the success of traditional crime prevention programs, the reduction in the number of crimes at adopter airports was not a surprise, and the results were expected.

Research Question 2

To examine research question 2, chi-square, a "goodness-of-fit" test, was conducted to assess if there is a difference in the routine activity between general aviation airports that have adopted the program and those that have not. Several variables were examined, including the location of the airports, type of police coverage, and observed population increase. Most of the airports were located in a rural area and did not have local police coverage. In the rural areas of Pennsylvania, there is not much local police presence, and since most of the airports were rural, the research confirmed very little local police presence. There was negligible increase in the population near the airports (see Table 4).

Several variables were explored that addressed research question 2, the Routine Activity theory. This included examining changes in the routine activity at the airports in the use of security lighting, locking of buildings, use of alarm systems, and use of security patrols. Based on the research, the results were insignificant because there was no significant change in the daily routine at any of the airports in how they were operated. This change in daily activity is a critical premise of the Routine Activity theory.

While there was very little difference in the routine activity between the adopter and non-adopter airports, there were some security behaviors that distinguished the two groups. The adopter airports tended to use physical security measures as compared to the non-adopter airports. The most common physical security measure utilized was security lighting and locks, which could have been a key factor in deterring a perpetrator as described by the routine activity theory, resulting in the reduction of crime at the adopter airports.

Chapter 5

Results, Conclusions, and Recommendations

RESULTS

This study arose from the observation that there has been no research related to crime prevention programs at general aviation airports. Traditional crime prevention programs have been studied to assess the impact of crime in neighborhoods such as the Seattle, Washington, Neighborhood Watch Program. The Seattle study examined the impact of a crime watch program on burglaries committed against homes and found that the crime watch program did reduce crime in the Seattle area. The university crime prevention program, to alert students about the risk of rape and date rape on campus, resulted in a reduction in sexual assaults on campus (Brevard, 1995).

Another study conducted in 2005 examined the security regulations that were mandated for the commercial aviation industry after the terrorist attacks of September 11, 2001. That study only explored if individuals felt more secure as it relates to commercial aviation, but not the impact of crime on commercial or general aviation. The study found that individuals did feel safer with the new security procedures. This feeling of being safe had nothing to do with the crime rate because that was not the focus of the research effort (Wiencek, 2005).

The research conducted in this study examined the Aircraft Owners and Pilots Association Airport Watch program between 2002 and 2004 to determine if the program, where implemented, prevented and/or reduced crime at general aviation airports. Based on the results of the completed research in this study, there was a reduction in crime against people,

295

property, and aircraft at the airports that adopted the Airport Watch program and an increase in crime against people, property, and aircraft at the airports that did not adopt the Airport Watch program.

This study confirmed what the previous research has shown. The utilization of a crime prevention program in a housing community, at a university, or even at a general aviation airport has a positive impact in the reduction of crime. The completed research also highlights the need for general aviation to continue to be proactive in increasing security at the airports in light of continued terrorist incidents that have occurred in the United States. This includes recent plots against military installations, the shooting of military staff at Fort Hood, Texas, and the use of a general aviation aircraft that was crashed into the Internal Revenue Service building (Straw, 2010).

While few incidents have been related to general aviation aircraft or airports, it does create a sense of fear in the mind of the public and is of concern to the Department of Homeland Security Transportation Security Administration. Continued terrorist incidents involving general aviation aircraft could lead to new security mandates for general aviation airports. One of goals of the Aircraft Owners and Pilots Association Airport Watch program was to avoid such mandates (AOPA, 2003). The completed research has demonstrated that the airport watch reduced crime and can prevent future security mandates.

Routine Activity Theory

The Routine Activity theory was developed by Lawrence Cohen and Marcus Felson in 1979 and has been used in analysis of crime watch programs and the impact on crime (Cohen & Felson, 1979). The Routine Activity theory is based on the assumption that a perpetrator seeking to commit a criminal act will study the routine or day-to-day activity of the target. An individual seeking to take part in criminal activity will then use these predictable behaviors of individuals at the target site to their advantage in taking part in criminal activity. Another premise of the Routine Activity theory is the use of capable guardians such as physical security measures at the target location that may reduce the possibility of crime (Vold, Bernard, & Snipes, 2002). The most comprehensive study dealing with the Routine Activity theory was the research conducted by Cohen and Felson. The research examined social changes and trends in crime through the lens of the Routine Activity theory. The research showed that the combined use of capable guardians and altering the routine activity of the target location did have an impact on the reduction of crime. The study did not make a distinction as to what aspect of the Routine Activity theory had a more significant impact in crime reduction, the use of capable guardians or changing the daily activity (Cohen & Felson, 1979).

Results of the Routine Activity Theory Research

In this completed study, the relationship between the Aircraft Owners and Pilots Association Airport watch program and the Routine Activity theory was examined. The adopter airports used more capable guardians or physical security measures, such as signs, locks, and lighting, compared to the non-adopter airports. There was no significant change in the daily routine at any of the airports in how they were operated. This change in daily activity is a critical premise of the Routine Activity theory.

This study confirmed what previous research has indicated: that the Routine Activity theory is valid in the reduction of crime. Based on the fact that both adopter and non-adopter airports in this study did not make significant changes in the daily activity or routine and adopter airports had more capable guardians, this research indicates that the use of capable guardians is more significant than a change in routine activity in the prevention of crime as it relates to the Routine Activity theory. Based on the observations of the study and hypotheses, the results were not unexpected.

Other Variables

In this research of the Aircraft Owners and Pilots Association Airport watch program, other variables were examined, including location of the airports, rural or suburban, population changes, and the type of police presence in the area. Most of the airports are located in rural areas with an insignificant change in population. With regard to police presence, a majority of the airports have state police presence. This is consistent with the rural location of the airports in Pennsylvania. The completed research also shows there was no impact to the airport operations or security based on changes in federal security guidelines and insignificant impact on airport operations and security due to government grants for aviation security. The airports that were studied, both adaptor and non-adopter airports, were of the same size and had the same crime before the development of the Aircraft Owners and Pilots Association Airport Watch program.

CONCLUSIONS

The hypothesis as presented in the completed research was that the Aircraft Owners and Pilots Association Airport Watch program would have an impact on crime against people, property, and aircraft at the general aviation airports in the Commonwealth of Pennsylvania. The completed research shows that the general aviation airports in the Commonwealth of Pennsylvania that adopted the Aircraft Owners and Pilots Association Airport Watch program experienced a reduction in crime against people, property, and aircraft. Crime increased against people, property, and aircraft at the general aviation airports that did not adopt the Aircraft Owners and Pilots Association Airport Watch program. The Airport Owners and Pilots Association Airport Watch program works and is an effective tool in the reduction of crime at general aviation airports.

This is important to the continued use of crime prevention programs in the criminal justice and aviation security profession and to the future of aviation security. The completed study reaffirms the success of crime prevention programs regardless of the environment that they are implemented, be it in community neighborhoods, on the campus of universities, or at general aviation airports; they do have an impact in the reduction of crime.

The completed research shows that crime prevention programs, specifically the Aircraft Owners and Pilots Association Airport Watch program, can be a useful tool in general aviation security in the Commonwealth of Pennsylvania and across the United States in the reduction of crime. In light of the fears and concerns after 9/11 and the evolving Homeland Security initiatives to counter new aviation security threats, the completed study establishes that the Aircraft Owners and Pilots Association Airport Watch program is an important asset in the aviation security protocol in the reduction of crime and homeland security of the aviation infrastructure. It also allowed the general aviation community to be proactive in aviation security by developing and implementing a volunteer security program. This proactive approach was a key factor in the avoidance of new security mandates from the Department of Homeland Security Transportation Security Administration that could have been costly to the general aviation airports in Pennsylvania and the United States.

RECOMMENDATIONS

This was the first research effort that examined crime at general aviation airports and the Routine Activity theory. It was also the first study to explore the relationship between crime at general aviation airports and the adoption of the Aircraft Owners and Pilots Association Airport Watch program. The results of this study indicate the Aircraft Owners and Pilots Association Airport Watch program did reduce crime against people, property, and aircraft at the general aviation airports that adopted the program. These results could be projected nationwide to provide an indication of the success of the Aircraft Owners and Pilots Association Airport Watch program.

It is recommended that this research be used as a baseline to expand research nationwide to examine the Aircraft Owners and Pilots Association Airport Watch program and the possible impact it has on crime at general aviation airports across the United States. The association of the Routine Activity theory and the impact of the Aircraft Owners and Pilots Association Airport Watch program with regard to crime prevention may produce more significant results from a broader nationwide study of general aviation airports. This first study of general aviation security could possibly direct future research efforts toward many different facets of general aviation security and commercial aviation security in the United States, benefiting the security and aviation profession as well as the academic community.

REFERENCES

Aircraft Owners and Pilots Association. (2003). *AOPA Airport Watch*. Frederick, MD: AOPA

Barkan, S. E. (2006). *Criminology: A social understanding* (3rd ed.). Upper Saddle River, NJ: Pearson.

Bartol, C. R., & Bartol, A. M. (2005). *Criminal behavior: A psychosocial approach* (7th ed.). Upper Saddle River, NJ: Pearson/Prentice Hall.

Beeler, K. J., Bellandes, S. D., & Wiggins, C. A. (1991). *Campus safety: A survey of administrative perceptions and strategies*. Washington, DC: National Association of Student Personal Administrators, Inc.

Bennett, T. (1989). An assessment of the design, implementation, and effectiveness of neighborhood watch in London. *Howard Journal of Criminal Justice*, 274(4), 241–256.

Bisignani, G. (2006). Airlines [Electronic version]. *Foreign Policy*, 6, 22–28.

Boetig, B. (2006.) The routine activity theory: A model for addressing specific crime issues. *FBI Law Enforcement Bulletin*, June, 32–46.

Bohm, R. M., Reynolds, K. M., & Holmes, S. T. (2000). Perceptions of neighborhood problems and their solutions: Implications for community policing. *Policing: An International Journal of Police Strategies and Management*, 23(4), 439–465.

Brevard, R. (1995). *Crime prevention at Tufts University*. Hartford, CT: International Association for Campus Law Enforcement Administrators.

Bullock, J. A., Haddow, G. D., Coppola, D., Ergin, E., Westerman, L., & Yeletaysi, S. (2006). *Introduction to homeland security* (2nd ed.). Burlington, MA: Elsevier Butterworth-Heinemann.

Burling, P. (2003). *Acquaintance rape on campus*. Washington, DC: National Association of College and University Attorneys.

Carter, D. (2002). *The police and the community*. Upper Saddle River, NJ: Prentice Hall.

Champion, D. J. (2006). *Research methods for criminal justice and criminology* (3rd ed.). Upper Saddle River, NJ: Pearson/Prentice Hall.

Clarke, R. V. (1992). *Situational crime prevention: Successful case studies*. Albany, NY: Harrow and Heston.

Clarke, R. V., & Cornish, D. B. (1983). *Crime control in Britain: A review of policy and research*. Albany, NY: State University of New York Press.

Cohen, L. E., & Felson, M. (1979). Social change and crime rate trends: A routine activity approach. *American Sociological Review*, 44, 588–608.

Cohen, J. (1992). Quantitative methods in psychology: A power primer. *Psychological Bulletin*, 112(1), 155–159.

Commonwealth of Pennsylvania Bureau of Aviation. (2007). *Regulations for general aviation airport operation*. Harrisburg, PA: Commonwealth of Pennsylvania.

Cornish, D. B., & Clarke, R. V. (1986). *The reasoning criminal*. New York: Springer-Verlag.

Criswell, J. W. (2003). *Research design qualitative, quantitative and mixed method approaches* (2nd ed.). Thousand Oaks, CA: Sage.

Cronk, B. C. (2006). *How to use SPSS*. Glendale, CA: Pyrczak.

Culp, R. F., & Bracco, E. (2005). Examining prison escapes and the Routine Activities theory. *Corrections Compendium*, May–June, 1–5, 25–27.

Curran, D. J., & Renzetti, C. M. (2001). *Theories of crime* (2nd ed.). Boston: Allyn and Bacon.

Emerson, S. (2006). *Jihad incorporated*. Amherst, NY: Prometheus Books.

Farrington, D. P., & Welsh, B. C. (2007). *Saving children from a life of crime: Early risk factors and early intervention studies on crime and public policy*. New York: Oxford Press.

Fischer, R. J., & Green, G. (2004). *Introduction to security* (7th ed.). Burlington, MA: Elsevier.

Groff, E. (2007). Simulation for theory testing and experimentation: An example using routine activity theory and street robbery. *Journal of Quantitative Criminology, 23,* 75–103.

Hope, T. (2005). The anti-social bias and the Maryland Method Scientific Methods Scale. *European Journal on Criminal Police and Research, 11,* 275–296.

International Association of Campus Law Enforcement Administrators. (2004). *University crime prevention survey.* Hartford, CT: International Association of Campus Law Enforcement Administrators.

Jackson, A., Gilliland, K., & Veneziano, L. (2006). Routine activity theory and sexual deviance among male college students. *Journal of Family Violence, 21,* 449–460.

Lindsay, B., & McGillis, D. (1986). Citywide community crime prevention: An assessment of the Seattle program. In D. P. Rosenbaum (Ed.), *Community crime prevention: Does it work?* (pp. 46–67). Beverly Hills, CA: Sage.

MacKenzie, D. L., & Hickman, L. J. (1998). *An examination of the effectiveness of the type of rehabilitation programs offered by Washington State Department of Corrections.* College Park, MD: University of Maryland.

Martin, G. (2006). *Understanding terrorism: Challenges, perspectives and issues* (2nd ed.). Thousand Oaks, CA: Sage.

Meadows, R. J. (2007). *Understanding violence and victimization* (4th ed.). Upper Saddle River, NJ: Pearson/Prentice Hall.

Moore, K. C. (2000). *Airport, aircraft and airline security.* Burlington, MA: Elsevier Butterworth-Heinemann.

Morgan, D. (2006). *Femicide: The impact of victim/offender relationships on crime.* New York: University of New York Press.

Neuman, W. L. (2006). *Social research methods qualitative and quantitative approaches.* New York: Pearson.

Nyatepe-Coo, A. A., & Zeisler-Vralsted, D. (2004). *Understanding terrorism: Threats in an uncertain world.* Upper Saddle River, NJ: Pearson/Prentice Hall.

Pennsylvania Bureau of Aviation. (2008). *Directory of Pennsylvania general aviation airports.* Harrisburg, PA: Commonwealth of Pennsylvania.

Pizarro, J., Corsaro, N., & Violet, S. (2007). Journey to crime and victimization: An application of routine activity theory and environmental criminology to homicide. *Victims & Offenders, 2,* 374–394.

San Miguel, C. (2005). *An analysis of neighborhood watch programs in Texas.* Huntsville, TX: Sam Huston State University.

Savage, M. (2003). *The enemy within.* Nashville, TN: WND Books.

Schmalleger, F. (2007). *Criminal justice today* (9th ed.). Upper Saddle River, NJ: Prentice Hall.

Sherman, L. W., Farrington, D. P., Gottfredson, D. C., & Welsh, B. C. (2002). *Evidence-based crime prevention.* New York: Routledge.

Simonse, C. E., & Spindlove, J. R. (2007). *Terrorism today: The past the players the future* (3rd ed.). Upper Saddle River, NJ: Pearson/Prentice Hall.

Smith, B. W., Novack, K. H., & Hurley, D. C. (1997). Neighborhood crime prevention: The influence of community-based crime prevention and neighborhood watch. *Journal of Crime and Justice, 20(20),* 69–86.

Sperry, P. (2005). *Infiltration: How Muslim spies and subversives have penetrated Washington.* Nashville, TN: Nelson Current.

Straw, J. (2010). The evolving terrorist threat. *Security Management.* 4–10, 46–49.

Swanson, C., Territo, L., & Taylor, R. (2005). *Police administration.* Upper Saddle River, NJ: Prentice Hall.

Sweet, K. M. (2009). *Aviation and airport security.* Upper Saddle River, NJ: Pearson/Prentice Hall.

Turney, A. M., Bishop, J. C., & Fitzgerald, P. C. (2004). Measuring the importance of recent airport security interventions [Electronic version]. *Journal of Air Transportation, 9,* 3.

Turvey, B. (2001). *Criminal profiling: An introduction to behavioral evidence analysis.* San Diego, CA: Elsevier Academic Press.

Vold, G. B., Bernard, T., & Snipes, J. B. (2002). *Theoretical criminology* (5th ed.). New York: Oxford University Press.

Wiencek, D. (2005). Open skies? *Journal of Counterterrorism and Homeland Security International, 11,* 12–24.

Zhao, J., He, N., & Lovrich, N. P. (2003). Community policing: Did it change the basic functions of policing in the 1990s? A national follow-up study. *Justice Quarterly,* 20(3), 697–724.

SURVEY QUESTIONS

Aircraft Owners and Pilots Association
Airport Watch Program Questionnaire

Survey Questions

1. What is the location of your general aviation airport?
   a. Located in a suburban area?   Yes   No
   b. Located in a rural area?   Yes   No
   c. Observed population increase?   Yes   No
   d. Observed population decrease?   Yes   No

2. What type of police presence do you have at the airport?
   a. Local police presence in area?   Yes   No
   b. Only state police presence in area?   Yes   No
   c. Crime prevention training by police?   Yes   No
   d. Number of observed police patrols each week? _____

3. How many aircraft are based at your airport?

   Number of based aircraft? _____

4. Changers in state or federal security guidelines?

   Yes   No

5. Availability of federal or state grant money for security improvements?

   Yes   No

6. Did your airport adopt the AOPA Airport Watch Program in 2003?

   Yes   No

7. Does your airport utilize any of the following physical security measures?
   a. Intrusion detection systems   Yes   No
   b. CCTV   Yes   No
   c. Security lighting   Yes   No
   d. Access control (card access/locks)   Yes   No
   e. Fencing   Yes   No

8. Does your airport conduct security awareness training?
   a. To staff   Yes   No
   b. To pilots   Yes   No
   c. To aircraft owners   Yes   No

9. Does your airport utilize security patrols? Yes No

10. Has your airport made changes to the routine activity at the airport to prevent crime?
    a. Security patrol schedules   Yes   No
    b. Times security lights are turned on   Yes   No
    c. Times hangars and buildings are locked Yes   No
    d. Times alarm systems are activated   Yes   No
    e. Times when CCTV is monitored   Yes   No
    f. Hours of operations of the airport   Yes   No
    g. Schedules of airport staff   Yes   No

11. What are the numbers [sic] of crimes at your airport by year against
    a. People?
       1. 2002 _____
       2. 2003 _____
       3. 2004 _____
    b. Property?
       1. 2002 _____
       2. 2003 _____
       3. 2004 _____
    c. Aircraft?
       1. 2002 _____
       2. 2003 _____
       3. 2004 _____

INDEX

.